Teacher's Manual to accompany

CRIMINAL LAW AND ITS PROCESSES

Seventh Edition

SANFORD H. KADISH
Alexander F. & May T. Morrison Professor of Law, Emeritus
University of California, Berkeley

And

STEPHEN J. SCHULHOFER
Julius Kreeger Professor of Law and Criminology
University of Chicago

ISBN 0 - 7355 - 1991 - 9

This manual is made available as a courtesy to law teachers with the understanding that it will not be reproduced, quoted or cited, except as where indicated. In the event that anyone would like to cite the manual for thoughts drawn from it, a reference to the relevant page number of the materials text (with the formula "suggested by") may be appropriate.

Copies of this manual are available on computer diskette. Teachers who have adopted the casebook may obtain a copy of the diskette, free of charge, by calling the Aspen Law and Business sales assistant at 1 – 800 – 950 – 5259.

Permissions
Aspen Law & Business
A Division of Aspen Publishers, Inc.
1185 Avenue of the Americas
New York, NY 10036

1 2 3 4 5

TABLE OF CONTENTS

INTRODUCTION

A. The Goals of this Manual

There is no single way to teach criminal law. Nor is any single approach the only appropriate one for teaching the particular materials we have assembled in *Criminal Law and Its Processes.* For many years we hesitated to offer a teacher's manual, out of concern that such a step would unduly constrict the handling of cases, notes and problems that so many teachers around the country have used successfully for so long. We believe that suggestions offered by those who have prepared the materials can be beneficial, but only if they are seen as just that: *suggestions* intended to indicate one or two among several worthwhile approaches, rather than a definitive path of attack. We hope that a teacher's manual offered in this spirit will prove useful not only to new teachers but also to our more experienced colleagues, just as their suggestions about teaching and about the use of our book have proved invaluable to us over the years.

Teacher's manuals often seek to preserve flexibility by offering lengthy sets of questions for the principal cases and by raising numerous themes that an instructor may wish to pursue. We have tried to resist the temptation to follow this approach. The leading criminal law cases already raise, on their face, more issues than a teacher can handle in an hour, and our Notes and Questions, like those of many casebooks, add more grist for the mill. The instructor will seldom need to worry about having too little to say. Rather, the principal problem in teaching criminal law, we find, is to structure and focus discussion so that each class hour has a manageable set of objectives and builds toward a useful conclusion.

With this problem in mind, we have chosen to be rather selective. In this Manual, we attempt to show how we think one (or a few) themes that we consider important can be introduced, developed and brought to a conclusion during the course of an hour's discussion. We include the specific problems and hypothetical cases that we have found useful for stimulating student interest and for moving the analysis in a constructive direction. We also include actual cases that can serve the same purpose, often more vividly than a law professor's "hypo." At the end of each section we suggest, more briefly, some of the supplementary problems or themes that can be pursued if time permits.

The teacher's manual reflects the distillation of our teaching experience and that of many others who have used our book, but as we have indicated, it does not purport to constitute a definitive statement of *the* proper approach to criminal law teaching. The two of us do not always handle material the same way, and each of us varies his approach somewhat from year to year. We have sought to develop a usable guide by focusing on some of the important themes and on the ways we think they can be effectively developed within the framework of an individual class hour.

B. The Organization of the Course

Consistent with the diversity of criminal law curricula in contemporary law schools, the Casebook is designed for flexibility. It can be and has been used in a variety of teaching contexts, ranging from the year-long, five- or six-hour first-year course to the three-hour upper-level elective.

In preparing the present Teacher's Manual, we have had primarily in mind the three- to four-hour first-year course, consisting of 45-60 class hours. The core of such a course will be Chapters 2-3 and 5-8, which can be taught straight through, with few if any deletions. At the end of this Introduction we provide an outline of the recommended sequence of assignments, and then two samples of a specific class-by-class syllabus, one for the typical three-credit course and another for the typical four-credit course.

The Manual, organized in accordance with that sequence, provides more specific comments on recommended assignments as part of the discussion of each major section. Instructors who have only 45 class hours available (or who teach students that have already studied criminal procedure) can consider skipping the material in Chapter 1 (except for pages 35-50). Other possible omissions for instructors pressed for time are suggested in the discussion of Chapters 2, 7 and 8. Teachers who have more time at their disposal, or who choose to use the book for advanced courses or seminars, will probably wish to be less selective in treating the materials on corporate liability and conspiracy (Chapter 7) and to include most or all of the material on theft (Chapter 9).

Our recommended sequence for a 60-hour first-year course is as follows:

> a. Introduction:
> > Chapter 1, Section A: pp. 1-12, and Section
> > B: pp. 12-22 (as background reading)
> > Chapter 1, Section B: pp. 22-50, 50-55
> > (optional), 55-73, and 73-93 (optional)
>
> b. The Justification of Punishment:
> > Chapter 2

c. Elements of Just Punishment:
>   Chapter 3

d. Rape
>   Chapter 4 (with pp. 371-386 primarily as
>   background reading)

e. Homicide:
>   Chapter 5

f. Harm:
>   Chapter 6

g. Group Criminality:
>   Chapter 7

h. Justification and Excuse:
>   Chapter 8

i. Conclusion:
>   The latter part of Chapter 8 (pp. 929-949) provides
>   appropriate material for a concluding class that can draw
>   together the themes and problems of the substantive
>   criminal law. Following such a class, if time permits, the
>   instructor can usefully focus on the ethical problems that
>   are constantly lurking in law school class discussions and
>   that will concern all the students directly in their careers
>   and in their lives, whether or not they practice criminal
>   law. For this purpose, we find that the material in
>   Chapter 1, pp. 73-93 provides an appropriate and highly
>   effective concluding topic for the course.

C. Specific Class-by-Class Assignments

The following pages present two samples of a detailed class-by-class syllabus of assignments, one for a three-credit course (45 class hours) and the second for a four-credit course (60 class hours). Our reasons for the specific inclusions and exclusions suggested in each syllabus are discussed in the corresponding sections of this Manual.

The syllabus for the three-credit course lists 47 classes, of which five (designated by an asterisk) are optional, readily severable classes; two of the five can be dropped in accordance with the preferences of the instructor. Similarly, the syllabus for the four-credit course lists 66 classes, of which 15 (designated by an asterisk) are readily severable; six of the 15 can be dropped in accordance with the preferences of the instructor.

Three Credit Course
(45 class hours)
SYLLABUS

Notes: (1) Bkg = Background reading: to be assigned but not
discussed in detail in class

(2) The asterisk (*) designates five optional classes. At least two
of the five should be dropped, in accordance with the
preferences of the instructor

---

[a] For alternatives, and more detailed suggestions, see pp. 237-238 infra.

Four-Credit Course
(60 class hours)
SYLLABUS

Notes: (1) Bkg = Background reading: to be assigned but not discussed
in detail in class

(2) The asterisk (*) designates 15 optional classes. At least
six of the 15 should be dropped, in accordance with
the preferences of the instructor

---

[b] For alternatives, and more detailed suggestions, see pp. 237-238 infra.

<u>Chapter 1</u>
<u>How Guilt is Established</u>

A. <u>The Structure of the Criminal Justice System</u>, pp. 1-12

This section can be assigned as background reading, to be completed before or during the first week of classes. The students should use their reading to acquire a familiarity with the organization of the criminal justice process, the procedural steps involved in a criminal case, and the vocabulary of criminal procedure.

Several of the prominent organizational features of the American criminal justice system have consequences that students will need to bear continuously in mind during their study of substantive criminal law. Prominent among these features are: (1) the intensive filtering process that winnows out the great majority of cases before trial (p. 10), (2) the heavy reliance upon guilty pleas, (3) the importance of official discretion in deciding what charges are filed and which cases are prosecuted, and (4) selection and training of police, prosecutors and judges, a factor which influences the quality of that all-important discretion.

B. <u>The Process of Proof,</u> pp. 12-93

Students studying criminal law, especially in the first semester of law school, usually have only a rudimentary knowledge of trial procedure and the process of proving facts in court. In order to put substantive criminal law problems in a concrete trial context and to discuss intelligently the case for expanding or contracting any of the required substantive elements (e.g., intent, knowledge, etc.), they will need familiarity with the process of proof. Chapter 1 offers an introduction that is worthwhile for its own sake and provides a concrete framework for the substantive criminal law materials that follow. The chapter can be covered in roughly three to four classes devoted to the following topics: the presentation of evidence (pp. 20-35), proof beyond a reasonable doubt (pp. 35-50), the jury (pp. 55-73), and ethics (pp. 73-93). The ethics material can, alternatively, be deferred until the end of the course.

1. <u>Overview</u>, pp. 12-20

The introductory material at pp. 12-20 should be assigned as background reading in preparation for the opening class. Although class discussion will probably focus primarily on close analysis of the first case (<u>Zackowitz</u>, p. 22), the principal themes of the introductory material can be mentioned or briefly discussed.

Pp. 18-20 summarize the stages of trial procedure and provide a vocabulary that students will need throughout the course. Pp. 12-18 raise questions about concepts that are both central to the "fact-finding" process and much more problematic than students often suppose:

(a) What is a "fact"? Students need to bear in mind throughout that the facts they and the appellate courts recite do not arrive pre-packaged on the attorney's desk or in court. They are just malleable as the law (Younger, p. 12), and bear only a much-diluted connection to the original facts of the event (Marcus, p. 13). (b) How do the "fact-finders" choose among conflicting versions of the facts? Credibility determinations are vastly more important to the outcome of most lawsuits than decisions resolving disputed questions of law. But how does a jury know which witness is telling the truth? The materials at pp. 13-15 raise troubling questions about the reliability and impartiality of decisions about credibility. (c) How are the "facts" determined in cases that do not go to trial? The materials at pp. 15-18 underscore the importance of plea bargaining to the fact-finding process and raise questions about the ways that negotiated outcomes may differ from outcomes reached after trial. Because up to 90% of all criminal cases are resolved by plea, students need to remember throughout the course that most often the importance of a legal rule is not so much in its influence on the formal trial process as in the way it affects plea agreements through its impact on the bargaining position of the plea negotiators.

2. <u>The Presentation of Evidence</u>, pp. 20-35

This section serves to familiarize students with the order of proof at trial and with the concepts of relevancy and prejudicial effect. In addition, the rules of evidence relating to "other crimes" provide insight into basic concepts of criminal responsibility.

Zackowitz, p. 22. Students should be clear on the facts and on the procedure below. What was the alleged error? What is the specific testimony to which the defendant objects? (See p. 23, last ¶). Was this evidence relevant? What element of the crime did it tend to prove? Students should see that the principal issue at trial was whether the killing was deliberate rather than impulsive. Is the specific evidence (the fact that defendant kept a small armory of weapons in his house) relevant to this issue at all? Note Pound's argument in dissent: The defendant made a selection from a group of weapons and therefore was deliberating his deed. Is this tenable? Was any evidence offered to show that the defendant was "making a selection"? If there is no evidence that the defendant actually made a selection, and the evidence consists only in his ownership of the weapons, how is ownership relevant to the question of deliberation? Note that the court's majority concedes that the person possessing such an arsenal was more likely to be a deliberate killer than a person who did not own any such weapons (and that a quarrelsome defendant is more likely to start a quarrel, p. 24, middle of first full ¶). The connection, if it exists at all, is very slight, but that is all that is required to satisfy the law's requirement of "probative value."

If the evidence does have some probative value (i.e. if evidence of bad character does tend to show that the defendant was more likely to have acted in conformity therewith), why should it be excluded? Consider the following problems:

a. The Clean Slate. Once a defendant has been convicted and served his sentence, shouldn't he be regarded as having paid his debt to society? Is it fundamentally unfair for a previous offense to be used repeatedly against him? Consider the situation of a defendant recently convicted of a series of four gas station hold-ups. Shortly after his release from prison another gas station is robbed. Doesn't the defendant become a prime suspect? Should his prior convictions be enough (by themselves? together with slight circumstantial evidence?) to convict the defendant of the fifth robbery? Note Cardozo's statement (p. 24, first full ¶) that the defendant should be able to "start his life afresh" when he faces a new criminal charge.

b. Should we try people for their acts or for their character? If character alone is a legitimate issue, how could the defendant effectively defend himself against it? Note the excerpt from the Lynch article (p. 30) and Cardozo's comment that instead of having to answer "a specific charge" the defendant was called upon to answer "another, more general and sweeping, ... pervasive and poisonous" (p. 25, lines 3-5).

If time permits, the applications of the "other crimes" rule are worth considering:

Case 1. The "Brides in the Bath" Case (p. 29). Is this case an exception to the other crimes rule? The point is that the other crimes are not offered to show that the defendant had a bad character and therefore acted in conformity therewith. Rather, the other crimes are offered to prove that the defendant had a unique modus operandi that identifies him as the killer. Consider the application of this rule in the two test cases on p. 30. Does the evidence show a unique modus operandi or does it simply show a bad character? Note that in all three cases the trial judge admitted the evidence. In practice the signature exception opens many opportunities for getting bad character evidence before the jury.

Case 2. Suppose that defendant D has two prior convictions for sexually molesting young children. A five-year-old child has been molested by a stranger at a school-bus stop, D is suspected of being the attacker, and one eyewitness tentatively identifies D as looking very much like the attacker. D denies any involvement. Assuming that the prior crimes do not suggest any distinctive modus operandi, should the prior offenses be admissible anyway? Is prior sexual misconduct a strong predictor of future behavior? Even if it is, does such evidence also carry unusually powerful prejudicial effects? Students should consider the merits of the special evidentiary rule for sex offenses enacted as part of the 1994 Violent Crime Control Act (p. 30).

Case 3. Suppose that in a rape prosecution, the district attorney offers evidence, as part of her case in chief, that S had previously committed a similar rape. The trial judge rules this "other crimes" evidence inadmissible because it does not establish a distinctive modus operandi. S takes the stand in his defense and claims consent. Now can the prosecution get S's earlier offense admitted into evidence? Students should see how the impeachment exception comes into play.

What is the theory of the impeachment exception? Note that the evidence comes in only for a limited purpose -- not to show that the defendant committed the crime but only to show that his testimony should not be believed. In practice, is this a meaningful difference? Even in theory, does the impeachment exception make sense? Note the assumption that the defendant, because of his bad character, may be disposed to commit perjury. But if a perjury conviction is not admissible, as part of the prosecution's case in chief, in a prosecution for a subsequent perjury, why should previous convictions for rape be relevant to show that the defendant may be disposed to commit perjury??

Apart from the theoretical vulnerability of the impeachment exception, note its practical effect. Is it likely that the jury will consider impeachment evidence only for the limited purpose for which it can be introduced? Once the other-crimes evidence is before the court and in the mind of the jury, can they ignore its general implications? To help insure that they can, the judge will give the jury a cautionary instruction (see p. 33, top). Will the jury (can the jury) actually follow this instruction? For that matter, to what extent does the jury follow any of the complex instructions that they receive during the course of a criminal trial? The note on pp. 32-34 explores the problem. Given doubts about the effectiveness of cautionary jury instructions, wouldn't it make sense to abolish the impeachment exception entirely? But what of all the other areas in which we rely upon the jury to follow instructions from the judge? What is the value of careful definition of substantive law concepts, if instructions about such concepts have only a marginal influence on jury behavior?

Discussion should make clear the tensions surrounding the fact-finding process and the many technical limitations on the kind of evidence that the prosecution can adduce in order to establish guilt at trial. The criminal law appears committed to focus on the particular event rather than the defendant's general character, but in practice this commitment is eroded by pressures to admit as much relevant evidence as possible, and by the administrative difficulties that flow from the complex fact-finding machinery of the American adversary system.

3. Proof Beyond a Reasonable Doubt, pp. 35-55

This section should bring out the nature of the prosecutor's burden, indicating both the difficulties faced by the prosecution and the circumstances under which the burden is less difficult to satisfy than might otherwise appear. In addition, discussion of the reasonable doubt requirement helps bring out the ways in which the criminal sanction is unique. In a first-year course, pp. 35-50 can be covered in one or one-and-one-half classes. The material on presumptions (pp. 50-55) can be skipped, or assigned as outside reading for students who wish to pursue a particularly difficult problem.

Winship, p. 35. Why does the Court hold that proof beyond a reasonable doubt is so fundamental that this requirement is implicit in the meaning of "due process"? The Court stresses the goal of reducing the risk that convictions may rest on factual error (p. 35), but pursuit of this goal will inevitably increase the risk that acquittals may rest on factual error. Why is the former risk less acceptable than the latter? Why is it, as Justice Harlan says (p. 36), that "it is far worse to convict an innocent man than to let a guilty man go free." The answer given by both the Court and Justice Harlan focuses on the important interests of the defendant that are at stake in a criminal trial. Conviction can lead to stigma and also the possible loss of liberty. But what interests of society at large are at stake? Consider:

> Case 1. The defendant is accused of robbing and brutally beating an elderly shopkeeper. What harms to society will occur if the defendant is guilty but nevertheless found innocent? Note both the loss of general deterrence and the costs of leaving this particular robber at liberty. Is it so clear that the harm of convicting an innocent person is "far worse" than these harms which society will suffer from acquittal of the guilty?

Students should see that this sort of balancing analysis (what Justice Harlan calls a "assessment of the comparative social disutility") is essentially indeterminate. Nonetheless, there is a strong tradition in favor of the proposition that it is better for a guilty defendant (or ten guilty defendants) to go free than for an innocent person to be convicted. Why is this? Consider first the Winship Court's reference to the "moral force of the criminal law." Why is it "critical that the moral force of the criminal law not be diluted"? Note how the deterrent effects of the criminal law can depend on its moral force and its stigmatizing effect. If we admitted the possibility of conviction even when guilt is in doubt, would the loss of deterrence offset the deterrence benefits that might otherwise flow from minimizing the risk of acquitting the guilty? By minimizing the risk of convicting the innocent, the reasonable doubt rule may actually enhance the security of society in the long run.

But what if one is not persuaded that this trade-off argues in favor of the reasonable doubt requirement? Suppose that society would on whole be better off with a lower standard of proof, such as the preponderance of the evident standard? Would that fact suffice to render punishment under the preponderance test justified? Consider:

> Case 2. Slavery. Would it be just for society to choose certain children at birth (orphans, perhaps) and make them slaves for life? Would the answer depend on "an assessment of the comparative social disutility" of having or not having such an arrangement? Suppose that a comprehensive analysis showed that the benefits of such a slavery system for society were greater than its costs. Students may object to some of the details of such a cost-benefit calculus, but are such objections the fundamental ones? Isn't it conceivable that such a system could be economically beneficial under some circumstances?

The more fundamental objection may be that such an arrangement would violate the right of each human being to equal concern and respect. A utilitarian analysis may seem unsatisfactory because it suggests that any individual can be made to suffer, if this would make others in society better off. An alternative approach would focus on the personal rights of each individual. If suffering can be justified only when deserved, then the individual defendant may have a right not to suffer punishment, except when his guilt can be shown beyond a reasonable doubt.

If time permits, other facets of this problem can be explored:

> Case 3. What burden of proof would be appropriate in a proceeding to civilly commit a person on the ground that he was retarded and therefore unable to care for himself? Does the prospective loss of freedom argue for a high standard of proof, so as to minimize the risk that a person not requiring institutionalization might be erroneously subjected to it? Note, on the other hand, the risk of erroneously denying such treatment to a person who needed it. Is it relevant that such a

proceeding does not result in stigma, or at least not the same kind of stigma of moral blameworthiness associated with a criminal conviction? If so, is a somewhat lower standard of proof justified in terms of the rights of the individual affected?

The discussion of the basic reasonable doubt requirement should bring out the unique nature of criminal proceedings: Society's own law enforcement objectives require preservation of the notion of moral condemnation; that can be accomplished only if there is solicitude for the rights of the individual defendant. In addition, moral condemnation implies that the defendant <u>deserves</u> his punishment, and therefore carries with it the obligation to confer on the defendant certain rights, independent of their overall social utility.

<u>Applications of the Reasonable Doubt Requirement</u>. Students need to develop an appreciation of what the reasonable doubt standard means in practice. It may be helpful, before discussing <u>Patterson</u>, to begin with simple cases such as the following:

> <u>Case 1.</u> The defendant is charged with robbing a bank at gunpoint. The robber was wearing a mask which he tore off as he left the bank and jumped into a getaway car. One of the bank tellers, who saw the man after he removed the mask, has identified the defendant as the robber. The defendant says that on the day of the robbery he was visiting his sister in a town 150 miles away. The sister confirms the defendant's story. In addition, a gas station attendant in that town has testified that a man resembling the defendant bought gas from him that day. Should the judge let such a case go to the jury? Is there sufficient evidence to prove guilt beyond a reasonable doubt? What would be your decision as a juror? As an appellate judge called upon to review a conviction? (What if the prosecution's evidence had included impeachment evidence, offered after the defendant's testimony, to the effect that the defendant had previously been convicted of an armed bank robbery?)

> <u>Case 2.</u> The defendant is charged with rape. The testimony shows that the defendant and the complainant met at a mutual friend's house, and then returned to the complainant's house where they played cards and drank beer with the complainant's brother until late in the evening. The complainant then went upstairs to her bedroom. The complainant testifies that she fell asleep and that the defendant entered the room, held a knife to

her throat and proceeded to rape her. The defendant testifies that before going upstairs, the complainant invited him to follow, led him to her bedroom and consented to intercourse there. Both parties testify with apparent sincerity. Is there sufficient evidence to prove guilt beyond a reasonable doubt? What would be your decision as a juror? As an appellate judge called upon to review the conviction? (What if the defendant has two prior convictions for rape?)

Discussion of such cases can be used to bring out the dangers of convicting an innocent person, and also the concern about releasing a person who may be guilty of a serious crime. In addition, the student should understand that proof beyond a reasonable doubt does not necessarily require what the layman would consider overwhelming evidence. In both cases the testimony of the prosecution's witnesses, if believed, is sufficient to establish guilt beyond a reasonable doubt. Since credibility matters are exclusively for the jury, an appellate court probably could not properly reverse a conviction in either case (see Curley, p. 36).

Patterson p. 38. Students should be clear on the nature of the charge and the defendant's defense at trial. Was the jury permitted to find guilt by a standard lower than that of beyond a reasonable doubt? (Note that the trial judge's instructions, p. 39, require that the prosecution establish an intentional killing beyond a reasonable doubt). What, then, was the defendant's argument on appeal? Compare the defendant's objection to that raised by the defendant in Mullaney. Note that the objection is essentially the same. But there the defendant won. What is the difference? Students should understand the difference between the statutory definitions of murder in New York and in Maine. The Court distinguishes the Maine statute on the ground that there murder is defined as a killing with "malice aforethought." But is this distinction simply "formalistic," as Justice Powell charges in his dissent? Consider:

> Case 3. Suppose that after Mullaney, the Maine legislature sought to keep the burden of proving provocation on the defendant? Could you advise the legislature whether there is a way for them to achieve this result? (Obviously, a simple restructuring of the statute would do the trick.)

> Case 4. Can a state place the burden of proving self-defense in a murder prosecution on the defendant? What does it depend

on? Note the various decisions considered on pp. 45-46, note 2(a). The answer appears to turn on whether the word "unlawful" appears in the statutory definition of murder. Is there any reason why the constitutional result should depend on such a technical matter of draftsmanship?

Case 5. Suppose that a state statute provides that it shall be considered murder for any person to cause the death of another person, but that it shall be an affirmative defense if the defendant can prove that the killing was unintentional. Doesn't this statute meet the formal requirements laid down in Patterson. The Court says that there are "limits beyond which the states may not go" (p. 41, last 5 lines). But what are those limits? One answer may be that the state does not have constitutional power to punish an accidental killing as murder; thus, lack of intent unlike the defense in Patterson, is not a "gratuitous defense" that the state might abolish entirely. But doesn't this argument also apply to Case 4 (self-defense)? See pp. 48-49. If Patterson is not limited to gratuitous defenses, as Martin v. Ohio (p. 48) implies, then what kinds of "limits" did the Court have in mind? After Patterson and Martin, how much is left of Winship?

What should the Court have done in Patterson? Would it be better to hold that any factual issue relevant to guilt or to the severity of punishment must be established beyond a reasonable doubt? What are the disadvantages of such an approach? Consider what might happen in the New York legislature if Patterson had come out the other way. Isn't it possible that the legislature would have abolished the "extreme emotional disturbance" defense entirely? If so, would defendants be better off under such a statutory scheme than under the law as it stands with Patterson? Moreover, if the legislature has power to abolish the requirement entirely, how can it be unconstitutional for the legislature to provide the defense but only in diluted form (by requiring the defendant to bear the burden of proof)? Note Underwood's arguments against the greater-includes-the-lesser approach, p. 47-48. On the other hand, the all-or-nothing approach might in practice pose a substantial barrier to legislative reform of the criminal law.

What alternative approaches are feasible? The analysis suggested by Jeffries and Stephan (pp. 46-47) would apparently prevent the states from shifting the burden on "gratuitous" defenses (e.g. self-defense).

Will this "substantive" test really help? Note that the need for ameliorative reform may apply just as much to the self-defense area as to the "gratuitous" justifications and excuses. Is the Jeffries and Stephan approach too restrictive with respect to defenses that are substantively required? Is it insufficiently restrictive with respect to the many justifications and excuses that are not constitutionally required?

How would Justice Powell handle these problems? Students should see that under his test a defendant would have to show not only that the defense in question makes a substantial difference to guilt, the degree of punishment, and stigma, but also that "in the Anglo-American legal tradition the factor in question <u>historically</u> has been held that level of importance" (p. 43, last 3 lines). Note that this latter requirement helps preserve flexibility for legislatures to adopt new ameliorative defenses. But why should history and tradition be constitutionally significant? Does the due process clause enact all the historical common law definitions of crime? In any event, suppose that the issue on which the state shifts the burden of proof does not involve a substantially <u>expanded</u> defense, but that in the absence of the shift in burden of proof, the traditional narrow defense would have been repealed entirely? See p. 46, Note 2(c). Isn't the concern about preserving legislative flexibility equally applicable, whether or not the defense in question involves a significant expansion of the traditional common law test?

Discussion should bring out that the all-or-nothing approach, together with other alternatives to the Court's position, involves the potential for inhibiting legislative reform. On the other hand, the Court's position leaves the legislatures with all but unlimited freedom to evade the force of the reasonable doubt requirement.

Presumptions, pp. 50-55

<u>Patterson</u> permits the state explicitly to shift to the defendant the burden of persuasion on certain issues. The presumption device enables the prosecutor to ease her burden of persuasion on issues that the state has chosen not to shift (and perhaps <u>cannot</u> shift) to the defense. Presumptions doctrine is of course quite detailed and beyond the scope of a first-year criminal law course. Students will encounter it again in Evidence. For present purposes, students should understand how the presumption device eases the prosecutor's burden (see bottom

of p. 51) and should understand the use of presumptions in areas of recurring importance in the proof of crimes -- possession and knowledge (p. 52, Note 3), intent (p. 53, Note 4).

Problem 1, p. 53: The presumption sounds commonsensical, but to determine its validity, students must be clear on the applicable test. People with blood alcohol over 0.1 probably are (more likely than not) intoxicated. Is this fact, if true, enough to sustain the presumption? It would be, if the judge's instruction creates only a permissive inference. See County Court, p. 52, Note 2(b). But is the wording of this instruction permissive only? Students should see that the instruction, as worded, creates a mandatory (though rebuttable) presumption and that the presumption is constitutional only if the factual relationship holds true beyond a reasonable doubt over the generality of cases. The connection between 0.1 blood alcohol and intoxication is strong, but not _that_ strong, so the judge's instruction is not constitutionally permissible. The court in Leverett (p. 54) so held.

Problem 2, p. 54, provides a way to test students' understanding of the basic issues. Was the trial judge's instruction permissible? Consider first whether the state could have invoked Patterson to place the burden of persuasion on the intent issue overtly on the defendant. (No: this statute is of the Mullaney type and "malice" (here intent to kill) was an express element of the offense. See p. 54 n.1.) Since the prosecutor must prove intent beyond a reasonable doubt, did the instruction impermissibly shift the burden of proof to the defendant? Students should focus on the next-to-last sentence of the instruction. What is the effect of this statement? Because it presumes intent unless "rebutted" this sentence implies that the defendant must carry the burden on the intent issue. It therefore violates Sandstrom, p. 53, Note 4. Any argument for the prosecution here? Note the last sentence of the instruction -- an accurate statement of the law. Does it cure the error in the preceding sentence? Four justices in the Supreme Court thought so. The majority thought, perhaps more realistically, that the two directly contradictory sentences (note that such contradictions in jury instructions are not uncommon) might leave the jury to assume that the defendant had to carry the burden of persuasion. The majority therefore correctly found a violation of Winship here.

4. The Role of the Jury, pp. 55-75

Jury trial exerts a fundamental influence on the structure of the criminal law and on the framework within which substantive law issues arise. This section provides a basis for understanding the American commitment to jury trial and the consequences of that commitment for both substantive law and procedure.

Duncan, p. 55. Students should be clear about the factual episode, the offense charged, and the potential punishment that the defendant faced. Note also the actual sentence imposed (60 days in jail), a rather severe punishment under the circumstances, even as alleged by the prosecution. Does that tell anything about the fairness of the trial and the judge who was the fact-finder? What is the court's holding? Note its two distinct parts: (1) the right to a jury in criminal cases is so fundamental that the 14th Amendment incorporates the jury trial right granted under the 6th Amendment; and (2) the charge of simple battery, because punishable by two years in prison, is a serious crime, not a petty offense for which a jury trial would be unavailable under the 6th Amendment.

The first part of the holding should be the focus of attention. Why is the right to jury trial so fundamental? The Court stresses its value in preventing oppression, a "safeguard against the corrupt or overzealous prosecutor and against the compliant, biased, or eccentric judge" (p. 56, second full ¶). Is this the only purpose of the jury? Why can't improper behavior by prosecutor or judge be corrected on appeal? Does the jury ever have a role to play if the prosecutor and judge are both highly professional and adhere scrupulously to the letter of the law? A more complex argument in favor of the jury can be read between the lines of the Court's opinion: note the Court's reference to the defendant who may prefer "the common-sense judgment of the jury to the more tutored but perhaps less sympathetic reaction of the single judge" (p. 56, middle of the second full ¶). (The same appeal to the equity-dispensing value of the jury appears implicit at p. 56, text at n. 26: When juries differed from judges in the Kalven and Zeisel study it was not because the judges were found to be biased or eccentric -- the study was based on information supplied by the judges themselves. Rather, the differences were based on jury sentiments about the law being enforced, or similar equitable considerations. See pp. 61-62.

Is the Court persuasive in arguing that the two goals (protection against oppression and affording a mechanism for flexibility and equity) justify the institution of the jury? Note that most other countries, presumably valuing the same goals, do not use juries in order to achieve them. In fact, given the much greater exercise of judicial control over the jury in England (pp. 60-61), it may be that the United States is the only country in the world in which the jury's fact-finding function is so carefully protected. Aren't there other ways to achieve the Court's goals without reliance upon an institution that creates such a cumbersome and uncertain process? Does the relative absence of careful training and supervision of prosecutors and judges in the United States, see Chapter 1, section A, suggest that Americans have a rather unique need for a safeguard like the jury?

In any event, is the equity-dispensing function of the jury a good thing? Note that in the American system, once a jury brings in a verdict of acquittal in a criminal case, the judge may not set aside that verdict, no matter how much it may be unjustified in light of the evidence. Is this really sensible? Why not allow the judge to order a new trial, or even to enter judgment NOV, as he could in a civil case? The acquittal of Peter Zenger (p. 63, first full¶) offers the classic example of a situation in which jury nullification was a good thing. But how relevant is the Zenger case today, when the laws on the books presumably have the support of a majority of the people? Why does a law remain on the books, if it is truly unpopular? (Note the problem of legislative inertia. But is haphazard jury nullification the remedy for that problem?).

Suppose that Duncan is murdered by KKK terrorists in reprisal for his alleged insult to the four white boys. Suppose that the KKK killers are prosecuted in state court but acquitted by a jury, against the weight of overwhelming, uncontradicted testimony. This the "two edged sword" to which Broeder refers (pp. 58-59). Does this dark side of the equity-dispensing function arise less often than the beneficial aspects? Apart from the relatively extreme examples of highly politicized nullification, why is flexibility and the common-sense judgment of untutored jurors a better guide to the result than strict adherence to the enacted rules of law? (Kalven and Zeisel nicely state the dilemma at p. 59.)

Discussion should bring out the tension, existing in all legal systems, between the desire for clear rules and predictability on the one hand, and the desire for flexibility and equity on the other.

Duncan appears to give constitutional status to the jury's equity-dispensing power. The effort to provide scope for flexible departures from the rules, and yet at the same time to keep such departures from getting out of hand, generates our elaborate trial structure of exclusionary rules of evidence, detailed instructions to the jury on the law and so on. The overwhelming complexity of our trial system can be seen in part as a consequence of our unwillingness to opt for either a system of strict rules or a system of unbounded discretion. Is there some satisfactory but simpler way to strike an appropriate balance?

To the extent that time permits, the class should examine the working out of this tension between rule and equity, in the context of two specific legal doctrines: nullification instructions and inconsistent verdicts.

Dougherty, p. 62. Does the jury have the right to disregard the trial judge's instructions on the law? Note that the judge will tell the jury what the legal rules are and instruct them that they must follow these rules. In what sense, then, is there a "right" to nullify the law?

> (a) Is nullification always undesirable in principle but accepted because it is simply impossible to stop (Ragland, p. 65, Note 3)? Why couldn't we stop nullification if we really wanted to? Couldn't we impose sanctions on jurors who disregard their oath? Or couldn't we simply provide judges the power to set aside verdicts for the defendant that are against the evidence (just as we routinely do in civil cases)? Consider the collateral hearing and juror-removal techniques approved by the court in United States v. Thomas (pp. 67-68). If judges can force adherence to their instructions in this way, why bother to have jury trial at all?
>
> (b) If, in contrast, jurors do have the right to nullify, and if it is good that they have this right, why shouldn't the judge tell them about it? Is the result in Dougherty hypocritical, or is it appropriate to make sure that we do not get too much of a good thing? If the judge does not tell the jury about the right to nullify, shouldn't other groups be free to spread accurate information about the jury's nullification power? Compare efforts to restrict the activities of the FIJA (p. 68, Note 4(c)) with the Dougherty court's assumption that citizens can get information about the legal system from voices other than the judge's (p. 63, last 6 lines).

(c) If nullification is sometimes a beneficial safety valve for the legal system, is it appropriate for jurors ever to take race into account in deciding whether the defendant deserves a nullifying verdict? Consider Professor Butler's arguments for limited use of race-based nullification. If racially integrated juries are important to legitimate the verdict in a criminal trial, then isn't it unjustified and contradictory to constrain African-American jurors to support a verdict that violates their conscience?

DeSacia, p. 72, line 1. Is it appropriate to set aside the inconsistent conviction? If so, wouldn't the prosecution be entitled to an instruction, in a case like DeSacia, that the jury must either acquit on both counts or convict on both counts? Wouldn't such an instruction constrain the jury's equity-dispensing function? Is it better, in fact, to constrain that function (e.g. Dougherty and United States v. Thomas) than to permit an illogical verdict to stand?

5. The Role of Counsel, pp. 73-93

In a one-semester, first-year course, one or two classes normally can be made available for this material. The section on the ethical responsibilities of defense counsel raises questions of pervasive importance for the study and practice of law, and it therefore warrants sustained attention, particularly in a first-year course. The material can be assigned at one of two points, either: (a) in the normal sequence after the section on the role of the jury; or (b) at the very end of the course, as a conclusion to the criminal law material and an introduction to the responsibilities and dilemmas of the practicing lawyer. Where two classes are available, the first can be devoted to the problem of conflicting responsibilities and the difficulties, particularly for the criminal defense attorney, of staying within "the bounds of the law" (pp. 73-87). The second class can be devoted to the questions that arise even when the attorney is within the bounds of the law -- including the ethics of whether and how to represent the defendant known to be guilty (or more generally the client known to be in the wrong) (pp. 87-93).

Client perjury. Consider first the Freedman article (p. 73) and especially the hypothetical posed at the bottom of p. 74. What is Freedman's solution? Is his approach morally appropriate? Is it permissible under the Model Rules of Professional Conduct? Note

first the attorney's obligation under Rule 3.3(a)(4), p. 78. This
provision bars the attorney from presenting the evidence. But won't
that reveal a confidence, in violation of Rule 1.6, p. 78? Do the Model
Rules impose conflicting obligations here? Students should note Rule
3.3(b), which would permit the disclosure. Thus, under the CPR, the
lawyer must avoid presenting the evidence, even it results in the
disclosure of a confidence.

Is the approach of the Model Rules a reasonable solution to the
problem? What is Freedman's critique? Consider first how the lawyer
can in fact prevent presentation of the evidence.

(a) The attorney can try to dissuade his client. Nix, p. 79, illustrates
the implications of this approach. The Court holds the attorney's
conduct constitutionally permissible. But was it also ethical? wise?
The Court viewed the attorney's actions as ethically obligatory. Is that
correct? Note that under both the Model Rules and the earlier Code of
Professional Responsibility (p. 81) it all depends on the Court's
assumption that the client's proposed story was false. How did the
lawyer know (how do we know) that it was? (Note the nature of the
client's explanation for his new recollection -- p. 80, second full ¶. This
seems tantamount to an admission of perjury. Nix may be somewhat
unusual in that regard. In most cases it is hard for the attorney to be
sure.) Or what happens if the attorney is convinced that his client will
be lying, but that the client insists that this is not the case. Can the
attorney act on his convictions without having a fair determination of
whether the testimony really is false? But how can such a
determination be made? Shouldn't the client be entitled to a hearing?
If so, shouldn't the client have (new) counsel at the hearing?

(b) Nix may be unusual in that the attorney's effort to dissuade the
client succeeded. But what should the attorney do if the client
persists? Presumably he should attempt to withdraw. But how? If the
lawyer does not fully explain the problem to the presiding judge, will
he be permitted to withdraw? If the lawyer is not permitted to
withdraw, note what happens: he will probably be forced to
participate (at least indirectly) in the presentation of the perjured
testimony anyway. What does he do then? Note Chief Justice
Burger's conclusion: he must reveal his client's crime to the court. P.
82, first full ¶ & n.6.

(c) Alternatively, what if the attorney does disclose the reason for
his request to withdraw? Doesn't this disclosure jeopardize the

defendant's right to a fair trial? The danger is clear when the judge is trier of fact. See Lowery, p. 85, Note 1(a). But are there possibilities for unfair prejudice even in a jury trial? See p. 86, Note 1(b). Note Noonan's solution: assign a new attorney and a new judge (see p. 78, lines 3-4). Does this really solve the problem? Won't the perjured testimony be presented anyway? Hasn't the first attorney still participated in its creation. Noonan gives an answer: see p. 78, second ¶. Is it convincing?

(d) Consider a fourth possibility, the "passive" approach (illustrated by the attorney's behavior in Lowery, p. 85). What was the Lowery court's objection to the passive approach? Note the implicit disclosure to the trier of fact. Do the court's objections to implicit disclosure to the judge also apply when a jury is the trier of fact? If not, then does it follow that explicit disclosure is permissible when the judge is not the trier of fact? This is the approach favored by the Chief Justice in Nix. See p. 82 & n.6. What are the criticisms of the "passive" approach? See the second paragraph of the ABA Comment at p. 79. What is the ABA's preferred solution? Under Rule 3.3(a)(4), p. 78, what are "reasonable remedial measures"? Does the Commentary imply that the remedy must include revealing the perjury to the court? See the fourth paragraph of the Comment at p. 79. Is the Comment a binding interpretation of the Rule? If so, does the attorney have an obligation to inform the client, at the outset of the representation, of the limitation on confidentiality? Does this suggest that Rule 3.3 is unworkable? Compare the advantages of the "passive" approach, discussed in the Lefstein excerpt, pp. 84-85.

Discussion should indicate the difficulty of satisfying simultaneously the lawyer's obligations of truthfulness and confidentiality. The difficulties are aggravated, in criminal cases, by the barriers to withdrawing from the case. If truthfulness and confidentiality unavoidably clash, which should be sacrificed? If confidentiality is sacrificed, will that promote (or impede) the long-run accuracy of the adversary system? Consider especially p. 79, Note 2.

Defense of the Guilty, p. 87. Is it unethical to seek an acquittal by entirely permissible methods (e.g. arguing reasonable doubt) when the attorney knows the client to be guilty. Note Samuel Johnson's answer at pp. 87-88. Is this persuasive? Does it assume equally effective advocacy on both sides? Does it assume that with such advocacy, the legal system will produce the just result? Are these assumptions always valid? If not, does the attorney who urges an unjust result bear some personal responsibility for it? Or do the overall advantages of zealous advocacy justify, on balance, the "unjust" result in the particular case?

Assuming that it is not per se unethical for an attorney to defend a client who is known to be guilty, are there limits on the means that an attorney should use in such a case? Consider Professor Freedman's hypothetical at pp. 88-89. Is it ethical for the defense attorney to use the information supplied by Jones to impeach the testimony of the victim? What is Chief Justice Burger's analysis, p. 89? Doesn't the approach favored by Chief Justice Burger in effect perpetrate a fraud on the court? Can it be argued that the attorney's behavior in such a situation is even worse than permitting the client to testify falsely? See Freedman's analysis (bottom of p. 89, 5th full ¶). But whether or not an attorney is troubled by presenting such impeachment evidence, can he or she ethically choose not to present it? Note the applicable provisions of the Model Code and Model Rules, p. 87 n.37. One solution may be for the attorney to avoid taking such a case from the outset, when a problem of this kind can be anticipated. But what if the attorney doesn't realize that the victim is telling the truth until long after agreeing to take on the case? (Note the facts of the hypothetical at pp. 88-89).

Even if it is ethically permissible to represent the guilty client, should a morally sensitive attorney agree to take such a case? One answer may be that the attorney does not know at the outset whether the client is guilty; once he or she finds out, it may be too late to withdraw. But suppose that the client admits guilt from the very beginning. Is it morally permissible to bargain for a low sentence in such a case? Is it morally permissible to work for an acquittal? Why would a conscientious, morally sensitive individual ever agree to do so? The importance of vigorous challenge for the effective functioning of the adversary system and for the long-term protection of civil liberties can be mentioned at this point. Is the attorney therefore free of moral responsibility for the outcome of a case, not only when she chooses not to withdraw after learning of a client's guilt, but even when she agrees to accept a client known to be guilty? Is the attorney's position like that of the doctor, whose efforts to heal need not imply moral approval of the patient? Note how the roles of doctor and lawyer are significantly different. See p. 93 & n.b. Given the differences between doctor and lawyer, doesn't the attorney necessarily retain some moral responsibility for an outcome that she persuades a court to accept?

Is Wasserstrom correct in arguing that the role-differentiated position of the attorney is "a very comfortable one to inhabit" (p. 91, 4th full ¶)? In what ways might that role be morally uncomfortable? What does Wasserstrom mean in saying (p. 93, last line of the excerpt) that by becoming a lawyer, one incorporates ways of thinking that "shape the whole person"? Does Wasserstrom mean that role-differentiated ways of thinking and acting, and the amorality associated with them, might spill-over into non-professional areas of the lawyer's life? In what ways can this occur? If the danger is serious, what can we do about it? One answer may be simply to avoid a criminal practice. But do these problems arise for attorneys in civil practice as well? Consider:

> Case 1. An attorney representing an insurance company learns that a compensation claim for very serious injuries is entirely justified, but that the complaint is barred by the statute of limitations. Should the lawyer plead the statute of limitations? Or should the insurance company lawyer vigorously cross-examine and attempt to discredit a key witness whom she knows to be telling the truth? In both instances, wouldn't it be unethical not to take these steps (unless the client specifically agreed to waive such defenses)? Doesn't the civil lawyer have essentially the same problems as the criminal defense attorney?

> Case 2. What about the role-differentiated position of the American law professor? Is it ever justified for a teacher to express, with apparent conviction, a viewpoint with which she actually disagrees?

Discussion of such questions can provide a background for students to think about the choices they will have to make and the values they will import into their practices (and into their lives), even when they stay fully within the bounds of the disciplinary rules and other legal requirements.

Chapter Two
The Justification of Punishment

This chapter is designed to familiarize students with the principal purposes of punishment, the empirical and philosophical debate surrounding each of them, and the difficulty of bringing them to bear on the resolution of concrete cases. The material provides an essential foundation not only for discussion of grading and sentencing, but also for analysis of all the doctrinal issues that determine whether imposition of a criminal punishment is justified.

In a one-semester, first-year course, roughly 2-3 class hours will be available to introduce this material.

A. <u>What is Punishment?</u>, pp. 95-101

The sense of this material is conveyed in the Introductory Note, p 95. This material provides a useful way to make concrete just what it means to inflict punishment. The material can help sharpen understanding of why utilitarian arguments for imposing punishment are often felt to afford an insufficient justification. The material can be assigned as background reading but need not be covered in class.

B. <u>Why Punish?</u>, pp. 101-156.

The material is presented in two parts: first, a number of textual extracts (organized according to the goal of punishment being considered) that directly address and take stands on the general issues, and second, a number of concrete cases and situations. How to deal with this material in class will vary with the tastes of the instructor. Some will prefer to emphasize the first part, taking up the theoretical issues as such, and using the concrete cases of the second part as illustrations. Others will prefer to do the reverse, confronting the cases of the second part as problems to be discussed, with the extracts of the first part being brought in as the instructor and students find them helpful. In the following paragraphs we offer suggestions on how some of the principal cases and extracts might be addressed, whichever approach the instructor adopts.

The three statutory statements of purpose (p. 102) vary considerably. Students should note the differences. Note especially the emphasis on social protection in the New York provision, with no reference to desert. In contrast, the California provision states that the only purpose of imprisonment is punishment (presumably independent of its utilitarian effect), and it emphasizes uniformity and proportionality to the seriousness of the offense, with no direct mention of social protection or other utilitarian goals per se. Are these differences important? How helpful is it for the legislature to set forth the purposes of criminal punishment? What happens when the purposes conflict?

1. Perspectives on Punishment (textual discussions), pp. 102-35.

Why should any defendant ever be punished, under any circumstances? Consider the following:

Case 1. Two business partners - - Honest and Corrupt - - are driving to meet a client. Corrupt decides to kill Honest and does so, in order to get sole control over the profits of the business. Is it justified to punish Corrupt? The answer seems an obvious "yes,", but why?

The first problem, perhaps, is whether punishment requires any special justification. Case 1 is clearly a murder, and the law specifies a punishment for murder. In a democracy, is that enough of a justification? Of course, we often criticize particular laws or social institutions as unfair; implicitly, we recognize that laws must have some justification, apart from the fact that a majority of the people supported them. In other words, we are looking for a substantive and not just a procedural or institutional justification for a particular law; we are questioning whether it was wise or just to have adopted it.

The need for substantive justification becomes particularly pressing in connection with punishment, which entails the deliberate infliction of suffering and stigma on an individual member of the community. How is society justified in choosing to inflict pain on one of its members? This is the subject of the various readings excerpted in this section. Each of the traditional justifications is worth detailed examination.

a. Retribution, pp. 102-15.

The notion advanced by Kant and Morris seems to be that punishment is good, good in itself, just because the defendant deserves it, and not because good consequences will follow from punishing the guilty. See especially Kant's island example (top of p. 103, last 8 lines).

This conception of retribution should be distinguished from justifications of punishment that may seem retributivist but really are not because they find the justification in some social good that will be produced by punishing the guilty. The Moore excerpt at p. 107 lays this out, but it can be helpful to ask students to state and compare each of the justifications of punishment given here; i.e., that of Kant (p. 102), Stephen (p. 104), the Royal Commission (p. 104), Feinberg (p. 105) and Durkheim (p. 106).

Turning to retribution, properly so called, Moore's variation on the Chaney case (p. 115) shows how plausible a retributive response can be in a particular situation. Many students will agree that the defendant rapist should be punished, even if no possible deterrent or incapacitative purpose could not be served by the punishment. But why? Moore argues (p. 115) that such intuitive responses themselves go some distance toward justifying retributive punishment. Is that persuasive?

Morris argues that punishment serves to restore an equivalence, to erase an unfair advantage (pp. 108-10). Does this make sense? Consider the following:

> Case 2. The defendant steals $10,000. What punishment should be imposed? Wouldn't a $10,000 fine be sufficient to erase the advantage? Presumably, the fine must be adjusted to take account of the probabilities of apprehension: If the defendant can commit such a crime five times and be caught only once, then a $50,000 fine would be necessary to erase the advantage. But this still is not the proper punishment, is it? Such a punishment simply leaves the defendant indifferent between committing or not committing the crime. Don't we want to make sure that he doesn't commit it? And if so, doesn't this require a punishment that will be more than sufficient to erase the advantage?

> Case 3. Suppose that the defendant has tortured his victim before killing him. What would be the proper punishment? Wouldn't the death penalty be insufficient? Kant says (p. 103, middle of last ¶) that the death of the criminal "must be kept entirely free from all mistreatment." But why? If Kant is serious about this limitation, doesn't imprisonment itself become suspect? In any event, if equivalence is required, is there any logical basis for Kant's limitation?

Discussion of such cases should make clear that erasing the defendant's advantage, or reestablishing equivalence, can lead to an intuitively insufficient or intuitively excessive punishment. If we are not really paying the defendant back, or redressing the balance, then why should we feel obliged to punish the defendant at all (apart from questions of pragmatic consequences such as deterrence)? Consider one further problem with the notion of redressing the balance:

> Case 4. The defendant, a young man, unemployed, the product of a broken home and alcoholic parents, steals a watch from a wealthy banker whom he encounters on the street. Should the defendant be punished? If so, is the reason for punishment that the defendant has acquired a "unfair advantage?" What assumptions are necessary in order for Morris's argument to hold?

Note that at the outset Morris says "let us suppose that men are constituted roughly as they now are" (p. 109, 2d full ¶). The assumption seems innocuous, but what departures from social reality may enter through the word "roughly"? On this point, see especially the Murphy article, p. 110.

Cases 2-4 illustrate some of the difficulties of accepting retribution, if that term implies an <u>obligation</u> to punish, regardless of social consequences. But then, what social goals justify punishment. Deterrence, reform (rehabilitation) and incapacitation should be considered.

The <u>Mackie</u> excerpt (p. 113) is a strong denial of the justice of purely retributive punishment. To Moore's claims based on the intuitions most of us share, his answer is that these are "sentiments that have grown up and are sustained partly through bilogical processes, and partly through analogous sociological ones." In short, anthropology rather than morality explains our retributive impulses. What do the students think of these opposing viewpoints?

> b. <u>Prevention</u>, pp. 115-25.

How can we determine how much punishment is appropriate? If the purpose and justification of punishment is to deter either the offender (special deterrence) or the population in general (general deterrence), then what punishment should be imposed in the following cases:

> Case 5. The defendant, a chronic alcoholic, kills his wife in a drunken rage. While awaiting trial, he is completely cured of his alcohol problems, and shows all evidence of an ability to lead an

exemplary life. How much punishment is justified here, for special deterrence? For general deterrence? Even if the defendant should receive some prison time, is this an appropriate case for life imprisonment? In this case, special deterrence would seem to warrant a short prison term, at most. If the defendant were to receive a longer term for a general deterrence, he is being made to suffer, in order to deter others. In effect, he is being "used merely as a means to promote some other good" (Kant, p. 102, last ¶). Is this fair?

Case 6. Suppose that it is extremely difficult for the telephone company to detect and catch individuals who deposit counterfeit coins into a pay phone. The telephone company is losing millions of dollars each year because of this kind of fraud. The legislature accordingly passes a statute providing for twenty years in prison for anyone caught using a counterfeit coin in a pay phone. The defendant is caught using such a coin to make a 25¢ call. How much punishment is justified? Would a twenty-year sentence be fair? Why not? Under which, if any, of the statutory statements of purpose (p. 102) would a twenty-year sentence be problematic?

Discussion should bring out the difficulty of treating deterrence (or related public safety goals) as the sole justification for punishment. Such a policy can lead to punishment wholly out of proportion to desert. The New York statute, without any proportionality requirement, provides no basis for objecting to a twenty-year sentence in Case 6. The MPC formulation indicates the importance of considering the seriousness of the offense. (The California statute even appears to make this the exclusive criterion).

Are deterrent sanctions effective, and if so, when? The answer depends in part on the extent to which potential criminal offenders respond in rational ways to the threat of criminal sanctions. (See p. 117.) Are the street hustlers described by Fleisher (p. 118) behaving rationally? (apparently they are - at least from a very short run perspective. They seem to select targets based in part on the chances of getting caught). But will increases in the severity of punishment or conventional strategies to increase the chances of arrest influence the behavior of offenders like these? What about the offender who rationally pursues "irrational" preferences - in the sense that he prefers death or severe punishment to accepting the humiliation of enduring disrespect (Gilligan, pp. 117-18)? What part of overall criminal behavior reflects patterns like these rather than a rational response to conventional conceptions of self-interest?

When deterrence is an appropriate goal, <u>what form</u> should a deterrence sanction take? The contemporary debate over shaming penalties (pp. 120-22) poses this problem in an especially controversial way.

- - Is there an intuitive revulsion against the idea of shaming penalties? But is that revulsion misplaced if the sting of a shaming penalty can satisfy society's retributive urges and give us the same deterrent effect at lower fiscal cost and with a less destructive impact on the offender (Kahan, p. 121)?
- - Could a shaming penalty ever backfire? Consider especially the Massaro and Gilligan excerpts, p. 121. If it is dangerous in some cases to undermine an offenders self-esteem, can we identify the kinds of cases in which shaming penalties won't present this risk?
- - Are child molesters, prostitution customers or alcoholic drunk drivers good candidates for shaming penalties? Note that these sorts of violations often occur precisely <u>because</u> the offenders in question already suffer from diminished self-esteem and feelings of shame. Which kinds of offenders would be better candidates for shaming penalties?

   c. <u>Rehabilitation</u>, pp. 125-30; together with
   d. <u>Incapacitation</u>, pp. 130-35

Both reform and incapacitation raise similar problems:

<u>Case 7.</u> The defendant, an eighteen-year-old, is arrested for shoplifting a candy bar from a drugstore. Background investigation shows that the defendant is a drug user and has frequently been involved in fights and gang activity. Probation officers conclude that to effectively "rehabilitate" this prisoner will require at least ten or fifteen years of incarceration and treatment. Similarly, in order to effectively incapacitate this defendant from committing future crimes (including shoplifting) he should be incarcerated at least until he reaches the age of thirty-five. Is a fifteen-year sentence justified?

Even if empirical evidence could establish the value of a fifteen-year sentence for rehabilitation or incapacitation (and could clearly overcome the problem of false positives, p. 133, before note 3), would a fifteen-year sentence for stealing a candy bar be fair?

Again, the social protection rationales appear inadequate to justify punishment. Some link between punishment and retributive notions of seriousness or desert seems essential to accord with our intuitive notions of when punishment is fair. But, as previously discussed, retribution is problematic as well. Does this mean that there is no satisfactory justification for punishment? That it is not fair to punish, even in the case of a cold-blooded killing (Case 1)?

Part of the answer may lie in seeing that retribution can be used in two senses: (a) It may imply a moral obligation to punish blameworthy conduct, regardless of the social purposes that such punishment might serve. (b) Alternatively, it may imply a moral obligation not to punish when conduct is not blameworthy or when punishment would be out of proportion to the blameworthiness. Kant advocates both of these propositions -- (a) in his island example, bottom of p. 103, and (b) in stating at p. 102, last 3 lines, that the offender "must first be found guilty and punishable" before any consideration is given to the utility of this punishment."

Students should note that we can accept (b) without necessarily accepting (a). Perhaps we cannot accept retribution as the aim of punishment (a), but we can accept retribution as a constraint upon what we can justifiably do in pursuit of other social goals (b). In this view, both social protection and desert are necessary conditions of just punishment, but neither alone is a sufficient condition; in other words, the general justifying aim of punishment is social protection, but this aim can be pursued only to the extent that retributive boundaries are respected. This is the "mixed theory" that Moore discusses at p. 114, his first ¶. The usefulness of this framework should be tested against the various hypothetical cases considered during the class hour, and against the other cases considered throughout the course.

Note the problematic empirical foundations of rehabilitation. But students often accept too quickly the claim that with respect to rehabilitation, "nothing works"? How good is the empirical evidence supporting this view? Why do ordinary citizens accept that premise so uncritically? (Consider the Mair and von Hirsch/Maher excerpts, pp. 127-130.)

Incapacitation is one goal that hardly seems to require empirical support -- it seems obvious that an offender in prison cannot commit more crimes. (Not strictly true -- he can assault guards and other prisoners, but "a thug in prison can't shoot your sister" (p. 131, lines 1-2)). Nonetheless, is money spent to incarcerate offenders really a good investment? Have we reached the point where the cost of imprisoning new offenders, especially long term imprisonment for property and drug offenders, exceeds the social cost of the crimes they would commit if free? (See p. 131, Note 1.) Even if an incapacitation strategy yields net crime-control benefits, could we achieve even greater crime-control gains by investing the same money in crime prevention through education, drug treatment and health care for young children and pregnant women? (See p. 134, Note 4).

     2. <u>Case Studies</u>, pp. 135-56.

The cases in this section provide an opportunity for students to apply the principles of punishment in the context of both unusual and rather typical cases. The material indicates the difficulty of legal decision-making when knowledge is uncertain and when equally desirable goals prove irreconcilable in practice. It also introduces the problem of designing appropriate institutions for legal decision-making under such circumstances.

<u>Dudley and Stephens</u>, p. 135. Should the defendants be punished? Did they do anything that they should not have done? Note the various possibilities: (a) They should never have killed the boy under any circumstances. (b) They could have killed him if they had waited long enough to make certain that help would not arrive; note that the court says there was some chance of rescue. (c) They could have killed someone, if he had been selected by a fair procedure (suppose that all the passengers had agreed to draw straws in order to determine which one was to be sacrificed); compare the American case (<u>Holmes</u>) discussed at the top of p. 138.

Which of these is the court's ground of decision? Which, if any, of them is sensible? It is arguable, of course, that the defendants did nothing wrong. To have waited longer would have exposed everyone to a greater risk that all the passengers would die. To have drawn straws might have meant that one of the stronger men, with a chance of survival, would have to be killed, while Richard Parker, who was about to die anyway, would be temporarily spared. If it is proper to take action to maximize the saving of lives (even at the cost of sacrificing the individual interests of one passenger for the benefit of the group), then the defendants' action is arguably justified.

     Even if the defendants should not have done what they did, for any of the reasons indicated, is that sufficient reason to justify punishing them for a crime? Note the court's statement that the prisoners were "subject to terrible temptation" (p. 136, last ¶) and the judges' admission (p. 139, 9 lines from the bottom) that they have "set up a standard we cannot reach ourselves." How can the judges declare the behavior to be criminal when they admit they themselves might have done the same? Is this fair to the defendants? What can it accomplish? Note that the sentence was commuted to six months' imprisonment. Does that make the result more palatable? Or, does it make the conviction and sentence utterly pointless -- how can such a mild sentence serve any purpose at all?

The discussion should make clear that in considering whether to punish any particular defendant, two questions are involved: (a) Is the conduct justified -- socially desirable; (b) if not, is the defendant's undesirable conduct nonetheless excusable. Both justification and excuse are examined in detail throughout the course.

<u>Bergman</u>, p. 140. Students should be clear about the specific offenses to which Bergman pleaded guilty, the maximum sentences available (five years and $10,000 for conspiracy to defraud and three years and $5,000 for filing the false tax return), and the defendant's personal background. How does the court justify the sentence imposed (four months in prison)? Are the court's reasons convincing?

With respect to <u>rehabilitation</u>, the court says that this can never be the ground for a sentence of confinement. Why not? Problems concerning rehabilitation can be covered at this point if they have not previously been discussed. With respect to <u>incapacitation</u>, the court says that the defendant is most unlikely to commit any offenses in the future. Is this so clear? Is there any data to indicate the likelihood of recidivism for a defendant in Bergman's situation? How do we know that he might not engage in some sort of fraud or dishonest dealing if he is released after only a short prison term? Does the court mean that a need for incapacitation cannot be based simply on speculation; that in effect the burden of producing data on the incapacitation question is on the prosecution?

With respect to <u>general deterrence</u>, is this likely to be effective for these types of crimes? Intuitively, one is inclined to think so. Is there really any evidence on the deterrence point? Why is the court less insistent on data with respect to deterrence than it is with respect to incapacitation? Is <u>retribution</u> playing a role here? Note the observations on p. 142, first full ¶, making explicit that it is. Retribution in what sense? The court implies that it is imposing a punishment <u>beyond</u> what is required for deterrence (and the other social protection goals). Isn't this unjust? Or, can we say that by not "depreciat[ing] the seriousness of the [offense]" (p. 142, line 5) we are really pursuing, indirectly but significantly, the goal of effective deterrence? (See Andenaes on the moralizing effect, p. 122, and Robinson & Darley, p. 123).

Assuming the need for some significant punishment for deterrence and retribution, what is the appropriate sentence? Why did the court reject the "constructive" sanctions proposed by the defense (p. 142, 2d full ¶)? Aren't they more beneficial and less costly for society than simply putting the defendant in prison? If so, why reject them? Do the prison sentences indicate retribution for its own sake? Or is there a sense in which retribution is necessary in order to promote effective deterrence? (See again the Andenaes excerpt, p. 122).

If something more painful than the "alternative" sanctions is required, why not consider a big fine? Note that the maximum fine available in the Bergman case was only $15,000. Would it make more sense to authorize very large fines, so that imprisonment could be avoided in cases like Bergman? Or is incarceration appropriate in any event, in order to avoid an unfair disadvantage for the street criminal who cannot pay a large fine? Why can't fines be made large enough to make them just as painful as imprisonment?

Jackson, p. 146. The defendant, a dangerous and incorrigible recidivist, clearly should get a very long sentence, but what is the right term? Is life without parole justified? If so, for what purpose?

Many students will feel that a life term makes sense. Jackson is a far more serious criminal than many who are subject to the recent "three-strikes" statutes described at p. 148, Note 3: Note that the present offense was Jackson's sixth "strike" (!!) and it, like all the previous "strikes," was for armed robbery, not just for any felony (p. 146, 2d ¶ of the opinion). Apparently there were also several other armed robberies on his record, not to mention an attempted murder (p. 148, Note 1). If the "three strikes" approach ever makes sense, Jackson seems a prime candidate for such treatment.

But what, precisely, is the purpose and justification for a life sentence? What are Judge Posner's reservations? Each of the possible rationales can be discussed: retribution? (Compare Posner at p. 147, 2d full ¶.) Incapacitation? Is this really needed after Jackson turns 60 or 70? How will the costs of his incarceration compare to the benefits when Jackson is an elderly man? (See Posner at p. 147, 3d ¶.) Deterrence? Again, what are the real gains (and costs) of adding additional time to the 20- or 30-year sentence that Jackson would otherwise get? (See Posner at p. 147, last 2 ¶'s.)

In the end, what sentence do all the relevant concerns suggest for Jackson? What is the right sentence for a bank robber who has "only" two prior felony convictions, one for unarmed robbery and one for burglary? What about a drug seller with two prior drug felony convictions? Should mandatory minimum sentences be set by statute for such cases (at what level?) or should sentencing in "three strikes" cases be left to the discretion of the sentencing judge?

Problem, p. 148, Note 4. What is the appropriate sentence for this case? For what purpose? Here deterrence appears to call for a substantial prison sentence. But doesn't rehabilitation argue strongly against any prison sentence? Note that in Bergman the social protection objectives were not inconsistent with one another. But here a deterrence sentence is likely to defeat hopes for rehabilitation, and vice versa. With respect to the clash between deterrence and rehabilitation, which goal is more important? Who should make that decision? Does it make sense to leave the choice to individual judges on an ad hoc basis? Concerns about potential inconsistency in how individual judges would resolve such basic policy issues were an important part of the background of the sentencing reform movement explored at pp. 150-56.

Note that assessments of rehabilitative needs may differ too. If the rehabilitation question is important, how can it be decided, when the necessary information remains unclear?

Sentencing reform; Federal Sentencing Guidelines, pp. 150-56

The preceding discussions will have focused primarily on the substantive problem of determining the right punishment for each of the cases considered. Procedurally, the answer in a traditional sentencing system is that the decision is made (with few constraints) by the trial judge alone. Typically the appellate court lacks the power to set aside a sentence, even when it thinks that the sentence is far too severe. See Jackson, at p. 146, last ¶. Is this a fair and sensible way to organize the sentencing system?

Questions of procedure and institutional organization have been considered previously, in Chapter 1. We do not permit a single judge to decide guilt: That judgment must be made (if the defendant so desires) by a jury, and even the jury's judgment is not final, but is subject to searching examination on appeal. Why should the sentencing power be left to the unchecked discretion of the judge? What problems does this arrangement present? Students can consider - - by recalling the cases just discussed - - the possibilities for widely divergent views about the merits in each case, and the resulting risks of permitting divergent decisions by judges acting independently in individual cases. The specific problems of disparity and arbitrariness are summarized in the Frankel excerpt at p. 151, Note 2.

This background of disaffection with the traditional discretionary approach has spawned the determinate sentencing movement described at p. 152, Note 3. "Determinate" regimes include those eliminating parole, those imposing mandatory minimums set by legislation, and most importantly, sentencing guidelines set by an administrative agency. Guidelines systems have now been adopted in many states, and they have become a crucial part of criminal practice in the federal courts.

An overview of the federal sentencing guidelines (p. 152, Note 4) is useful to introduce students to this increasingly important area of practice. In addition, much of the course will be concerned not only with doctrines that determine the difference between guilt and innocence, but with doctrines that determine the kind and degree of guilt for defendants who are undoubtedly guilty of something. The latter doctrines are in effect concerned with an aspect of sentencing, and it is important for students to have, as background, some familiarity with the way that a finding of guilt of a particular offense (in itself a somewhat abstract conclusion) is translated into an actual, concrete punishment.

Johnson, p. 153, gives students an opportunity to see the way in which the federal sentencing guidelines system operates in a concrete case. The process of determining sentence proceeds step-by-step through a determination of the seriousness of the offense, with various adjustments up and down (p. 153, last ¶), and once the offense level is determined, the sentence range (a very narrow one) is drawn from a grid that provides a different sentence range for each offense seriousness level, depending on the prior record of the offender. (Johnson was a first offender, so this last aspect of the grid was not at issue.)

Is this whole idea too mechanical and inhumane? Does it make sense to sentence simply by the numbers, rather than fitting the particular punishment to the infinitely various circumstances of each individual offender? Or does the guideline approach provide a useful way to bring order and consistency to the resolution of recurring issues?

Johnson also makes clear two respects in which the guidelines retain some degree of flexibility. First, the judge can "depart" from the offense level indicated by specifically authorized guideline adjustments, provided that the statutory test for departures (§3553(b), p. 154, last full ¶) is met. Secondly, the sentencing judge's guideline calculation and the reasonableness of any departure decision are subject to appellate review. (Compare Jackson, p. 146, denying appellate review in the tradiitonal system.)

Was the departure in this case justified? Johnson's family situation certainly appears to call for some moderation of the sentence that would otherwise be imposed; a prison sentence would inflict great harm on the five young children who are dependent on Johnson's care (p. 154, indented quote). Through the impact on the children, society itself would suffer serious direct and indirect consequences as well. But according to what theory of punishment should Johnson get a lower sentence?

Traditional purposes (retribution, deterrence, etc.) do not seem to suggest any reason why Johnson's family situation is at all relevant. Yet the intuition remains strong that the family situation is relevant. One possible reason may be that deterrence, incapacitation, rehabilitation, etc., do not exhaust the relevant utilitarian considerations; harm to Johnson's family may be a cost that should be factored in.

On a retributive theory, does justice require that Johnson get the sentence she deserves, even if this means inflicting serious injury on her innocent dependents and on the rest of society? Compare Johnson's sentence, six months home detention, to the 27 month prison sentence imposed on her co-defendant Purvis, whose offense conduct and prior record was essentially identical to Johnson's (p. 156, Note 2). Was Purvis a victim of sentencing disparity?

If family circumstances like Johnson's do justify a lower sentence, what result in Problem 3(b), p. 156. Is this family circumstance (pregnancy) unusual enough?

What result in Problem 3(a), p. 156? Is it fair for a white collar defendant supporting a family to avoid a prison sentence that would be imposed on an otherwise identical defendant who is poor? Or will a sentence reduction for family circumstances just perpetuate class discrimination in sentencing outcomes?

C. <u>What to Punish?</u>, pp. 156-171.

This section makes for a provocative class, but in a one-semester course we recommend skipping these pages in order to ensure that adequate time is available for the difficult substantive criminal law material that follows.

Those with time and interest to cover this material can begin with <u>Bowers</u>, p. 158. It may make sense to put aside the doctrinal issues specific to American constitutional law and simply ask whether a statute punishing consensual sodomy is morally justified. If the Court is right that such a statute is constitutionally permissible (is there a persuasive distinction between <u>Bowers</u> on the one hand and cases like <u>Roe v. Wade</u> or <u>Meyer v. Nebraska</u> on the other??), we still need to face the question whether it is nonetheless right for England, Australia or an American state to enact such a statute and to punish consenting adults who violate it.

Is past social custom or present opinion enough to provide a <u>justification</u>, as distinguished from a mere description of existing social practice? Shouldn't individuals have an intrinsic right to choose their own way of life, except to the extent that their activities harm others? Many students will likely feel that the requirement of social harm makes a statute like that in <u>Bowers</u> intrinsically unjustified. But what constitutes social harm? Is there an objective way to determine when the activities of consenting adults cause indirect harm to others? See the Harcourt excerpt, p. 166, Note 6. What, precisely, is the social harm on which Lord Devlin (pp. 163-65) attempts to rely? Isn't it circular to define "society" as a community of ideas (p. 164, 2d ¶), if those ideas are not universally shared by its inhabitants?

Even if there is no logically tight objection to laws that prohibit various forms of activity between consenting adults, what are the practical barriers to the effectiveness of such laws? What are their distinctive pragmatic costs? See the Kadish excerpt at pp. 167-69.

Chapter Three
Defining Criminal Conduct

This chapter develops the principle elements of just punishment -- notably, culpability, proportionality and legality. The culpability section (pp. 173-278) is best taught straight through. The proportionality section (pp. 278-290) ordinarily can be skipped in a one-semester course. The legality section (pp. 290-312) considers problems of vagueness and strict construction which appear in other forms throughout the course; it too can be omitted if time constraints require.

B. Culpability, pp. 173-278

In introducing this material, it may be helpful to provide a summary of the essential elements of a criminal case. Traditionally, the elements are broken down, see MPC § 1.13 (9), into the forbidden conduct, attendant circumstances and a result, each accompanied by some level of intentionality -- purpose or knowledge, recklessness or negligence. More fundamentally, and of particular importance in Chapter 3, the law is concerned with establishing what each of these elements means and with the question when or whether they must be proved. (No one of these elements is invariably required for criminal liability.)

It may also be helpful to comment on where the principles of criminal liability come from. Many states have enacted comprehensive codes (often patterned on the MPC) that specify the relevant principles of interpretation and provide operational definitions of all (or nearly all) of the important terms used. But in other states the "penal code" is still a collection of archaic common law terms and provisions for punishment that sometimes lack a definition of operative terms ("conspiracy shall be punished by five years in prison"). In such states interpretation usually requires heavy reliance on precedent and on traditional common law principles of interpretation. Chapter 3 is devoted to developing the elements of that tradition and to illustrating the application of the corresponding MPC principles. With respect to each of the cases and problems in this chapter, students should not only seek to understand the result under the law of the particular jurisdiction, but should regularly refer to the appendix of the Casebook in order to work out the resolution of the issues under the MPC.

1. <u>Actus Reus</u> -- <u>Culpable Conduct</u>, pp. 173-203.

   a. <u>Positive Actions</u>, pp. 173-82

This class develops the meaning of the voluntary act requirement and the reasons for it.

<u>Martin</u>, p. 173. What are the elements required by statute? Are they satisfied here? Students should note that the required conduct (the defendant must "appear" and "manifest") and the attendant circumstance ("while intoxicated") are all satisfied here. To reverse the conviction, the court must read into the statute a requirement of voluntariness. Where does this requirement come from? No legislative history is referred to. The court is apparently drawing on common sense and the common law tradition.

What is the reason for requiring that the act be voluntary? Note the MPC explanation, pp. 176-77, indented quote. Is this persuasive? Aren't there some situations in which involuntary movements can be indirectly deterred? (Why can't a defendant avoid situations in which he might be compelled to commit an involuntary movement? Martin could have avoided drinking at all.) Is the primary problem that the law cannot hope to deter, or does the voluntariness requirement spring more fundamentally from a sense of unfairness about punishing someone for a particular act that she had no choice about committing? But why is it unfair if she could have avoided putting herself in the general situation?

How would <u>Martin</u> come out under the MPC? The language of § 2.01(1) needs to be examined carefully. Doesn't Martin's conduct <u>include</u> a voluntary act (e.g. his use of loud and profane language)? One answer may be that loud and profane speech by a drunk person is itself an involuntary act. Is this a possible argument under the MPC? (§ 2.01(2)(d) suggests not). Then would the Code permit conviction in <u>Martin</u> (his conduct does "include" a voluntary act)? Or should the MPC be interpreted (despite its language) to mean that <u>all</u> the required acts must be voluntary? Consider the following:

> <u>Case 1.</u> The defendant, in a bar, drinks seven or eight martinis. As the drinks begin to take effect, he chooses to go out on the street. Weaving and swaying, he gets to the street, then starts to lose his balance, feels very nauseous and finally vomits on the street. Would the MPC permit a conviction here? Would the Alabama court? Note that now the defendant's act in manifesting his drunken

condition (i.e. vomiting) would have to be considered an involuntary act. But his appearance in public is perfectly voluntary. Under those circumstances, doesn't a conviction seem fair, even though one of the proscribed acts occurred involuntarily? (Note that enforcement of public drunkenness laws will not be very effective if the court is compelled by a voluntariness requirement to reverse a conviction in a case like Case 1.) Presumably the Alabama court would convict, and the same result could be reached under the MPC. Thus, it appears sufficient for a conviction that the conduct include one voluntary act. But then, why is the conviction in Martin reversed?

Case 2. Decina, p. 179, Note 4. Is Decina's conduct while driving voluntary or involuntary? Presumably the latter. Does he have a defense against conviction, on the ground that his conduct includes an involuntary act? Presumably it is sufficient for a conviction that his conduct, though partly involuntary, also includes a voluntary act -- his decision to drive in the first place.

Given the Decina type of analysis, can we say that Martin's drunken appearance is not really involuntary, because it resulted from the earlier voluntary decision to drink in the first place? Most students will see that we cannot turn back the clock in Martin, as we can in Decina, because of the way the elements of the offense are defined; Decina was driving recklessly before his involuntary seizure occurred, but Martin did not "appear in any public place" until forced to do so.

A more perplexing aspect of Martin is that although the defendant's appearance was involuntary, his use of profane language was not. Since his conduct includes a voluntary act, why is the conviction reversed? Was it sound for the court to conclude that the appearance itself must always be voluntary? The court may have been influenced by the fact that Martin was taken from his own home by the police. Would the court insist on a voluntary appearance under other circumstances? What if Martin had caused a disturbance in a bar and had been ejected by a bouncer, so that he was responsible for his being forced out into a public place? It can be seen that the common law voluntariness requirement, though very important, is a quite narrow one. It is satisfied if any one of the proscribed acts is committed voluntarily. (But Martin might still have a defense in the preceding hypothetical if after his involuntary appearance, his only manifestation of a drunken condition were also involuntary, e.g. vomiting).

Newton, p. 175. How would this case be decided under the MPC? If the jury believes Newton's testimony, his reflex reaction presumably would qualify as an involuntary act under MPC § 2.01(2)(a). Thus involuntariness can be established not only by overwhelming external force, as in Martin, but also by claiming internal reactions that may be less obvious and harder to refute. (Incidentally, which side has the burden of proving the voluntariness or involuntariness of the act? Presumably, under Patterson (p. 38) and Martin v. Ohio (p. 48, Note 4), the prosecution must prove this required element of the offense beyond a reasonable doubt).

How far does the notion of an involuntary act extend? Does the MPC give an answer? Note that § 2.01 does not define what a voluntary action is, although subsection 2(d) seems to imply a definition. Consider the following cases:

> Case 3. Newton alleges that he has a deep psychological aversion to the police. Due to unfortunate childhood experiences, he completely loses control of himself when stopped or ordered about by a police officer. Psychologists support his claim that under such circumstances he cannot control himself and if a weapon is available he will uncontrollably reach for it and shoot to kill. Is Newton's action voluntary under these circumstances? Apparently under the MPC it is, because it is "a product of the effort or determination of the actor." In the common law tradition, the same result would be reached: Note Lord Dennings statement (p. 177, Note 2): "nor is an act to be regarded as an involuntary act simply because the doer could not control his impulse to do it."

To consider Newton's act voluntary in Case 3 involves an odd usage of language. Why should Case 3 be treated any differently from the Newton case itself? Aren't both defendants are equally undeterrable? Are there differences in moral culpability? Perhaps, but if you really believe the testimony, moral culpability seems more or less absent in both. Is there any difference from the viewpoint of incapacitation or rehabilitation? The person who has uncontrollable muscle spasms when shot in the abdomen (the actual Newton case) poses no special problem for society; the defense raised in Case 3 suggests that the defendant poses a serious threat (all the more serious if you are fully persuaded that the defense claims are true). If there is a defense in Case 3, it would presumably need to be a more limited and qualified one than the automatic exclusion of liability in the case of involuntary acts.

Case 4. Hypnosis, p. 178. Does the hypnotized subject meet the MPC standards for an involuntary act? Is it clear that "the law cannot hope to deter" the action of someone under hypnosis? Numerous experiments have shown, as the MPC commentators appear to admit (p. 178, indented quote), that "the hypnotized subject will not follow suggestions which are repugnant to him." If the hypnotized subject is in fact subject to the influence of consequences, why shouldn't he or she be punished? Is the "dependency and helplessness" (p. 178) simply a symbolic matter? Does punishment offend our sensibilities simply because we are fooled about the nature of hypnosis?

Case 5. Cogden, p. 178, Note 2(d). What result under the MPC? Presumably under § 2.01(2)(b), her action is not "voluntary." But is Cogden really "asleep"? She is not randomly tossing and turning in bed; her perceptions are quite acute. (Note the accuracy of her aim.) In law, as Morris says (p. 179), the killing is not regarded as her act at all. But whose act was it? The episode appears impossible to understand, except as a product of Mrs. Cogden's own personality and psychological needs. In terms of the purposes of the criminal law, does the acquittal make sense? (a) Is Mrs. Cogden deterrable? (What might have happened if the night before the killing, Mrs. Cogden had read in the paper the story of a sleepwalker who, after killing a member of her family, had been convicted and executed for the crime?) (b) Does the acquittal make sense in terms of needs for incapacitation? (How does Mr. Cogden feel about the acquittal? What if there is another daughter at home?) In terms of social protection, some restraint and involuntary rehabilitation clearly could serve a useful purpose. (d) Isn't the notion of blameworthiness therefore essential to explain the Cogden result?

Cogden suggests that we normally locate blameworthiness in the operations of the conscious mind. But then why doesn't the blameworthiness requirement pose a barrier to punishment in a case like Case 3? Following the MPC analysis (pp. 176-77), it could be said that Newton in Case 3, like Cogden in Case 5, presents a public health or safety problem calling for a therapy or even custodial commitment, but does not present a problem of correction. The criminal law (and the MPC) apparently remain much influenced by a view of personality under which people are morally responsible for action that is the product of conscious (or habitual, see p. 177 note 2(a)) effort or determination, but are not responsible for actions prompted by the unconscious.

b. <u>Actus Reus</u> -- <u>Omissions</u>, pp. 182-203.

<u>Pope v. State</u>, p. 183. Why was the conviction reversed? Because Pope was neither the parent of the child nor legally responsible for supervision of the minor child as required by the first part of the statute. Then, implicitly, the conviction of physically abusing a child would have been affirmed if Pope was found to be responsible for the supervision of the child. But does this mean that a person can be said to abuse a child by simply refraining from taking any action? That, of course, is what the court is saying. Is there anything wrong with this position conceptually? Does it constitute a fair interpretation of the child abuse statute?

Was the court correct in finding that in the circumstances Pope was not responsible for the supervision of the child? Were the reasons given by the court persuasive? How might a contrary position be argued?

The court concedes that the failure of Pope to protect the child from the insane attack of its parent was morally outrageous. Why should the statute have been drafted as it was, restricting liability to designated persons? The English and American legal tradition is to deny criminal liability if the only fault of a person is that he or she failed to act to prevent criminal harm to another, even if the person could have done so without danger to herself. Is this defensible? Do the incidents described in the Kiesel extract (p. 185, Note 1) suggest otherwise? Do the possible explanations of why people refuse to help another (see the Yaeger extract, p. 186, Note 2) warrant the law's hands off policy? Here the arguments canvassed by Kleinig in the excerpt at p. 187 can appropriately be taken up.

<u>Jones</u>, p. 190. Why is the conviction reversed? Under appropriate instructions, could the defendant be convicted, even in the absence of proof of any act? Note that the court holds a conviction would be possible if the jury finds a legal duty, resulting for example from a contract. Thus, criminal liability does not always require an act, in the sense of some "bodily movement" (MPC § 1.13(2)).

Then why isn't Jones liable? Note that a helpless infant was starving in Jones' house. Why should Jones' liability depend on the existence of a contract? Is the contract important to show Jones' awareness that the baby was in danger? Not really: the medical evidence showed the baby was "shockingly neglected," and for a manslaughter conviction the prosecution presumably had to show that the defendant was or should have been aware of the danger to the child. (More on this in Chapter 5, Homicide).

Suppose that Jones was perfectly well aware that the baby was dying and _purposely_ chose to let it do so. Could she be convicted in the absence of a contract, or other appropriate status relationship? No. But is there any good reason why she should not be liable? Is the argument against conviction in Jones simply that the law as it presently stands does not impose a duty, or is the argument that it would be undesirable for such a generalized duty to be imposed? A variety of possible reasons for rejecting a generalized duty to aid might be cited (students will be helped by the material in the Kleinig exerpt):

a. Priorities: Resources are limited; arguably enforcement should be concentrated on the affirmatively dangerous individual rather than the one who is merely insensitive or uncharitable.

b. Vagueness: Citizens might have difficulty knowing when they were obliged to act. Query whether the common law standard in Jones or the MPC standard, §2.01(3), is any clearer.

c. Overreaction: If there is a generalized duty to rescue, victims might be overwhelmed by the aid of hundreds of rescuers all obliged to act by the criminal law. But does the common law position avoid this problem?

d. Laissez-faire: In some political theory, the role of the government is limited to preventing positive harms; it is not the government's business to encourage citizens to help one another. At an extreme it might even be argued that it is not even desirable for government to do so: If the welfare of society is maximized by the actions of individuals each pursuing their own personal self-interest, and if free market forces (the invisible hand) are expected to guide these selfish efforts to maximize the welfare of society as a whole, then compelling altruistic assistance might be viewed as "inefficient." What assumptions are necessary to justify this highly individualistic, laissez-faire conception of the role of government?

e. Where do you draw the line? If there is a generalized duty to rescue, then is the wealthy person required to give his money to prevent starvation of a beggar? For that matter, is even a person of very modest means required to give the beggar what little money he has?

Which of such arguments, if any, is applicable in the Pope case previously discussed? In the Jones case? Would it have been too expensive for Jones to feed the baby? Note that she could simply have called the welfare department; she could even have called collect. Note that European statutes commonly impose a duty to rescue upon those who can do so without serious risk to themselves. Similar statutes are rare in the U.S., but the Vermont statute (p. 189, Note 1) provides an appropriate example. Are the above arguments sufficient to justify rejection of such statutes? Consider:

> Case 1. The defendant is walking through a park when he sees a stranger drowning in the middle of a lake. If the defendant is known to be a good swimmer, is there any good argument against requiring him to rescue the stranger? Suppose that a life preserver is nearby so that the defendant need not even jump in the water, but simply must toss the life preserver and pull the stranger in. What accounts for the refusal of our law to impose a duty to rescue in this situation? Is it enough that the rescue effort might render the defendant late for an important appointment? For a trivial appointment? Can the common law preference for individualistic self-reliance be justified in the case of this kind? Don't we also believe that "no man is an island..."

If a duty to rescue in Case 1 is too broad or too burdensome for the common law mind, what would be wrong with a statute imposing a duty to rescue whenever the defendant can do it without any inconvenience to himself. Even such a duty, much more limited than that imposed by the Vermont statute, would have obliged Jones to act. Why does the common law (and the MPC) refuse to go even this far?

Given the common law approach, liability depends on application of the standard indicated in Jones. Is the MPC standard any different? Note that the vagueness of §2.01(3) seems simply to leave the matter to preexisting common law principles. Application of these principles to a variety of cases should be considered. To what extent are such problems as vagueness and overreaction equally present under the common law approach?

> Case 2. Beardsley, p. 194, Note 1. How would this case be decided today? Would a modern court be less offended by the notion that Beardsley should be treated "as if" he were the deceased's husband. But the defendant was not in fact the deceased's husband; would a conviction deprive the defendant of fair warning? Is there some other common law category that could be invoked here? There is apparently no common law duty of one lover to another. Could the

court imply such a duty? What about the fact that the woman was a weekend guest in Beardsley's home? Shouldn't there be a duty of homeowner to guest?

Case 3. Suppose that your roommate falls in the bath tub and knocks himself out, blood gushing from an open wound in his head. Can you let him bleed to death? Or do you have a duty, as his roommate, to come to his assistance?

Apparently, a common law category such as invitee or co-occupant could provide a rubric for liability based on a status relationship. But the question is: would a court treat those kinds of statuses as sufficient? Jones itself appears to give an answer: the baby was a guest in Jones's home, but that status relationship was insufficient. On that theory there is no liability in Cases 2 & 3; Beardsley would come out the same even today. Once again, is there any sound reason for such a result? Is Oliver p. 195, Note 3) contrary to Jones and Beardsley?

The pool example (pp. 196-97) provides an opportunity for testing the students' understanding of the common law categories. Adam surely has a duty to act. But what if Adam thought the child was a good swimmer, and afterwards, knowing that the child was about to drown, chose not to come to her aid? A murder prosecution based on Adam's act of pushing would fail because he did not have a culpable mental state accompanying that act (assume for this purpose that Adam's "reckless" running was not dangerous enough to make him criminally negligent with respect to the risk of killing someone). He could be convicted of murder or manslaughter only if it were established that he had a duty to rescue the child after she had fallen in the water. Could such a duty be based upon his earlier act of innocently or playfully pushing the child in? Consider Jones v. State, p. 196, Note a. If so, can Tina be held on the same basis?

Note that the requirement of linking each act or omission to the accompanying mental state gives the omissions rule much of its significance. It is always possible to find that at some point in time the defendant committed an act (in the sense of some bodily movement). But if the necessary mental state can be shown only at a later time, when the defendant does not carry out any bodily movement, then it becomes crucial to show that he was under a duty to act at that later time. (The solution proposed by Professor Smith at 197 may profitably be analyzed at this point.)

A bystander in the pool situation, of course, would not be liable under common law principles. Could he be liable under the Vermont or the German statutes (p. 189, Note 1)? Presumably yes, at least if the necessary aid was not provided by others. Does the common law approach avoid problems of ambiguity or the potential for imposing the duty to rescue on an excessive number of rescuers? Note that even under the narrow common law tests, Adam and Tina both might have a duty to rescue. As a practical matter which danger is greater: That persons in peril will be overwhelmed by too many rescuers or that persons in peril will be ignored?

Examination of the euthanasia problem raised in Barber (p. 198) and the materials that follow probably will require at least part of an additional class hour. The material can be profitably explored by student reading and discussion outside of class, but if time permits, careful examination in class is worthwhile.

Barber v. Superior Court, p. 198. Does the physician who pulls the plug commit an act or is his behavior simply an omission? Students should see why it makes a difference in determining his liability. What is the court's holding? If the cutting off of "heroic" life-support measures is not an affirmative act but rather an omission (as the court holds), then isn't it also an omission to disconnect a tube providing intravenous fluid to a comatose patient. (Apparently the court agrees that its reasoning must carry it that far.) If pulling out tubes that provide ordinary nutrition and fluids is merely an omission, why doesn't the physician have a duty to provide such ordinary, inexpensive life-sustaining assistance? What if the patient still has some (though a small) chance of survival? With respect to the scope of the doctor's duty, consider the following:

Case 4. A is dying. If he can be attached to very expensive life-sustaining equipment, he can live another two days. Is it murder if a doctor refuses to attach him to such a machine? The answer may depend upon whether the doctor has a duty to aid. If the doctor has no duty to aid in a "hopeless" case (see Williams, p. 200, first full ¶), refusal to attach A to the machine might not violate the doctor's duty to aid. But under Williams' analysis wouldn't this conclusion hold true even if there were no competing use for the machine?

Case 5. Same situation, but a previous doctor has already attached A to the machine. If the doctor now decides to unhook A, is he guilty of murder? Why is this situation any different from Case 4?

<u>Case 6.</u> Same situation as Case 5: A is attached to the machine and has at best only two days to live. The doctor learns that patient B has a chance of complete recovery, but only if he can be attached to the machine immediately. There is no other machine available. If the doctor detaches the machine from A in order to give it to B, has he murdered A? More specifically, does the doctor, in detaching A, commit an "act" or an omission, and in the latter case does his omission violate a duty to act? If the doctor has committed a culpable act or omission he might (or might not) have an affirmative justification. Can we avoid the difficult choice of evils problem by deciding that the doctor has not committed an act? If so, then what result if the doctor detaches the machine from A in order to give it to C, a more wealthy patient whose survival chances are poorer than A's?

The decision whether to characterize the physician's conduct as an "act" or an "omission" can appear arbitrary. But shouldn't that decision depend on the reasons why we require an act in the first place? If act is required because of our desire to focus on those who cause positive ill effects on others, then the decision in <u>Barber</u>, <u>Airedale NHS Trust</u> (p. 199), and the position of Professor Williams (p. 200) make sense. But then suppose some intruder disconnects a patient's life-sustaining machine in order to witness the suffering and death of the patient. Would we have to say that the intruder has committed a mere omission? If our reasons for requiring an act are to confirm evidence of mens rea, and to confirm that the defendant is a person prepared to <u>act on</u> his thoughts (see p. 181, Note 2), then isn't there an important difference (morally and otherwise) between failure to restart a machine and actually unplugging the machine? From this perspective doesn't it make sense to say that both the physician and the intruder have committed "acts"?

The discussion can provide a vehicle for showing how the interpretation of a legal requirement such as the "act" doctrine depends upon developing the reasons underlying that doctrine. Beyond this, the euthanasia problem obviously raises independent policy questions that ideally should be the subject of specific legislative treatment. But when such issues do not receive specific legislative attention (and given the volatile nature of the issues, it is easy to understand why they do not), then the courts are forced to grapple with them, using the common law categories at their disposal. Note that the straightforwardly legislative problem of whether physician-assisted suicide or physician euthanasia should be treated by the law as an instance of justifiable homicide is considered at p. 832, but the instructor might plausibly wish to take that material up at this point.

2.a. <u>Mens Rea</u> -- <u>Basic Conceptions</u>, pp. 203-224.

This introductory section serves to familiarize students with mens rea terminology and with the kind of analysis necessary to identify the required mental state when, as so often happens, statutes or courts leave the matter unclear. As already seen, criminal responsibility requires a choice (i.e. a voluntary act or omission when the act could have been performed). But choice alone is normally insufficient; a defendant ordinarily is not considered culpable unless she acts intentionally or is aware of the consequences of her choice. As a result, it becomes crucial to the justification of punishment, and to describing the kind of conduct we want to punish, to identify the particular state of mind necessary to establish a given criminal offense.

If schedule constraints require the introduction to be completed in just one class, the instructor can assign and cover pp. 203-17 in a single hour and then move straight to the mistake of fact material at p. 225.

We believe it far preferable, however, to allow the time for two classes on the introductory material. Such an allocation of time is often necessary to insure familiarity with terms and to consolidate analytic skills that are crucial for all of the course material that follows. We therefore believe that the additional class hour is time well spent. With this strategy in mind the casebook supplements the overview material (pp. 203-13) with specific problems (pp. 212-24) that will give the students practice in using mens rea vocabulary and working with the concepts. The first class (pp. 203 through 212 Note 2) should focus on <u>Cunningham</u>, the explanatory notes and the statutory exercises that follow. The second class (pp. 213-25) can focus primarily on the problems of defining "intent" (<u>Neiswender</u>, p. 217 and Holloway, p. 218) and willful blindness (<u>Jewell</u>, p. 220)

<u>Cunningham</u>, p. 204. Students should be clear on the facts and the statutory language. Did the defendant know that Mrs. Wade was in the house? (Yes.) Was he hoping to injure or kill her? (There is no evidence that he was.) What are the elements of the offense? Note that the defendant must administer the poison "maliciously." What does this mean? Suppose there is evidence that the defendant actually liked Mrs. Wade and was a close friend. Would such evidence, if believed by the jury, preclude liability? The court makes clear (p. 206, just after the 1st and

2d indented quotes) that the term "maliciously" in the statute is not being used, as in ordinary speech, to refer to some particular grudge, spite or ill will. Malice often exists when such animus is absent. Then is it sufficient to prove that the defendant committed a wicked act by stealing the gas meter? Should malice simply mean, as the trial judge had instructed, something which is "wicked" or "which the defendant has no business to do"? Originally malice did mean wickedness in general. But note how this seemingly simple approach creates problems for the courts. What is the appropriate penalty for administering poison maliciously? Doesn't it depend on the particular kind of wickedness that the defendant displayed? What are the various kinds of wickedness that could be present? The following are among the principal possibilities:

a. The defendant wanted Mrs. Wade to inhale the poison gas because he wanted her to suffer. (Or because he wanted her to die so that he could inherit her fortune.)

b. The defendant hoped that by some miracle Mrs. Wade would not inhale the poison gas, but he knew that it was virtually certain she would do so.

c. The defendant did not know for sure that Mrs. Wade would inhale the gas, but he considered the possibility that she might do so and decided to take the chance.

d. The defendant did not think of the possibility that Mrs. Wade might inhale the gas, but if he had used his common sense he would have realized that this was a significant risk.

e. The defendant didn't realize the risk to Mrs. Wade and probably couldn't have done so, even if he had used ordinary common sense (e.g. the gas leaked into her room through a small crack in an apparently solid wall).

These are not the only possibilities but they provide some of the principal distinctions. Even in the last case the defendant might still be considered "wicked" because he was doing something "which he had no business to do," but he neither foresaw nor should have foreseen the particular injury to which the statute speaks. Note that the preceding possibilities correspond respectively to what the MPC would call purpose, knowledge, recklessness, negligence and strict liability. Which kind of mental state did the trial judge in Cunningham consider sufficient? (Arguably (d) - - negligence, because he says that the defendant must

-47-

have known perfectly well what would occur.) But don't his instructions permit the jury to convict even without finding negligence, simply because the defendant did something that he had no business to do? What mens rea does the appellate court require? (Note the court's insistence on actual foresight - - possibility (c) - - or what the MPC calls recklessness.)

Why shouldn't strict liability be sufficient, at least where the defendant has clearly committed an illegal act? Consider <u>Faulknor</u> (p. 206) in this connection. Note that the defendant is already subject to punishment for theft or attempted theft. The question is whether punishment for an additional crime is also justified. The courts found the original broad meaning of malice, i.e. wickedness in general, too crude to answer this question. The term had to be given a more precise meaning, in order to determine whether a defendant, however wicked, deserved the additional punishment specified for the particular offense.

Discussion of <u>Cunningham</u> and <u>Faulknor</u> should bring out that blameworthiness is not a simple either-or concept. Courts must analyze mental states carefully to identify the precise kind of blameworthiness involved in a particular case. If the blameworthiness entailed in commission of a crime could suffice to establish blame for some other result that the defendant could not reasonably foresee (the position of the trial judge in <u>Cunningham</u> and of the prosecutor in <u>Faulknor</u>), then criminal liability would not remain tied to the kind and degree of the defendant's fault. For that reason courts generally reject the notion of "wickedness in general." (Felony murder, to be considered in Chapter 5, is an important exception). Thus, when a statute requires that a result be produced with "malice," the prevailing common law position, reflected <u>Cunningham</u> and <u>Faulknor</u>, is that such a statute requires actual foresight of the possible consequences.

<u>Santillanes</u>, p. 211, provides a vehicle for the student to understand the important difference between a mere accident for which no one is culpable; an act of negligence for which the actor is liable only for damages in torts; and finally an act of negligence that is so extreme that it may suffice for criminal liability.

How does the <u>Santillanes </u>court interpret the term "negligently" in the statute? In effect, the court holds that negligently does not mean negligently; it means something <u>more than</u> negligence. See p. 211, last 3 lines of the opinion. Is this a legitimate interpretation of the statutory language? What is the justification for it? Negligence, in the sense of inadvertent creation of a risk of harm, is widely used in the criminal law, but it is a controversial basis for criminal liability. To insure that the degree of fault is sufficiently great to warrant "moral condemnation and social opprobrium" (p. 211, end of 1st full ¶), not to mention the severe deprivations of a prison sentence, the court requires that the degree of negligence be substantial. For a statement of what criminal negligence might mean, see MPC §2.02(2)(d), and p. 210, last ¶. We explore the issue in more detail in the Homicide chapter.

The MPC should be examined as an alternative approach to the problems of identifying the appropriate mental state. What mens rea categories are established by the Code? What mental state does the Code require when the definition of a specific crime is silent or ambiguous concerning mens rea?

The statutory exercises, p. 212, Note 2, provide a vehicle for testing the student's understanding of the Code:

Burglary. Suppose that a defendant, intending to commit theft, enters a building that he believes to be a gift shop. It turns out that the owner of the store has a small apartment, at the side of the store, in which he lives. It also turns out that, although the defendant thought it was still daylight, in fact the sun had just set and is therefore legally "night." Is he guilty under the N.Y. statute? The California statute? Both statutes require an intent to commit a crime in the building, but beyond that there are problems. The N. Y. statute requires a knowing entry, but is silent with respect to the mens rea, if any, required with respect to the building's status as a dwelling and the time of the entry. The California statute is even less specific. Can we get answers by ordinary interpretation of language? By looking at the legislative intent? Students should see that even these relatively modern, relatively specific statutes are a mess when it comes to specifying the required mens rea.

What mental elements would be required if these statutes are interpreted in accordance with the provisions of the MPC? First, students should see that if a mental state is required with respect to any element, then the Code presumes that that mental state carries over with respect to all other material elements of the offense. § 2.02(4). In this instance that might mean that intent (i.e. purpose) would be required with respect to all the material elements. But isn't it absurd to limit the offense to cases in which the defendant's purpose is to enter at night? Assuming that we must disregard this implication of § 2.04(4), the N.Y. statute would require knowledge with respect to all material elements. In California, since no

mental state is required (other than the intent to commit a felony), §
2.02(3) tells us that recklessness is required with respect to each material
element.

Destruction of property. Suppose that a defendant rides through the
woods on a motorcycle and runs over and kills a growing vine. Can he be
convicted under the D.C. Code if he did not actually realize that he was
running over the vine? Students should see that the statute gives a clear
negative answer to this question (the defendant must "maliciously"
destroy the vine). But what if the defendant thought he was riding on his
own land? What if he thought the thing he was deliberately driving over
was a snake rather than a vine? What if he thought the vine was one of
trivial value, but it turns out that it was a rare plant worth $2,000?
Students should see that each of these factors involves a different material
element of the offense, and that some decision must be made about the
mental state, if any, required for each of them. Under the MPC,
recklessness presumably would be required with respect to each element.
What result under the N.Y. statute in each of the variations above? Note
that several different mental states are required: Intent to damage, but
only negligence with respect to whether the defendant had any right to do
so. No mens rea is specified at all with respect to the value of the property
damaged -- does this mean that there is strict liability with respect to this
element?

These exercises should help the students to see that crimes typically
consist a number of different material elements; that the same mental state
will not necessarily be required with respect to each of them; and that a
decision must nonetheless be made as to the mental state, if any, required
with respect to each material element. Legislation, even when relatively
specific, time and again leaves gaps with respect to these issues. The MPC
provides a way out of the morass by offering several general principles of
statutory interpretation. Under the Code conviction ordinarily requires
proof of at least negligence with respect to each material element (see
§2.02(1)), and in the absence of specific statutory language to the contrary,
the MPC requires at least recklessness (see §2.02(3)).

The meaning of the four crucial kinds of culpability under the MPC
is described in the MPC comments at pp. 208-11, but it may be worth brief
discussion in class.

Purpose: does it differ from "motive"? Note that a person may
desire one result as a way of getting another result, but he still desires (ie.
has a purpose) with respect to the first result. See Williams' example of

the burglar, p. 213, Note 4(a). Similarly, what if a traitor helps a foreign country not because he feels loyalty to its ideals, but solely to get money? He still has a purpose to aid, in order to achieve a further purpose.

Recklessness and negligence raise many problems. One concerns precisely what risk the defendant must be aware of. This problem is explored at p. 214, Note 6. How should the Shimmen case, p. 215, 1st ¶ of the indented quote, be resolved under the language of the Model Penal Code? Under a statute the student would propose? What is the proper analysis for the hypothetical at p. 215, 1st full ¶?

It may be helpful to note how the MPC concept of recklessness compares with that used by the courts in Cunningham and Faulknor. The Code attempts to be much more explicit about how great the risk must be, and about what would make a risk unjustifiable. Nonetheless, there are inevitable problems of judgment and degree. The homicide materials explore these problems in depth.

"Specific" and "general" intent, p. 215, Note 7. The confusions and perplexities generated by courts' use of the terms "specific" and "general" intent need to be brought to the attention of the student. Examples of cases employing these terms appear at various parts of the book. But even at this early point the student needs some guidance in preparation for confronting these usages. The material at pp. 215-217 provides an introduction.

Neiswender, p. 217. Note the statutory language. Did the defendant "endeavor" to impede the due administration of justice? Such a term seems to imply a desire to achieve a particular result, and the court itself appears to read the prior decisions as requiring a "specific intent" (p. 218, lines 1-2 of the indented quote) which might again imply the need for a true "purpose." But how does the Neiswender court interpret the "specific intent" requirement? What MPC term comes closest to describing the mental state which this court requires? Most students will see that while ostensibly requiring specific intent, the court is in fact requiring only negligence (i.e. reasonable foreseeability). Is the court's concept of "reasonable foreseeability" equivalent, in effect, to the Santillanes - MPC concepts of negligence? Students should see that the Neiswender standard, ostensibly an interpretation of the meaning of "specific intent," involves even less culpability than the Santillanes - MPC concepts of negligence.

Does the Neiswender result make sense? Why didn't the court simply say that a conviction under § 1503 requires only proof of simple negligence? That would be hard for the court to admit, but once we cut through the mystification of the court's legal fiction (p. 218, middle of the indented quote), it becomes clear that a mens rea of simple negligence is all that the court has required.

Apart from the analytic missteps in Neiswender, does the result make sense as a matter of policy? Should negligence (or gross negligence) be a sufficient basis for liability under §1503? What if a clerk carelessly spills hot coffee on the defense attorney, thus requiring a delay in the proceedings or making it harder for the attorney to "give it the full effect." Has the clerk violated §1503? (Presumably not.) But how is that case different from Neiswender itself? Neiswender is not a sympathetic defendant, but is that a legitimate basis to distinguish the case of the negligent clerk? If it is, what about Cunningham: should Cunningham be convicted of malicious injury that he didn't foresee, just because he intentionally committed another crime? Some students will want to distinguish Cunningham from Neiswender, but they should see the analytic parallel: In both cases the defendant intended to commit theft and in the process set loose forces that poisoned the atmosphere, risking injury to persons or to the administration of justice. If it is improper to convict Cunningham of an offense other than the one he was aware of committing, shouldn't the same principle apply to Neiswender?

In sum, Neiswender certainly should be convicted for the attempted fraud (presumably in a state court), but a conviction of the §1503 offense makes little sense in the absence of a purpose to obstruct justice.

Knowledge, pp. 220-24. The concept of knowledge seems clear, but the distinction between knowledge and recklessness can involve only a matter of degree, and courts often confuse "knowledge" with recklessness or even negligence. Jewell, p. 220, and the Notes following provide a way to make concrete the difference (at least in principle) between knowledge and mere recklessness. They also suggest reasons why a legislature might conclude, in some contexts, that mere recklessness (ordinarily a culpable subjective mental state) was not a sufficient basis for criminal punishment. Class discussion of this material can therefore be a useful way to enable students to develop a command of the issues, without getting bogged down in some of the abstractions of general definitions or the MPC Commentaries.

Jewell, p. 220. Was the defendant properly convicted? Was the result unfair? (Many students will have little intuitive sympathy for Jewell, but that, of course, does not necessarily mean that he got a fair trial.)

Note that the statute requires knowledge. Was there proof of knowledge on the facts of the case? (Only indirectly at best). Did the trial judge's instructions require the jury to find actual knowledge? (No, see p. 221, 1st indented quote.) How did the court get around this problem? MPC § 2.02(7) equates knowledge of a high probability with knowledge of the actual existence of a particular fact. But did the trial judge's instructions satisfy even the looser MPC standard? Note that the instructions permit conviction if the defendant's lack of knowledge was the result of a decision to avoid learning the truth. Two sets of questions can be posed about this:

- (1) Is the trial judge's standard in effect equivalent to actual knowledge, or to recklessness, or to something even less?

- (2) If the standard is not equivalent to actual knowledge, is it nonetheless substantively fair, and is it a legitimate standard under a statute in which Congress has chosen to require knowledge?

As to question (1), the dissent (by then-Judge Anthony Kennedy) poses a hypothetical that makes clear why a conscious decision to avoid learning the truth is not at all the same as knowledge: Does the person carrying a gift (p. 222, last full ¶) have actual knowledge? Clearly not; the decision not to see what is in the package is not even negligent. The dissent makes clear (pp. 222-23, last 3 ¶'s of the opinion) the three defects in the trial judge's instruction, and how the instruction would have to be remedied in order to identify cases in which wilful blindness can legitimately be equated with actual knowledge. Jewell himself probably could have been properly convicted under a lighter instruction but that, obviously, is not the same thing as saying that he was properly convicted in the case as actually tried.

Although a sloppy approach to willful blindness prevailed in Jewell, the fact that the dissent was by Kennedy helps give legitimacy to the more analytically rigorous approach. Subsequent decisions in the 5th and 7th Circuits (Farfan-Carreon, p. 223, next to last ¶, and Giovannetti, p. 223, last ¶) reinforce the more rigorous approach by holding that an "ostrich" intruction, even if properly formulated (as per MPC §2.02(7)), still should not be given to the jury unless there is both knowledge of a high probability of illegality and conduct contrived to avoid learning the truth.

If time permits, a good classroom hypothetical can be drawn from the facts of United States v. Civelli, 883 F.2d 191 (2d Cir. 1989). Note the facts and the trial judge's instructions on willful blindness. Should the conviction be upheld? Under the approach of the Jewell majority, the instruction apparently would be held proper, because it requires a finding of "a conscious purpose to avoid knowledge." How would Justice Kennedy decide this one? The first of the three Jewell defects (failure to require awareness of a high probability that drugs were present) is repeated here; presumably Kennedy would reverse. Likewise the 5th & 7th Circuit criteria apparently are not met, because Civelli was just proceeding in the ordinary course (he did not contrive to avoid knowledge) and because, again, there was no finding that Civelli thought it highly probable that the envelopes contained drugs. (But on the latter point, query the relevance of Bedoya's reputation, especially if Civelli knew of it.)

The actual outcome in the Civelli case is perhaps a surprise; the 2d Circuit affirmed the conviction. The court's reasoning is interesting as an illustration of the ways that willful blindness doctrines can distort the mens rea analysis. The court first held that a willful blindness charge is appropriate where the "surrounding circumstances were such that reasonable persons could have concluded that the circumstances alone should have apprised the defendants of the unlawful nature of their conduct." The court then said, reviewing the evidence, that "the delivery itself plainly was not a straightforward one" and therefore that "this evidence . . . tended reasonably to show that circumstances should have apprised appellant of the unlawful nature of his conduct" (emphasis added). As a result, the trial judge's instruction was permissible. What mens rea does this approach require? In effect the court is willing to permit the jury to infer knowledge simply from evidence of negligence. (The fact that, under the trial judge's instruction, this inference is merely permissive and rebuttable takes away some but not all of the sting; the 5th & 7th Circuit approaches would not permit a willful blindness instruction on so slender an evidentiary foundation.)

Question (2) above (p. 53 of this Manual) is an underlying concern in all willful blindness cases: that is, putting aside the issues of analytic purity or statutory strict construction, why should actual knowledge be required in these cases? One answer is simply is that Congress has chosen to do so, and it not legitimate for a court to override that judgment. But is the result really unfair?

For many students, strict insistence on actual knowledge may not appear to make much substantive sense in a cocaine case like Civelli or in the other cases considered. Is Congress just dense about this?

One point to stress is that Congress often requires knowledge because the penal prohibition, in statutes regulating business activity, for example, applies to conduct that is not culpable in the absence of actual knowledge; a willful blindness approach, once accepted, will presumably extend to knowledge requirements in such statutes. (See p. 223, Note 1, or the bank fraud in Barnhart, p. 223, Note 3.) What about Civelli and Jewell? Surely recklessness or perhaps even negligence seems culpable in those contexts. But what is the applicable penalty in a case like Civelli? Note that the mandatory minimum sentence was 10 years without parole. Presumably, Congress limited liability to cases of actual knowledge because the penalty would be way out of proportion to fault for defendants who were merely negligent. In light of the applicable penalties, does the slide from a knowledge requirement to negligence really make substantive sense?

b. Mistake of Fact, pp. 225-235.

This material provides an opportunity to develop further the student's analytical skills and to focus more specifically on the policy question of what mental state should be required.

Prince, p. 226. What are the material elements of the offense charged here? What mens rea is required with respect to each of them? Is the court holding that no mens rea is required at all? Consider:

Case 1. Suppose that Prince called at the Phillips' house while the parents were away. An aunt who was staying there told Prince that the girl had been left in her care and gave Prince permission to take her to France with him for the weekend. It turns out that the parents had not entrusted the girl to the aunt's care. Can Prince be convicted? With respect to the statute's requirement that the defendant be acting against the will of the parents, is this a matter of strict liability? Could Prince be convicted if he had been negligent in believing that the aunt had lawful care of the girl?

Note that the court requires actual knowledge that the defendant is acting without the parent's consent. (p. 226, 13-14 lines from the bottom). Once again, the mens rea analysis becomes multi-faceted: The court requires conscious awareness with respect to one of the material elements but a different mens rea with respect to another.

What mens rea does the court require with respect to the age of the girl? Does the prosecution at least have to show negligence? Note that the jury found not only that the defendant's belief was honestly held, but also that the belief was reasonable. In upholding the conviction, the court in effect holds that even negligence is not required with respect to this particular element. With respect to the age of the girl, the offense becomes one of strict liability.

What is the justification for this result? What reasons does Bramwell give? Is the result dictated by the fact that words of mens rea are not present in the statute with respect to the age of the girl? Is the court barred from reading in language which is not there? If so, then how can the court hold that knowledge of the father's non-consent is required? Clearly, the result cannot depend on the wording of the statute, but must instead depend on a decision to treat one element (the age of the girl) differently from another element (the consent of the parents) for reasons of policy. What are those reasons? Consider the following:

a. Mistake as to attendant circumstances. Should it make a difference that the defendant's defense can be characterized as one of "mistake"? Does it make a difference that his claim of ignorance relates only to one of the attendant circumstances? Note that the court stresses the importance of the prosecution's showing that the defendant knew he was doing the act forbidden by the statute, namely taking a girl from the possession of her parents without their consent. But why is the consent of the parents part of the forbidden act while her age is not? Why can't we say that the act is simply the taking and the lack of the parents' consent is (like age) an attendant circumstance? Why should the result depend on word games of this kind? Consider whether we can treat a defendant's claim of "mistake" as analytically separate from the question of what mens rea is part of the prosecution's affirmative case:

Case 2. Suppose that a defendant picks up a gun that he believes (negligently) to be loaded only with blanks. The defendant shoots at a friend, and the friend is killed. In a prosecution for murder by intentional killing, is the defendant's defense that he had no mens rea, or that he made a mistake of fact about whether the gun was

-56-

loaded? Could the defendant be convicted in Pennsylvania, on the theory that the statute (pp. 225-26) precludes reliance upon his unreasonable mistake of fact?

Students should see that this approach involves a contradiction in terms. If an offense requires knowledge, then a mistake of fact, even if unreasonable, by hypothesis negates that knowledge. (In Pennsylvania the statutory provision presumably would have to be ignored.) As a result, there is nothing about the structure of the statute itself, or the characterization of the defendant's claim as a "mistake" that in itself supports strict liability.

b. The defendant assumes the risk. But *why* should he be held to assume the risk? (1) Is it because of the desire to impose on the defendant a duty to exercise extreme care about the circumstances? If so, then why not impose the same duty of extreme care with respect to whether the defendant has the parents' consent? (2) Strict liability can also be seen as a way of deterring commission of the underlying behavior -- that is, the conduct which the defendant knows that he is engaged in.

We can identify three possibilities with respect to the underlying behavior. First, the conduct may, to all appearances, be totally innocent. (That would be the case if the defendant believed that he had the parents' consent.) Secondly, the conduct may be immoral but not illegal. (That would be the case if the defendant knew he was taking a girl without her parents' consent, but believed that she was seventeen.) Finally, the underlying conduct itself could be illegal. (That would be the case, for example, if the defendant had intercourse with a girl whom he knew was younger than the statutory age, but in fact the girl was so much younger that a more serious charge could be brought.)

In the first situation (underlying conduct appears wholly innocent), the court does not require the defendant to run the risk. But in the second case (conduct immoral but not illegal) the court requires that the defendant run the risk. Why is there a significant difference between the first two cases? For an argument that there is one, see the article by Professor Brett, p. 228, Note 1, and the White case, p. 227. But does that argument make sense? What is the source of the duty to which Professor Brett refers? Who should have the authority to define it? What punishment should be provided for it? On these points, the arguments of *Judge* Brett seem decisive: As a matter of institutional competence, the court has no authority to declare wrongful or to attempt to deter conduct that the legislature has not chosen to condemn as criminal.

Is there, however, a significant difference between the second and third situations? In the third situation, the underlying conduct is illegal; there is a statutory policy to condemn such conduct and deter it. In that context, does it make sense to say that the defendant should run the risk? Note that although Judge Brett dissented in Prince (the second situation), he did not question the assumption of risk approach in the situation in which the defendant knows he is committing some crime. Is this sound? Strict liability may discourage underlying conduct which has been declared illegal. But what is the proper punishment for that conduct? Does the defendant have the kind of blameworthiness which warrants the punishment prescribed for the underlying conduct, or the punishment prescribed for causing the harm that happened to occur?

Students should see that the assumption of risk analysis involves unfairness, even when the underlying conduct is itself illegal. Both the degree of blame and the kind of blame we impose (theft versus arson) must depend on the mens rea that the defendant actually had; otherwise decisions about labeling, grading, and punishing are thrown out of phase with the defendant's actual culpability.

Statutory rape (p. 234, Note) is worth separate discussion because it shows that the issues raised by Prince are of continuing importance as a matter of statutory analysis and practical results. A typical statutory rape provision provides: "unlawful sexual intercourse is an act of sexual intercourse accomplished with a person who is not the spouse of the perpetrator, if the person is a minor . . . under the age of 18 years" (California Penal Code §261.5, full text in Ch. 4, p. 320). What are the elements? What mens rea should be required with respect to the age of the victim?

Several approaches can be considered. Under the approach of the court in Prince, is strict liability appropriate? Assuming that the facts were as the defendant believed them to be (i.e. his partner was nineteen years old), is his act illegal? Note that generally fornication is no longer an offense. Do we even consider his act immoral? Analytically, some mens rea ought to be required, even under the approach of the court in Prince, in order to show that the defendant had some consciousness of wrongdoing.

Yet, where does the law stand? Cases like Hernandez, p. 232, are the exception. *In the United States*, the great majority of jurisdictions accept the strict liability approach, as the Court in Olsen points out (p. 232, n.10).

Is this fair? Is it justifiable even on utilitarian grounds? Note that strict liability does ease the prosecutor's burden and put a higher duty of care on the defendant. But what if the defendant has exercised the greatest possible care that anyone could imagine? Would a strict liability approach still lead to conviction? Perhaps no jury would be so harsh in practice. But is that clear? Note that strict liability is in part a <u>procedural</u> issue. If a reasonable mistake of fact is not a defense, then evidence tending to show that the defendant was reasonable can properly be <u>excluded</u> at trial; the jury will never have a chance to consider it. If negligence is required, then at least the evidence will get admitted; guilt will depend on whether the defendant should have done more (before or during the episode) to ascertain the victim's age, and the case can be argued to the jury in those terms.

Note that *in Britain*, <u>Prince</u> and the strict liability approach it endorsed have been expressly repudiated. In a decision rendered too late to be included in the casebook - - B (a minor) v. D.P.P., [2000] 1 All E.R. 833, [2000] Crim. L. Rev. 403 - - the House of Lords ruled that in interpreting criminal statutes, including statutes that prohibit sexual conduct with minors, courts must presume that knowledge or at least subjective recklessness are required with respect to all material elements (including the age of the minor), unless the legislature provides to the contrary, either expressly or by an implication that is "compellingly clear." Brief extracts from the opinions in this case are included as an Appendix to this Teachers Manual. See pp. 263-265 infra.

How would the typical statutory rape provision be interpreted under the MPC? Given the absence of mens rea language, § 2.02(3) requires at least recklessness. But note the special MPC provisions for statutory rape, p. 234, Note. Why the departure from the Code's usual emphasis on subjective cupability? Can it be justified in principle, or only as a concession to political palatability? Isn't the Code's burden of proof provision unconstitutional anyway?

<u>Olsen</u>, at p. 230, illustrates that courts continue to be drawn to the strict liability approach. How can the court distinguish its own decision in <u>Hernandez</u>? The wording of the statute authorizing probation may be crucial; but the court does not rely on that provision alone. What other arguments does the court offer? Note the theme that a defendant committing a lesser wrong should be held strictly liable if a greater wrong occurs (e.g. the discussion of <u>Lopez</u> on p. 232). <u>Lopez</u> indicates the

continuing influence of the lesser wrong theory, despite the more principled analysis of cases like Cunningham and Faulknor.

In any event, is the lesser wrong theory even applicable here? Focusing on the acts that the defendant knew he was committing, was his conduct illegal or even immoral? There was a serious allegation of forcible rape, and one can see why Olsen was prosecuted. But on this point the defendant's version of the facts apparently proved convincing at trial (see p. 232 n.7), and he was acquitted of forcible rape. Was he guilty of statutory rape? Maybe not, see the dissent at p. 233, n.2.

Another theme in Olsen is that the greater seriousness of the harm and the greater severity of the punishment authorized under § 288 argue for strict liability (p. 233, 1st ¶). Does this make sense? Note that the defendant received a three-year prison sentence on the § 288 charge, despite the absence of any proof of wrongdoing in that connection.

In the next section strict liability will be further examined in connection with regulatory offenses: there stigma is typically slight, penalties are usually (though not always) mild, and the underlying conduct usually carries no implicit flavor of immorality. The discussion of Prince and the statutory rape cases and other cases involving acts with minors below a certain age should familiarize students with strict liability approaches triggered by an underlying moral wrong or lesser legal wrong, and should bring out the moral and procedural consequences of the choice between strict liability and negligence in this context.

c. Strict Liability, pp. 235-255.

This material introduces the problem of strict liability for public welfare offenses, considers whether such offenses can or should be distinguished from traditional criminal offenses (for which a mens rea is ordinarily required), and finally provides a vehicle for summing up the debates about the role of moral fault in a system of criminal law.

Balint and Dotterweich, p. 236, establish the principle of strict liability in regulatory legislation. Discussion of these cases should bring out the absence of any wrongdoing charged in Balint or proven in Dotterweich. In both cases the absence of explicit mens rea language and the interest of the government in maximum enforcement of the law, even at the cost of convicting some non-blameworthy defendants, led to the imposition of strict liability.

Morissette, p. 237. Note that the statute makes it a crime to "knowingly convert." Isn't this language sufficient by itself to render defendant's honest mistake a defense? The problem is that by taking bomb casings that he thought were abandoned property, the defendant did "knowingly convert" them to his own use. The statute does not explicitly limit criminal liability to cases where this is done with "intent to steal," and the Court therefore treated the question as whether such an intent should be read in.

Was there authority against reading an additional mens rea requirement into the statute? Surely: Balint and Dotterweich. How could the Court distinguish these cases? See what Justice Jackson says concerning Balint and Behrman (p. 238, last full ¶). Note that the Court could have inferred an intent requirement from the wording of the statute in Morissette (whoever embezzles, steals, etc.) or could have limited Balint to cases where a congressional intent to impose strict liability could be specifically inferred (see the last two sentences of Balint at p. 236). What path does the Court actually take? Note that the Court appears to recognize two distinct categories of crime: traditional common-law crimes and new statutory offenses designed to regulate "activities that affect public health, safety or welfare."

Although the Court refuses to "set forth comprehensive criteria for distinguishing between crimes that require a mental element and crimes that do not" (p. 240, 1st full ¶), the Court in effect creates two strong presumptions: (1) criminal intent should be required for traditional common-law offenses; and (2) criminal intent should not be read into statutes in the public welfare category. The first presumption is by now familiar. (See MPC § 2.02(3)). But what is the justification for the second presumption?

Consider first how the court in Prince, p. 226, would have decided a "public welfare" case like Balint and Dotterweich, p. 236. Recall that in Prince, the court would allow a defense for any mistake that deprived the conduct of its immoral character (i.e. if the defendant thought he had the father's consent); in Prince itself strict liability was imposed only because the underlying conduct was "wrong in itself." Is this true in Balint and Dotterweich? Did the Court in those cases view the distribution of food and legitimate drugs as morally suspect activities? Note that the public welfare cases extend strict liability to situations where there can be no plausible legislative purpose to condemn or deter the underlying behavior.

What then is the justification for imposing criminal liability when the defendant is not at fault with respect to either the underlying conduct or with respect to the harm that subsequently occurs? The Canadian case, Regina v. City of Sault Ste. Marie, p. 249, which rejected strict liability in Canada, and the material following it, through p. 255, provide a basis for student consideration of this question.

Several possible justifications can be discussed:

a. The prosecutor can be trusted to prosecute only egregious cases. But if this is true, doesn't the same point apply to all offenses? Why do we ever require that mens rea be formally proved?

b. Juries will convict only when they sense actual culpability. Again, if this argument is valid at all, why doesn't it apply to all offenses? In any event, if we want to restrict conviction to cases of actual culpability, why should prosecutors escape the usual burden of proof? Finally, is this just a question of modifying the burden of proof? If the mens rea of the defendant is irrelevant, doesn't this have the effect of making evidence of due care inadmissible?

c. Strict liability, because it does render conviction easier, will be a more effective deterrent and will encourage defendants to exercise extraordinary care. The pragmatic advantages of strict liability are clear, but how can they be reconciled with the principle of fault?

At this point, Justice Jackson's reasons for treating the public welfare area as distinct (top of p. 239) should be explored. Aren't most of his reasons equally applicable to traditional offenses (e.g. "whatever the intent of the violator, the injury is the same")? The key point seems to be that "penalties commonly are relatively small, and conviction does no grave damage to an offender's reputation." But then why treat such offenses as "criminal" at all? Perhaps society uses the special stigmatizing effects of criminal punishment to gain additional deterrence; otherwise why resort to criminal sanctions in preference to the civil fines (for which procedural burdens are far easier)? But in that case, isn't the decision to apply criminal sanctions against those without fault clearly indefensible?

Staples, p. 241. Does it go even further than Morissette in rejecting strict liability? After all, is the public interest in controlling traffic in automatic firearms any less than the interest in controlling the drug trade or in protecting against impure food and drugs? What was faulty in the government's argument, p. 242, 1ˢᵗ full ¶, that "guns, whether or not they are statutory 'firearms', are dangerous devices that put gun owners on notice that they must determine at their hazard whether their weapons come within the scope of the Act"? Why doesn't the Freed case, concerning possession of hand grenades, p. 242, 2d full ¶, support its position? Both the majority and the concurring opinion stress that possession of guns, despite its general dangerousness, is an entirely legal activity. Does this approach, together with the more recent decision in X-Citement Video (p. 243, Problem), betoken the end of cases like Dotterweich?

If time permits the remaining material may be covered as follows:

Guminga, p. 244, presents the departure from the fault principle known as vicarious liability. Note that the waitress who serves the drinks to the minors can clearly be convicted, without any showing of mens rea, since the offense presumably falls in the public welfare category, where courts frequently permit strict liability. Given that starting point, how does the restaurant owner have any defense? How is his claim any different from that of the waitress? Note that in the case of the owner there is an absence not only of any mens rea but also of any actus reus. Thus, to punish him would not only impose strict liability but also vicarious liability for the acts of a third person.

Is vicarious liability justified? Don't the pragmatic arguments for strict liability apply with equal force with respect to vicarious liability? In theory perhaps yes, see the Guminga dissent. Does that mean that parental liability in the context of a case like Akers, p. 246, Note 2, is also justified? Logically, perhaps yes again, but note that personal responsibility for the socially harmful result is even more attenuated. The violation of the fault principle, already inherent in strict liability, becomes even more severe in the context of vicarious liability. The doctrinal difference between actus reus and mens rea requirements provides one way for a court like Guminga to limit the reach of pragmatically motivated incursions on the fault principle. Strict liability is quite common in regulatory offenses, by vicarious liability is rare.

Baker, p. 247, allows for the instructor to develop the interesting doctrinal turn which allows the defense of an involuntary action to defeat liability even under a strict liability offense. In some cases the doctrine applies in a clear cut way. E.g., p. 249, hypothetical 1(c). But in Baker what does absence of a voluntary act mean? The court concludes that if the brakes fail or if the throttle sticks, the defendant will be liable under the strict liability principle, because there would be voluntary actions of the defendant on which to ground liability. What actions? Presumably such acts as driving the car with these defects, failing to repair them, etc. But then how can the court successfully distinguish the case where the cruise control sticks? Is there a principled difference?

    d. <u>Mistake of Law</u>, pp. 255-278.

This material normally requires two to three classes. A full hour may be required for adequate discussion of pp. 255-63. The subsequent material, pp. 263-78 can be covered in one or one and one-half classes.

<u>People v. Marrero</u>, p. 255, serves as a basis for discussing the basic doctrine with respect to mistake of law, as well as a number of wrinkles. The defendant's conduct appears to be faultless. On the face of the statute it would appear altogether reasonable for him to read the definition of peace officer to apply to himself as a federal correctional officer. If he were correct in this interpretation he would have been doing nothing wrong. A trial judge agreed with his reading of the statute and dismissed the indictment on this ground. Two judges of the Appellate Division also agreed. Nonetheless, because a majority of the appellate judges read the statute differently, the defendant's conviction was upheld.

Two main issues are presented. (1) Applying ordinary principles applicable to determining the mens rea elements of an offense, shouldn't the defendant's mistake afford a defense? (2) Even if there is no defense under general mens rea principles, shouldn't the defendant have a defense under the special statutory reliance defense that had been enacted in New York?

As to (1): The result seems grossly unfair. On what ground was the conviction affirmed? Is the majority holding that this is an ordinary strict liability offense? What result if the defendant had claimed he was not aware that there was a gun in his briefcase? (The court is not explicit on this point, but under ordinary principles of mens rea, this mistake of fact presumably would afford a defense, even when the penal prohibition is silent as to any requirement of mens rea. E.g., MPC §2.02(3). <u>Staples</u>, p. 241, reaches the same conclusion in the specific context of firearms regulation. We can assume that the court here would likewise reject strict liability for a mistake of fact, because it does not invoke general strict liability doctrines but focuses instead on the particular kind of mistake involved here.)

If this is not a strict liability offense, and if defendant reasonably believed he was committing no crime, on what basis is the conviction affirmed? (On the basis of the classic doctrine that a mistake of law is no defense.) But how can doctrine which produces a result as unjust as the one in <u>Marrero</u> be defended? The majority opinion states the traditional arguments at p. 257, bottom, as does the extract from Holmes at p. 256, 3d full ¶. How persuasive are these arguments? What are the dissent's arguments against this view? Students should see that the conflict here is between the policy of facilitating the conviction of criminals by blocking defenses likely to be abused, and the policy of insuring justice and fairness to the individual accused of crime.

As to (2): Can the conflicting policies referred to in the preceding paragraph be mediated by tailored exceptions to the stringent common law rule? The New York Penal Law attempted to do so by §15.20; the interpretation of this provision is a central issue in the case. What was the likely intent behind this exception to the mistake of law rule? The majority opinion looks to the Model Penal Code, which was apparently the prototype for the New York provision. Could the appellant's argument possibly succeed under the MPC provision? No: the ruling "afterward determined to be . . . erroneous" was the trial judge's ruling dismissing the indictment (p. 256, lines 6-8), and this ruling obviously was issued <u>after</u> the defendant's conduct and was not what he relied on. What defendant relied on was his interpretation of CPL §§1.20, 2.10. These CPL provisions obviously were not "afterward determined to be invalid or erroneous"; all that was determined to be invalid or erroneous was defendant's interpretation of the provisions. Students should see that the point of the MPC was to give a defense when the defendant relied on an authoritative interpretation from some official source, not when the defendant himself read the statute to mean something different from what the court finds it to mean. Thus, defendant's argument is a clear loser under the MPC.

Does defendant fare any better under the N.Y. formulation? How was the New York statute different from the MPC formulation? (See p. 260, 1st full ¶.) Does the difference in statutory language warrant interpreting the N.Y. provision to allow a defense for reasonable reliance on a defendant's own interpretation of a statute? Compare the arguments of the majority and the dissent. The dissent's approach presumably produces a result more in keeping with fairness to the individual. How heavily should this consideration be weighed in interpreting a statute?

Under the dissent's approach, would anything be left of the doctrine that mistakes of law are not a defense? Students should see that the dissent's approach would (for better or worse - - maybe for the better) obliterate most of the traditional rule that even reasonable mistakes of law are not a defense. The principal remnant would be that complete ignorance of the existence of the law would still be no defense. But wouldn't that be a bizarre way to reform the mistake of law doctrine - - if reasonable misinterpretation of a known law is no defense (even though the defendant at least has some choice about whether to run the risk of being wrong), then shouldn't reasonable ignorance of the existence of a law be a defense a fortiori?

The scope of possible reliance defenses will be explored in more detail in the second mistake-of-law class, in connection with Albertini, p. 268. For now, students should see that the prevailing attitude toward mistakes of law creates strong momentum in favor of the majority's seemingly harsh interpretation of the N.Y. statute, and that in any case, other jurisdictions would very likely reach the same result under more precisely formulated provisions like MPC §2.04(3)(b).

Marrero implicitly raises a third issue: Absent an official reliance claim, are mistakes of law never a defense, or are there situations in which a mistake of law would be a defense just in the way that a mistake of fact would be? Consider Smith, p. 261, Note. The court allows a mistake defense where the mistake clearly relates to the defendant's understanding of what the law is. And the court allows the defense "whether or not [the belief] is a justifiable belief" (p. 260, last line of the indented quote), i.e., whether or not the belief is reasonable. This is consistent, of course, with the usual rule applicable to mistakes of fact; an honest, non-reckless belief is sufficient whether or not it is reasonable.

Is Smith simply inconsistent with Marrero? Note that the Marrero majority distinguishes People v. Weiss at p. 256, 2d full ¶. In Weiss the court allowed a mistake-of-law defense - - in that case the defendant's mistake in believing he had legal authority to seize the victim. Thus, Marrero acknowledges that some mistakes of law can be a defense (even without reliance on an official interpretation).

What is the distinction between mistakes of law which are a defense, as in Weiss and Smith, and those which are not, as in Marrero? The MPC Commentary (p. 262, 3d indented quote) attempts to explain the distinction, but most students, on first reading, find the explanation vague, unsatisfactory or incomprehensible.

To work through the issues, consider how <u>Smith</u> would be decided under the Code:

(a) Under §2.04(1) (p. 262, 2d indented quote), a mistake of fact <u>or law</u> is a defense if it negatives the mens rea required with respect to a material element. Is "property belonging to another" a material element under the Code? Students may want to argue this out in terms of plain meaning or what feels "material." This is a good time to call their attention to §§1.13(9) & (10), which define "material element" rigorously (and make clear that "property belonging to another" definitely is one).

(b) What is the mens rea required with respect to this material element? Since the statute is silent §2.02(3) applies; the answer is recklessness. Thus, an honest, non-reckless mistake of fact <u>or law</u> is a defense; the MPC result is identical to that of the <u>Smith</u> court.

Where does this MPC analysis leave the traditional mistake-of-law maxim? Does the analysis mean that Marrero would prevail under the Code? In other words, can Marrero argue that even though he has no defense under §2.04(3)(b), he nonetheless prevails under §2.04(1), which makes a mistake of fact <u>or law</u> a defense? He does prevail, <u>if</u> his mistake negatives the mens rea required with respect to a material element. Here is where §2.02(9) becomes important. The bottom line is that Marrero is going to lose because of this provision. But many students will not immediately see why. If "property belonging to another" is a material element in <u>Smith</u>, why not "peace officer" in <u>Marrero</u>? The drafting of §2.02(9) is cumbersome; when parsed rigorously it could be read to apply to both <u>Smith</u> and <u>Marrero</u> (or to neither).

The Commentary offers one crucial clue for distinguishing the domain where §2.04(1) permits a mistake-of-law defense from the domain where §2.02(9) denies the defense. The key is the Commentary language at p. 262, last 2 lines of the 2d ¶: there is no defense (i.e. §2.02(9) applies) when the mistake relates to "the law defining the offense"; conversely there can be a defense (i.e. §2.04(1) applies) when the mistake relates to "some other legal rule that characterizes the attendant circumstances." A simpler way to state the same basic thought is that the mistake-of-law doctrine denies a defense for mistakes about the <u>penal law</u> itself; mistakes of <u>other law</u> are treated just like mistakes of fact.

Applying this approach to Smith, it is clear he knew the penal prohibition - - that it was a crime to destroy property of another. He made a mistake about <u>other law</u> (property law), so §2.04(1) applies and his mistake of law is treated just like a mistake of fact. Applying this approach to Marrero, his mistake concerns the coverage of the <u>penal law</u> itself [we can raise a question about this in a minute], so §2.02(9) applies and his mistake is not a defense.

How should <u>Woods</u>, p. 262 ¶(a), be analyzed under this approach? Students should now be able to work through the steps of an MPC analysis to see the result: Here the mistake relates to other law (the law of interstate recognition of divorce); §2.04(1) therefore applies; the statutory silence about mens rea makes §2.02(3) applicable; and an honest, non-recklessly held belief that Shuffelt was not "another woman's husband" is therefore a defense, whether the mistaken belief results from a mistake about fact <u>or law</u> and whether the belief is reasonable <u>or unreasonable</u>. (The <u>Woods</u> court actually invoked the mistake-of-law rule to hold that the defendant had no defense; students should see that this was a misapplication of the rule because there was no mistake about the existence or coverage of the penal law.)

Note that there is now an added wrinkle in <u>Marrero</u>. Technically, the defendant's mistake was not in interpreting the Penal Code itself (Penal Law §265.02); rather he made a mistake about the interpretation of Criminal Procedure Law §§1.20, 2.10. If "peace officer" were <u>not</u> defined in the CPL or elsewhere, defendant's mistake would clearly be one of penal law; §2.02(9) would apply; and defendant would clearly lose under the MPC, as we have said above. But here "peace officer" is defined by a law outside the Penal Code. How should this situation be analyzed under the MPC? Is the CPL essentially part of the penal law, or is it more like "other law" that characterizes the attendant circumstances that the penal prohibition makes relevant - - the status as a peace officer being like property of another (or status as another woman's husband in <u>Woods</u>)?

The defendant evidently did not raise this issue in <u>Marrero</u>, and the court does not consider it. Possibly the court would have classified mistakes of crim. pro. law with mistakes of penal law, so that the defendant still would lose; or perhaps the penal law/other law distinction would have afforded defendant a winning argument. Either answer has to be arbitrary unless we know why we are drawing the penal law/other law distinction in the first place. If a mistake of other law can be a defense, why shouldn't the same approach apply to mistakes of penal law?

This question is perhaps the most fundamental and the hardest of the issues posed by the mistake of law material. The Code Commentary offers no help, and it may be that there is no fully satisfactory answer. A partial explanation is that a mistake of other law indicates no moral failing in itself, any more than a mistake of fact does; there is nothing morally culpable about a non-lawyer (or perhaps even a lawyer!) who fails to master property law doctrines governing the rights of landlord and tenant. In contrast, a mistake about penal law often is culpable; a man who thinks it legally justified to kill another person for a trivial insult is morally blameworthy for doing so, even if we are persuaded that he really thinks that his actions are not illegal.

Unfortunately this "explanation" is transparently inadequate, because it fails to cover cases like Marrero, where the conduct is *not* malum in se. And of course such cases, involving mistakes about the coverage of morally neutral regulatory statutes, are the only ones in which the mistake of penal law doctrine has any practical importance. Logically, the right line might be one between malum in se prohibitions and all other civil or criminal laws, not between penal and non-penal law. Perhaps we can view the MPC approach as something of a compromise, an effort to protect the fault principle by allowing a defense for some mistakes of law, while avoiding too much legislative opposition by preserving the rule in the domain where prosecutors are most likely to feel the need for it.

Students often wonder how the mistake of law doctrine works in the converse situation, i.e. when the defendant thinks that the law prohibits his action, when in reality it does not. The Taffee case, [1983] 2 All E.R.625 presents this unusual situation. The defendant arrived at a customs entry point in England, with some sort of contraband strapped to his back. He said that he thought the hidden packages contained currency, and he clearly believed that he was violating the law by illegally importing it. It turned out that the packages contained cannabis, a controlled substance, but it would not have been a crime to import currency. The court held that the defendant could not be convicted of importing cannabis (the statute punished only "knowing" violations, and he could not be convicted of any other customs violation, because what he thought he was doing was not a crime. In other words the case is to be judged according to the *facts* as defendant believed them to be, but not according to the *law* as the defendant believed it to be. Of course, thinking that you are breaking the law does not warrant convicting you if you are not. The result in the case make look odd at first, but the law here is consistent. Just as a mistake about penal law cannot exculpate, when the penal law does cover your conduct, likewise a mistake about penal law cannot inculpate, when the penal law does not cover your conduct.

Cheek, p. 263, presents another exception to the doctrine that ignorance of the law is no defense, viz., if the crime is so defined as to require that the defendant be aware that he is breaking the law. If the statute requires that a defendant be aware of his duty to pay a tax in order to be guilty of attempting to evade it, then his ignorance of his duty under the penal law is a defense, even when his mistake is unreasonable.

The hard question in Cheek and like cases is whether the statute should be interpreted to impose this requirement of knowledge of the penal law. In Cheek the only statutory language that directly bore on this issue was that the defendant "willfully" attempt to evade the tax. The Court found that this verb implied knowledge of the legal duty to pay the tax. Query: Were the Court's reasons persuasive? Does this language alone sufficiently convey this meaning? Note the refusal of courts in other kinds of cases to give the term "willfully" that interpretation. See pp. 266-68. What further considerations led this Court (and several earlier cases) to interpret "willfully" in the tax laws as requiring knowledge of the law? Note the Court's emphasis on the complexity of the tax laws as the reason for this interpretation of the term "willfully." In this and other cases of this sort (see particularly International Materials, Liparota, and Ratzlaf) the absence of clarity of statutory language leads the courts to assess the practical impact of the statute were it to be construed one way or another.

Another issue in Cheek is the Court's conclusion that while a good faith belief that the law does not impose a duty to pay a tax is a defense (even if unreasonable), a good faith belief that a statute imposing such a duty is unconstitutional is not a defense, even if that belief is reasonable. If the defendant does not willfully attempt to evade the tax in the first case, how can it be said that he does so in the second case? Isn't it true that in both cases he believes he is not under a legal duty to pay? Why should it matter whether his reason is an incorrect interpretation of the statute or an incorrect interpretation of the Constitution? What are the Court's answers to these questions? Are they persuasive?

United States v. Albertini, p. 268, provides a basis to pursue further the second principal issue in Marrero - - the exception to the mistake of law principle where some official body (here a court) has declared that the defendant's proposed action would not violate law, and where the defendant relies on that pronouncement. The scope of such an exception and the rationale behind it are stated in the MPC extracts at p. 270, Note 3.

Is this exception properly applicable to Albertini? The court held that it was. But is the reasoning of the court cogent? Was the defendant really "entrapped" (p. 269, 3d full ¶)? Consider the hypothetical at p. 269, Note 1. Would it be fair to say that the defendant that situation would necessarily be "entrapped" if he acts in reliance on the opinion of the intermediate appellate court? In Albertini itself, didn't the defendant know that the time for appealing the 9th Circuit decision had not yet expired? Why would it be unfair to hold him liable for repeating his conduct before the highest appellate court has a chance to speak?

Does the fact that the defendant's action in Albertini involved a political demonstration, which this very court had originally held to be protected by the First Amendment, serve to explain the result. Even if so, does it justify the result, if we accept the premise that, as the Supreme Court determined, the First Amendment in fact does not protect this sort of conduct?

What result in Albertini if the Supreme Court had granted certiorari before the defendant acted? The 9th Circuit states (p. 269, n.2) that it does not reach that question. But if the court would have considered denying a defense in that situation, why should it treat differently the case where the Supreme Court is still contemplating whether to grant certiorari?

One way to sort out such issues is to focus on the MPC requirement (§2.04(3)(b)) that the reliance must be reasonable. If the Supreme Court has not yet granted cert., but the government has announced its intention to seek cert., and if the defendant knows that all other circuits have ruled to the contrary, reliance on the 9th Circuit opinion might be unreasonable. Reasonableness presumably is highly context-dependent and would normally be a question for the jury under all the circumstances. Yet the 9th Circuit simply set aside the conviction, apparently holding that there is a good defense here as a matter of law. If Albertini means that reasonableness of the defendant's reliance under all the circumstances is not an element of the defense, the result would seem contrary to the MPC and perhaps to sound policy as well. The court's decision can presumably be understood as reflecting a determination that here the reliance clearly was reasonable under all the circumstances (see p. 269, 1st line of the 3d full ¶). The court therefore presumably would not allow the reliance defense in the variations presented at p. 270, Note 1.

Hopkins, p. 270, Note 2. Here the court rejected the defense of reliance on an official's declaration of the meaning of the law. Why was the defense not allowed? The court's reason is that such advice would then "become paramount to the law." Is the argument persuasive? Doesn't this confuse justification with excuse? The advice can't really supercede the law because such a defense is normally available only once. See MPC Comment, p. 271, indented quote.

Given the recognition of a reliance defense in <u>Raley</u> (p. 273), is the <u>Hopkins</u> result now unconstitutional? Or is <u>Hopkins</u> distinguishable? To explore this question, consider how <u>Hopkins</u> and <u>Raley</u> would be decided under the MPC. <u>Raley</u> presumably would come out the same way. But what result in <u>Hopkins</u>? Do we know whether the State's Attorney had official authority to interpret or enforce the statute? Do we know whether the advice rendered in 1944 was part of an "official interpretation"? Suppose the State's Attorney had been drinking with Hopkins in a bar, and had commented that he thought Hopkins' sign would be O.K. Discussion should make clear that under both the MPC and the constitutional principles reflected in <u>Raley</u>, reasonable reliance can constitute a defense. But reliance will be deemed reasonable only in certain narrowly defined situations that pose little danger to legitimate law enforcement.

<u>Lambert</u>, p. 271. The Court treats the mistake as one of purely penal law, but a defense is nonetheless allowed. Does the Court require that the mistake at least be a reasonable one? Note that the Court requires actual knowledge of the duty to register, or the probability of such knowledge. That seems an even broader defense than one of <u>reasonable</u> mistake of law.

When is this constitutionally mandated defense available? Note that Justice Douglas emphasizes that the defendant's conduct was "wholly passive" (beginning of the last full ¶). But why is the wholly passive character of the conduct crucial? Is it because acts are likely to alert the defendant to the likelihood of regulation? Consider these possibilities:

> <u>Case 2.</u> A commercial shipper ships dangerous products. Isn't it likely that the shipper has some knowledge of the possibility of regulation? Can't the failure to inquire be considered at least negligent?

> <u>Case 3.</u> A private householder ships furniture to another city in connection with a move. Is it fair to infer knowledge of applicable law in this case?

> <u>Case 4.</u> Suppose a "convicted person" takes a job as a babysitter in violation of a local ordinance. Can we infer knowledge of the law

here because the conduct, unlike that in <u>Lambert</u>, involves the commission of <u>acts</u>?

 <u>Case 5.</u> Is possession of a weapon "wholly passive"? Was Hutzell (p. 274, Note 2) fairly convicted?

 Discussion of such examples should make clear that the passivity of the defendant's conduct is a poor guide to the likelihood of reasonable notice. But then, what is "the generalization that underlines, and alone can justify" the <u>Lambert</u> decision (Frankfurter J. dissenting at p. 273, last ¶)? Would the appropriate generalization be that a mistake of law (or a <u>reasonable</u> mistake of law) is a constitutionally mandated defense to <u>all</u> crimes? For that matter, if a reasonable mistake of law is a constitutionally mandated defense, then why not the same (a <u>fortiori</u>?) for a reasonable mistake of fact? Consider:

 <u>Case 6</u>. In <u>Hopkins</u>, suppose that the defendant relied on an informal oral assurance of the State's Attorney, backed up by a written opinion from his own lawyer to the effect that his sign would not violate the statute. Assume that Hopkins is acting in good faith and has no reason to question the advice given to him. Should he have a constitutionally mandated defense? Is the case distinguishable from <u>Lambert</u>?

 <u>Case 7.</u> In <u>Lambert</u>, suppose that the defendant knew of the regulation, but thought that she was living outside the city limits. Assume again that she was acting in good faith and that her mistake was reasonable. Would a conviction be fundamentally unfair?

 Consider how Cases 6 and 7 are different from <u>Lambert</u>. In both cases, the mistake (of law in Case 6 and fact in Case 7) is reasonable. But in each case doesn't the defendant (unlike Lambert) at least have a chance to avoid the gray area? Why is ignorance of the *existence* of the law (i.e. <u>Lambert</u>) fundamentally different from mistake about either facts or the interpretation of law? Ordinarily in the former case there is a much stronger sense that the defendant had no opportunity to do otherwise. But courts have refused to extend <u>Lambert</u> to situations involving ignorance of the very existence of a law, when affirmative action is involved.

 How does the MPC deal with these problems? Consider particularly how Case 4 (the babysitter) would be resolved under the MPC. Note that the only Code requirement of reasonable notice, § 2.04(3)(a) is extremely narrow; publication alone is deemed sufficient. Presumably the babysitter would not have a defense, so long as the ordinance had been published. How would Lambert be decided? The Code itself does not appear to provide a defense. Thus, Lambert adds an additional lack of notice defense to those narrow situations contemplated by Section 2.04(3)(a). Note the possibilities for unfairness that remain. (Consider Cases 3 and 4.) Could a more general mistake of law defense be drafted without opening undue possibilities for abuse? Consider the California legislative proposal and the arguments for and against it developed at pp. 274-76.

All the material in this section brings out the tension between the blameworthiness requirement and the demands of effective law enforcement. The discussion should help students become familiar with the doctrines through which the law attempts to strike a compromise between these two conflicting demands and to see why those doctrines become complex and riddled with exceptions.

C. Proportionality, pp. 278-90

This material raises two kinds of issues. The first has to do with the significance of the principle of proportionality and its relation to the principle of culpability. These issues are introduced in the Introductory Note at p. 278 and are explored in the readings at pp. 279-83. The second has to do with defining that amount of punishment which is excessive and therefore disproportional. These kinds of issues are intrinsic to the task of constitutional adjudication concerning the meaning of cruel and unusual punishment and may be presented through a discussion of Harmelin v. Michigan, the latest decision of the Supreme Court on the subject. (p. 283).

D. Legality, pp. 290-312

This material constitutes an introduction to the nulla poena sine lege principle in its various applications. Shaw (p. 290) is interesting because of its fact situation and because there is scarcely any aspect of the nulla poena principle that is not threatened by the decision in the case: retroactive law making, law making by personal predilection, vagueness, and unlimited prosecutorial discretion. The case allows students to see the importance of the doctrinal limitations of the substantive criminal law. Keeler (p. 294), on the other hand, is a situation in which it is debatable to what extent nulla poena values are implicated. A little legal realism is appropriate here. What was the influence on both the majority and the dissent of the fact that the constitutionality of abortion was unresolved at the time of decision? To what extent were the judges taking positions in this case largely out of concern for preserving their positions in the abortion cases? <u>Nash</u> (p. 299, Note 3) introduces the problem of vagueness and the countervailing need to allow legislatures some degree of flexibility when language is inevitably somewhat imprecise.

<u>Morales</u> (p. 300) poses the same issue in an important contemporary context, and it adds two additional wrinkles - one analytic and one practical.

Analytically, as <u>Papachristou</u> (p. 307, Note 1) indicates, the void-for-vagueness doctrine rests on two concerns (p. 308, beginning of the 2d indented quote): that vague statutes fail to give "fair notice" to citizens, and that they encourage arbitrary arrests by police. (See also the "two independent reasons" articulated by Justice Stevens at p. 301, 3d full ¶.) Was the first concern implicated in Morales? Note possible arguments that the police officer's order to disperse might fail to indicate just how far a citizen must move, or how long he must remain away. But this problem apparently was not the <u>Morales</u> Court's main concern. Even if the officer's order to the citizen provides very clear notice, the ordinance is still vague, the Court holds, because it fails to constrain the discretion of the police in deciding when to issue such an order. In effect the Court seems to have held (perhaps for the first time) that criminal law must be made with some specificity by legislative bodies, not by executive officials, even if their decrees have only prospective application.

The practical problem involves the argument (Hill, p. 309, Note 4) that police need some degree of discretion in their order-maintenance activities, especially in high-crime neighborhoods. Is the argument persuasive? Why can't legislative bodies define clearly the minor misconduct (sometimes called "quality-of-life offenses") that they wish to prohibit? But does this approach really constrain police discretion, if there are hundreds of very specific offenses that police may or may not choose to enforce? Does police discretion of this sort pose the same problems of potential abuse and potential police-community tension as would the enforcement of an ordinance like that mentioned at p. 302 n.29?

Chapter Four
Rape

These materials are significant for their own sake, because rape prosecutions are complex and of obvious practical importance. In addition, the material serves broader objectives. It makes clear the way actus reus doctrines and administrative considerations condition the operation of mens rea requirements in practice. And it shows how substantive criminal law doctrines reflect deeply rooted social conventions and respond (or fail to respond) to pressures for social change. Intense controversy surrounding rape law makes this an area of major importance in the study of contemporary criminal law.

The very intensity of feelings concerning rape law requires special thought about how the material should be handled. Students care more deeply about these issues and think of them more personally than many other issues considered in the course. If classes are handled with conscious attention to this element, it can promote rather than hinder effective discussion. Criminal law is, after all, society's principal institutional mechanism for channeling responses to the most serious injuries that human conduct can inflict. This means that it must, by definition, confront and deal with the strongest of emotions, but at the same time that its task is to create an organized framework for dealing with the issues in as constructive and rational a manner as possible.

This tension -- between the need to be attentive to context and emotion while at the same time abstracting from them to create and administer doctrine -- is a problem not only for criminal law (and all law) but especially for the criminal law class. The tension can, however, be turned to pedagogical advantage if students are invited to see in the strong feelings unleashed by rape law both (1) the impossibility of severing doctrine from its complex social underpinnings and (2) the need for somewhat abstract concepts and categories to order social controversy, guide behavior and resolve disputes. Indeed, the very intensity and contentiousness of the debate about rape make attention to this subject (preferably early in the course) a very valuable way to understand the workings of criminal law.

For further discussion of problems posed by teaching the rape material, and suggestions for handling those problems, see the very helpful articles by Professors James Tomkovicz and Susan Estrich in 102 Yale L. J. 481, 509 (1992). Although these articles were written primarily for teachers, they also provide a context for students who might otherwise attribute their strong feelings and possible discomfort to their own classmates or their own professor. The articles may therefore be worth mentioning or excerpting for students, in order to give the class a more detailed basis for understanding the professor's pedagogical goals.

In terms of overall approach, two strategies seem viable. One is to begin with close, rigorous analysis of legal doctrine (the elements of the offense and ways of proving them), and from there to raise questions about the reasons for the legal categories, their fairness to women and their adequacy in capturing the relevant harmful aspects of the underlying behavior. Teachers who wish to proceed in this fashion can begin directly with a discussion of Rusk (see below). The second approach is to begin less analytically -- to discuss perceptions and feelings about rape first and then to move from open-ended discussion to a consideration of legal doctrine and whether it adequately captures the underlying dynamics of sexual misconduct. Although this second approach can lead to (and may encourage) the expression of strong, controversial feelings, it does help get those views out naturally (rather than in opposition to the teacher's doctrinal agenda); it can also make it easier for students to see why there is such a clash of perceptions about rape and why law (and lawyers) are needed to bring some order to the dispute.

For teachers who prefer this latter approach, Section A, Perspectives (pp. 313-18), provides an overview of some of the broader issues, and the excerpts in this section can be discussed explicitly in class. Those who prefer the former approach can assign pp. 313-318 as background reading and begin class discussion with close analysis of the facts and holdings of the first set of cases on actus reus (starting at p. 323).

A. Perspectives, pp. 313-318

One way to begin is to invite students to offer their own understanding (independent of what they might have read about legal doctrine) of what "rape" is. Does it include cases in which a woman forces or pressures a man to have sex? Does it include cases in which a stronger prison inmate violently compels another male inmate to submit to sex? (Until recently, and still in many states, rape can only be committed by a man upon a woman). Does rape (in ordinary, non-legal understanding) include cases in which a man induces a woman to submit by arguments and pressure, by threats to end the relationship, or by encouraging her to drink in order to reduce her resistance? Should rape encompass any or all of these cases? The objective of such questions can be to get students to think about the kinds of harm that such actions cause and the importance of criminalizing (or not criminalizing?) some or all of these sorts of cases.

The discussion can also be used as an introduction to the specific statutes reproduced at pp. 318-22. With respect to each of the cases considered, especially those that students may feel *should* be considered rape, are they in fact considered rape under the MPC or under current law in California, New York or Wisconsin?

Students often take it as a given that traditional rape law was discriminatory and unfair to women. It helps to ask students to be precise about the ways in which this was so. Enforcement practices were undoubtedly an important source of resentment. But what about statutes themselves and the legal definitions of rape? In what ways were they unfair to women? Consider as a typical example of the older statutes the California 1950 provision (pp. 318-19). Note that *only* a woman can be a victim of rape. At first glance, the statute seems to give *heightened* protection to women. But which kinds of women were in fact protected? (The social assumptions about "proper" and "improper" behavior can be mentioned here.) In one sense rape law discriminated against certain kinds of women, but can this amount to discrimination against all women as a class? Perhaps it can, to the extent that the law in effect enforced certain expectations and certain kinds of behavioral norms for women, thus arguably denying all women the option of certain forms of social and sexual independence.

Whether broadly or narrowly defined, what is the frequency of rape?

(1) How common are the cases in which a man induces a woman to submit by psychological pressure or by using liquor to weaken her resistance? If such cases are very common, is that an argument against extending the criminal law to cover them, or does that suggest a particularly strong need for a legal remedy?

(2) Consider the clearest sort of case, in which a man uses physical violence to force a woman to submit. How common is this sort of behavior? Note the difference between the NCS victimization survey, suggesting a rate of 0.14% of all women per year (p. 316, third full paragraph), and the Koss survey suggesting that 27% of all college women had been the victim of at least one completed or attempted rape since age 14 (p. 315, note 1). Does the discrepancy result from different definitions of rape, different survey methods or other factors? Note that 42% of the victims in the Koss study subsequently dated the men who had supposedly attacked them. Does this suggest that these women

were not "really" raped? Compare p. 315, Note 1, last full ¶. If male aggressiveness in ordinary dating situations is as prevalent as the Koss figures suggest, is that an argument against extending the criminal law to cover it, or does that suggest a particularly strong need for a legal remedy?

Do (some) women expect their dates to be somewhat assertive, to take the initiative, or to be sexually aggressive? Or do (some) men think that they are expected to behave in this way? Is sexual assertiveness ever "acceptable"? If so, what standards mark the line between permissible initiatives and harmful (and illegal) aggression. Consider the Stanko quote, p. 316, Note 3. Are her perceptions accurate? Some students consider them quite exaggerated (if not paranoid). Others strongly disagree. Discussion provides a way to bring out the subtle forms of intimidation that concern many women, as well as the reasons why such intimidation often is not noticed by men and women alike. (See also the Stanko excerpt at p. 328.) If such pervasive intimidation does exist, should the concept of "force" in rape be expanded to take it into account? Or is the pervasiveness of such male behavior a reason not to criminalize it?

C. Actus Reus, pp. 323-351.

   1. Force, pp. 323-46

      Rusk, p. 323. Note the elements of rape as defined in Maryland: (1) intercourse; (2) by force or threat; and (3) against the will and without the consent. Are they satisfied here? Given the complainant's testimony, the evidence of intercourse and non-consent is clear. But what about force? Is this just a factual question for the jury? On what evidence could a reasonable jury find force or threat here?

      (1) Consider the complainant's question "Will you let me go without killing me?" p. 324 (middle of the second indented quote). Why isn't this evidence sufficient to provide an open-and shut case of improper force? Given this testimony, how could Rusk possibly be a "close" case? Either the court is being incredibly scrupulous here, or it must be concerned about the lack of specific evidence that the defendant actually heard this question.

      (2) The victim described a "light" choking. Again, shouldn't this evidence be sufficient to provide an open-and shut case of improper force? Given this testimony, how could Rusk possibly be a "close" case? The complainant's choice of words here lends itself to different interpretations.

What was the real significance of the choking? But isn't this a question for the trier of fact?

(3) Taking the car keys, the strange neighborhood and the complainant's repeated requests to leave. Should these factors be enough (even without the fear of being killed and the choking) to show that the intercourse was by force? What is the court's position? Note that although the court ultimately affirms the conviction, its opinion reaching this result (by a slender majority) puts special emphasis on the "choking" testimony (p. 326, full ¶ of the majority opinion); apparently, without that testimony, there would not have been enough votes to uphold the conviction. But why should testimony of that sort be essential in order to establish "force"?

Suppose there had been no testimony about the "light" choking. Should the court still defer to the jury? Before analyzing this question, it may be helpful to focus on why force is required in the first place:

> Case 1. Suppose that Pat had gone voluntarily to Rusk's room. When he began to make sexual advances, she firmly and persistently said no, but he pushed her down on the bed, took off her clothes and had intercourse. Would Rusk be guilty of rape? Note the force requirement. Does his act of pushing Pat satisfy it? Rusk's behavior here could arguably be viewed as a customary way of taking the sexual initiative. Even if that is so, why shouldn't her firm, repeated refusal to consent be sufficient to render his behavior criminal? What kinds of assumptions could possibly justify the premise of statutes such as Maryland's, that non-consent alone is not sufficient to render the behavior criminal?

Several possible explanations may be suggested: (1) In the absence of force or resistance, can we be sure that the defendant himself knew of non-consent? This is the perennial problem of whether "no" really means "no." Shouldn't defendants be required to accept the victim's verbal protests at face value? Even if the "no means yes" attitude still survives among some (many?), is it appropriate for the criminal law to reflect and legitimate the position that "no" does not mean no?

(2) Once it is made clear that, legally, "no means no," are there any further reasons for retaining the force requirement? Suppose a woman acquiesces in her partner's demand for sex because she doesn't want him to break off their relationship, as he has threatened to do if she won't meet his sexual needs. Should her acquiescence here count as "consent"? (Compare the definitions in California §261.6 (p. 320) and Wisconsin §940.225(4) (p.

322, requiring "freely given" or "freely and voluntarily" given consent. If this situation involves nonconsent, should the man's behavior be punished as rape? Note the Rusk dissenters' stress on the point that rape is viewed (and graded) as a crime of violence (p. 327, last 6 lines of the 2d full ¶). If the force requirement makes sense for an aggravated felony offense, should there be a lesser degree of the offense for cases involving nonconsent without physical force?

Whatever the conclusion with respect to these policy issues, the problem in Rusk is that a statute punishing nonviolent intercourse had not been enacted, so that Rusk's behavior, however egregious, can be punished only if there is sufficient evidence of force. Assume that there were two degrees of non-consensual rape, one with force and one without. (The Wisconsin statute, p. 322, §§940.225(2),(3), is a helpful illustration of such an approach). Could Rusk have been convicted of the more serious offense? We can return to the evidence with this problem in mind.

Returning to the facts of Rusk, was there any evidence of resistance? The victim expressed her resistance verbally but apparently not physically. Is the court holding that verbal resistance is sufficient? Would it be appropriate to hold, under a statute like Maryland's, that verbal resistance is sufficient? Consider why resistance should ever be relevant at all. See pp. 329-30, Note 2(b), and especially the excerpt from the Anderson article.) Although some state statutes expressly require resistance - - see p. 329, Note 2(a) - - the Maryland statute, a common formulation, says nothing about resistance. So why is resistance relevant? How does the court in Rusk link resistance to the statutory elements? Note two themes in the court's opinion:

a. At one point (p. 326, first full ¶), the court says that "lack of *consent* is generally established through proof of resistance." Resistance presumably serves to corroborate that the non-consent was clear, genuine, and obvious to the defendant. But why should resistance be <u>necessary</u> to prove non-consent? Why can't other kinds of evidence (including verbal resistance) establish unequivocal non-consent?

b. A second theme emerges from the third indented quote on p. 325: Resistance (or a threat preventing resistance) is required because "force is an essential element." From this perspective, is it still clear that verbal resistance should be sufficient? Verbal resistance seems problematic if rape remains defined as a crime of violence. But why should <u>physical</u> resistance always be necessary; aren't there other ways to prove "force"? Note that physical resistance is *not* always necessary; resistance is excused if it is prevented by threats. See p. 330, note 2(c). Does the resistance requirement therefore boil down to the same thing as the statutory requirement of force or threat? Is there any difference between the two requirements? Analytically, perhaps not, but there seems to be a significant difference in emphasis. Does the resistance approach divert attention from the defendant's actions (about which the statutes speak) and refocus attention on the propriety of the victim's response? Why this odd shift of focus?

One other theme worth bringing out is the notion that resistance is excused only when the victim's fear is reasonable (p. 331, Note 3). Weren't the victim's fears reasonable in Warren, p. 331? Even if that is debatable, why should it matter whether the victim's fear is reasonable? One answer may be that if the victim's reaction is unreasonable, then the defendant may not have realized that his actions had put her in fear and prevented her from expressing resistance. But then why not focus directly on the defendant's knowledge? Consider the following:

> Case 3. The defendant knows that a woman W has a morbid fear of snakes. The defendant threatens to open a cage and release several snakes into the room unless W cooperates. If W then submits to intercourse, is the defendant guilty of rape? What result in Maryland? Under the MPC?

In Maryland, the result would probably depend on whether the victim's fears were "reasonable." If it were made clear that the snakes were not poisonous, wouldn't it be difficult to sustain a conviction? But why should reasonableness be relevant in Case 3? Is there any good reason why the defendant should not be convicted? Alternatively, consider the result under the MPC. Note the language of 213.1(1)(a); rape is limited to certain extremely serious kinds of threats. (Even a threat to inflict pain is insufficient unless the pain threatened happens to be "extreme"!) Less serious threats fall under §213.1(2), but even under this provision can there be a conviction in Case 3? Note that under both the Maryland and MPC approaches, a defendant may be acquitted, even when he is fully aware that his threat has put the victim in acute fear of serious harm.

Discussion should bring out that the "reasonable fear" or "ordinary resolution" standards are both too broad and too narrow to avoid unfairness to defendants. When the victim's fear is unreasonable, the defendant will be acquitted even if he is aware of those fears; if the victim's fears are reasonable, the defendant will be convicted even if he is unaware of those fears. Why not simply abandon the effort to focus on the response of the victim and concentrate solely on the question whether the defendant knew (or perhaps should have known) that his actions aroused fear.

If the victim's reasonableness is indeed the appropriate standard, what should reasonableness mean? Should the reasonableness standard reflect existing norms, or should the law be used to refine sensibilities and raise norms to a level that is more respectful of the dignity and autonomy of individuals? (Reconsider Warren, p. 331.) A forward-looking perspective may argue for use of the criminal law to change prevailing norms. Conviction might therefore be required even when the defendant did not deviate from cultural norms widely accepted by men and women alike.

But when criminal law works this way, is the defendant being *used* for instrumental purposes. Is punishment *just*? Arguably even commonplace behavior is sometimes *wrong*. But if the defendant can't be blamed, and therefore can't be punished, how can the prevailing standard of "reasonable" behavior ever be changed? Discussion should make clear that adoption of a "reasonableness" standard (from the perspective of *either* the victim or the defendant) does not solve any of the problems, but merely serves as a screen behind which we (or legislatures, or prosecutors, or courts or juries) must make the difficult judgments about what prevailing standards of behavior actually are or should be. The class should consider not only what the actual judgments should be but *who* should be making them, and who *will* be making them, if the legal standard is stated in terms of "reasonableness."

Coercion through implicit and/or nonphysical threats, pp. 332-38

Why should a rape conviction require proof that the defendant used or threatened *physical* harm? If a teacher demanded money in return for permitting a student to graduate (cf. Thompson, p. 333, Note 2), he would be guilty of extortion (MPC §223.4(7)), but if he demands payment in the form of sex rather than property, he is not guilty of rape, and in most states he probably would not be guilty of any criminal offense (unless the student was under the age of consent).

Why should consent to sex be considered valid when it is obtained in this way? Are the boundary problems in connection with sexual extortion different from those that arise in traditional extortion of money? The MPC punishes nonphysical threats only when they would prevent resistance "by a woman of ordinary resolution" (p. 336, Note 3(b)). Is this approach adequate to reach cases like Thompson? Is it sufficiently clear? Would it (should it) reach cases like that of the destitute widow (see Mlinarich discussion, p. 334, last 8 lines), or the liquor store manager in <u>Lovely</u> (p. 336, Note 4)?

Why shouldn't consent be invalid whenever it is obtained by threats of any sort? Is that the result (should it be) in states where rape statutes extend to any form of "coercion" or "duress" (p. 336, Note 3(c)). Does the solution proposed by Schulhofer (p. 337, Note 4(a)) go far enough? Or does it go too far? Would it make sense in these scenarios (as Bryden perhaps implies, p. 338, Note 3(c)) to say that the sexually attractive woman is also an extortionist - - or that neither party is? Can we solve this problem by specifying that only "unreasonable" threats are impermissible?

Students can be asked to suggest statutory definitions or tests that would address these issues without being underinclusive, overinclusive or too vague. The Model Statute proposed at p. 364, especially §202(c)(5), could be considered at this point. What are its benefits and shortcomings?

<u>M.T.S.</u>, p. 338. Students should be sure to understand the two different versions of what occurred here, and the trial judge's ultimate conclusion, which does not fully accept either party's story. On the facts as found by the judge, how can this conduct meet the statutory requirements for sexual assault? The preceding discussion will have suggested many of the policy arguments in favor of imposing criminal liability even without physical violence that coerces the victim's consent. Here it is worth pausing to consider the court's analysis as an exercise in statutory interpretation.

How does the court define force? (See p. 342, 2d full ¶). Given that definition, what does the statutory element of force add to the statutory element of intercourse? Given the court's interpretation, would a defendant violate the statute if he engaged in an act of sexual penetration with a fully willing partner? Students will no doubt understand that the court has read into the statute a requirement of non-consent; force, as defined by the court, exists when there is sexual penetration in the absence of freely given consent (p. 342, 2d full ¶). Note the net effect: a statute criminalizing intercourse committed by force, without regard to consent, is interpreted to prohibit intercourse in the absence of consent, without regard to force (other than that intrinsic to the act of intercourse).

Is the grading of this offense appropriate to cases not involving additional forms of physical violence? Note the mandatory minimum sentence, p. 340 n.a.

If existing criminal laws are inadequate or have significant gaps in coverage, should courts take the lead in reform (as in M.T.S.) or should they await initiatives from the legislature? Is the legislature likely to correct defects in the law more quickly when they involve penalties that are arguably too high (perhaps the net result of M.T.S.) or too low? Does the likelihood of legislative correction depend on whether it is men or women who are harmed by the gaps and anomalies?

Apart from the awkward questions of statutory interpretation, is there anything wrong with the substantive result reached by the court? Criminality under the court's holding depends entirely on the absence of consent, but what factors determine when consent is absent?

- First, the court makes clear that silence or ambivalence are not sufficient to show consent; consent must be affirmative. Is that is the right standard? The controversy over this point is explored at pp. 343-46, Note 3.

- Second, there remains, again, a concern about grading: when a defendant in a dating situation proceeds in the face of his partner's silence or ambivalence, or when he negligently believes that he does have affirmative permission signaled by his partner's conduct, should he be placed in the same grading category as the defendant who compels submission by threats of a severe beating?

- Third, assuming that consent is affirmatively expressed, when is such consent "freely given" (p. 342, 2d full ¶)? In other words, when does "yes" really mean yes? Reconsider the cases discussed in connection with the issue of nonphysical coercion, p. 84 above.

In Pennsylvania, criminality requires a showing of force, and force includes "moral, psychological, or intellectual" pressure, Rhodes, p. 336, Note 3(d). In New Jersey, the analytic framework looks different, but similar substantive issues arise: there is no requirement of force extrinsic to the act of intercourse, but consent must be "freely given." Precisely what kinds of pressures or constraints will render consent invalid in New Jersey? Consider what circumstances constitute force (in Pennsylvania) or "unfree" consent (in New Jersey).

- Would Thompson, p. 333, and Mlinarich, p. 334 be convicted under the recent New Jersey and Pennsylvania approaches? If so, does that mean that "economic duress" (p. 336, 1st indented quote) will constitute "force" or render consent "unfree"?

- What if a woman consents in response to a defendant's threat to break off a dating relationship, or a threat not to give his female subordinate a deserved promotion? Does the result change if such "threats" are re-characterized as "offers" (i.e., an offer to continue the dating relationship if the woman is willing to accept her male partner's sexual terms)? Should such questions simply be left to the jury (was consent "freely given"; was there "moral, psychological, or intellectual force"?) or should the questions be governed by specific rules of law? What criteria will be used to provide the answers?

2. Deception, pp. 346-51

Evans, p. 346. Even viewing rape as a crime of violence, shouldn't Evans be convicted? Under N. Y.'s statute, rape by forcible compulsion "a threat, express or implied" (§130.00(8), pp. 320-21). But wasn't there such a threat here? Note that the trial judge was the trier of fact. If a jury had convicted, could an appellate court properly reverse? Presumably a jury could conclude that the defendant's statement ("I could kill you") was intended as a threat. Is the trial judge's alternative interpretation (p. 348, 2d full ¶) sufficiently plausible to raise a reasonable doubt? Or is the trial judge as naive, psychologically, as Miss P.?

What result should be reached in Evans if the defendant had employed all the same devices, without making the statement "I could kill you ..."? Would there be any way to convict the defendant of forcible rape under such circumstances? (Consider the material on indirect intimidation, p. 332, Note 1) If not, should there be some other offense applicable to Evans's misconduct? Should he be subject to punishment on the basis of his deception and manipulation? Such behavior has not been thought of as "rape," but should there be some criminal offense for situations in which consent is procured by "artifice, deception, flattery, fraud or promise" (p. 347, last ¶). What problems would arise?

In this connection consider Boro, p. 348. Note that the deception employed here is obviously sufficient to support a theft charge (p. 349 n.a) but is held insufficient to support a charge of rape. What is the distinction between fraud "in the factum" and fraud "in the inducement"? Is conduct of the latter type punishable as rape? (No.) As any other offense? (Apparently not: if defendant had not taken money under false pretenses, he would have committed no crime at all.) Why are property rights more carefully protected than a woman's sexual autonomy? Why shouldn't Boro's conduct be punishable? Note the line-drawing problem, p. 350 n.5. But does this difficulty justify immunizing all deceptions, even the most highly egregious ones? Consider:

Case 1. Pat voluntarily goes to Rusk's room. During the course of the evening Rusk professes his love for Pat and tells her that he wants her to move in with him and live at his apartment starting the next morning. Persuaded of Rusk's sincerity, Pat agrees to intercourse. Subsequently Rusk drives Pat home and tells her he is married and won't be able to see her again. Evidence proves that the "move in with me" line is his standard ploy and that he never had any intention of carrying out the promise. Should Rusk be guilty of rape?

Note that the misrepresentations are clearly "material." If Rusk had induced Pat to part with property on the basis of analogous false representations, he could be convicted of theft by deception. See MPC §223.3. Should such a deception similarly invalidate Pat's consent to intercourse? Should women likewise be guilty of criminal sexual misconduct if they make material misrepresentations to their male partners?

If there are good reasons not to extend criminal liability to all misrepresentation of emotional attachment or other material facts in sexual relationships (this, of course, is highly debatable, see the articles cited at p. 351, Note 3), how can we distinguish situations that should not be subject to legal regulation from egregious abuses like Boro? Consider the California statute enacted after Boro (p. 351, Note 1). Could Boro himself be convicted under this provision? If this is too narrow, what kinds of deception should suffice to invalidate consent? Compare the MPC standard for theft by deception, §223.3. Is this test be appropriate for dealing with deception in sexual relations? Consider the standard proposed at pp. 364-65 in the suggested Model Statute §§202(c)(7),(8). Is this approach too narrow?

D. Mens Rea, pp. 351- 66

Sherry, p. 351. What mens rea standard is the court adopting here? Students should see that the court rejects the approach of requiring actual knowledge of nonconsent (this was the theory of the instructions requested by defendants at p. 353 n.8). Does this mean that proof of negligence is required for conviction? Although many American courts take this approach (Mayberry, p. 358, Note 2, is perhaps the leading case), students should see that the Sherry court (p. 353, last full ¶) does not commit itself to a negligence standard. In the companion case (pp. 353-54), Justice Brown expressly rejects a negligence defense and treats the consent issue as a matter of strict liability ("the person proceeds at his peril"), at least once an explicit "no" has been articulated. Is strict liability necessary for adequate protection of women? What if the woman does not articulate an express "No"? Is a defendant still subject to conviction for rape if his honest and reasonable belief in consent turns out to be incorrect? See <u>Ascollilo</u> and <u>Simcock</u>, p. 358, Note 1, holding in the affirmative. Is this a defensible position? Is the <u>Simcock</u> court's analogy to statutory rape sound?

Should the appropriate mens rea depend in part on the degree to which stringent requirements of physical force must be met as part of the actus reus element? A strict liability or negligence standard might not pose frequent problems of fair warning under statutes that require proof of physical violence or threats of serious bodily harm. But consider the Pennsylvania definition of forcible compulsion (p. 356, 2d indented quote). In the case of a college student who makes sexual advances to a date with whom he already has a sexual relationship, is it fair to hold that he must know at his peril when she feels compelled by "emotional or psychological force"?

Was a criminal conviction justified on the facts of <u>Fischer</u>, p. 354? If so, why? Is it because the defendant obviously knew he was abusing the victim and proceeded without her consent? That is certainly one possible reading of the facts. But was the jury required to reach that conclusion in order to convict? Presumably not. Though the trial judge apparently did not tell the jury (as in <u>Simcock</u>, p. 358, Note 1) that a reasonable mistake was no defense, but he also did not alert the jury that a reasonable mistake would be a defense. The appellate court assumes that the jury might have considered Fischer's mistake reasonable and then upholds the conviction nonetheless. On that view of the facts, is a felony conviction for rape (or IDSI) really fair?

What is the court's justification for the result? One of its reasons seems largely technical - - that trial counsel can't be faulted for failing to anticipate a possible challenge to existing law (pp. 357, last line, and top of p. 358). But what would this court do in a future case, on identical facts, if defense counsel had raised such an issue at trial and if the trial judge had rejected her request for an instruction on reasonable mistake? Note the point made at p. 357, next to last full ¶: because physical force was alleged, the strict liability approach should control. Does a strict liability standard nonetheless pose culpability problems and lack of fair warning on facts like those of Fischer? Or is Fischer a situation in which it is fair to require the one who initiates sexual advances to proceed at his peril?

As a reality check, it may help to consider whether the mens rea requirement actually makes any difference in practice. How can a defendant ever claim an honest mistake of fact about consent when, as in <u>Sherry</u>, the woman (by her testimony) has expressly protested? Is it still possible, in the 1990's, for a defendant to claim that "no" doesn't really mean know? Are there ever situations in which a woman might say "no" but not mean no?

Students now hesitate to articulate this view, though sometimes some will acknowledge that they know other people who think or act this way. If the class thinks that this kind of thinking is now totally non-existent, the data at p. 362, Note 7 can be referred to for contemporary evidence. In the 1988 study of Texas college undergraduates, 39% of the women said that they had sometimes said "no" when they wanted to have sex, and more recent studies in other parts of the country report similar findings (p. 362 n.20). If such thinking still exists, then mistakes about consent *are* possible. See the Weiner excerpt (p. 362). The Henderson and Friedland articles, cited at p. 362, are also helpful on this point.

(b) If mistakes about consent are possible, one way to provide greater protection for women is to punish defendants when their mistakes are unreasonable. But is this approach fair? Consider:

> Case 1. A defendant named Cunningham breaks off a gas meter to steal the coins inside, and allows gas to escape from the broken meter into the house. He honestly believes the gas cannot harm anyone, but his belief is unreasonable under the circumstances. Can he be convicted of causing malicious injury to a person who breathes some of the gas? Was the Cunningham decision wrong in requiring actual foresight of consequences? If not, in what ways is the Cunningham situation distinguishable from Sherry and Fischer?

> Case 2. When leaving the bar with F, M grabs a raincoat lying on the chair next to him. The raincoat is found in M's car when he is later arrested for the alleged rape of F. The raincoat belongs to a patron at the bar, but M claims that he honestly thought it was his, and in fact M does own a very similar raincoat. If the jury believes that M honestly (but unreasonably) thought that he was taking his own raincoat, can he be convicted of theft? No: See Kelly, p. 361. Consider a variation: Suppose that M had seen a patron at the bar walking off with that raincoat. Thinking that the coat was his own, M had rushed up to the other patron, pushed him, and grabbed the raincoat away. Can M be convicted of robbery? Just as M cannot be convicted of theft in the original Case 2, M would not be guilty of robbery in the variation. (He might, however, be guilty of an assault, since he knows that he is striking another person, and may not have a privilege to engage in self-help under these circumstances.)

Query: should the law of robbery and theft be extended to reach the situations in Case 2? If not, is there reason for treating a mistake about the owner's consent in the law of theft and robbery (Kelly) differently from a mistake about the victim's consent in the law of rape? There are two possible answers here (though both are debatable). First, in the context of rape, a failure to exercise reasonable care is <u>criminally</u> culpable (see the Estrich excerpt, p. 361, last indented quote, and the discussion of Case 3 below.) Second, the harm to the victim in rape is more serious and more permanent than the harm to the victim in theft. (But compare the harm to the victim in <u>Cunningham</u>, p. 204, where subjective culpability was required).

> <u>Case 3.</u> Return to the situation in which M and F leave the bar together. While they are driving, M and F are having an intense personal discussion, sitting close to one another and hugging. F is not resisting M's advances, and M is thinking about where he can find a secluded place to park. Suddenly, there is a loud crash. Distracted, M had failed to see a stop sign and had collided with a car entering the intersection from another direction, killing the driver. Has M committed a crime? If so, <u>what</u> crime? Query whether M's negligence is sufficiently gross to satisfy the requirements for negligent homicide or involuntary manslaughter (discussed in Chapter 5). Would it be appropriate to convict M for murder?

Discussion of Cases 1-3 can suggest two conflicting impulses with respect to the treatment of mistakes as to consent. First is the traditional doubt about whether negligence should ever be a sufficient basis for criminal liability. [The MPC limits negligence liability to cases of a "*gross* departure" and provides that even then, this is to be an exceptional basis of liability. See §2.02(3).] But, second, is such doubt sufficient to warrant exonerating M even in Case 3? Doesn't the social importance of encouraging due care apply not only in Case 3 but also in <u>Sherry</u>? If criminal liability is warranted, what should be the appropriate level of punishment? Note under the MPC that rape is a felony of the first or second degree, but negligent <u>killing</u> is only a felony of the third degree. Do we need a separate offense of negligent rape? (See the proposed Model Statute §203(b), p. 365.) Would this risk diluting the penalties now imposed on cases of *intentional* rape in social situations?

Discussion should make clear that mens rea requirements cannot be determined solely as a matter of logical analysis. Decisions depend first on social conceptions about the kind of behavior the community condemns or resolves to deter. Secondarily, but of great practical importance, such decisions also depend on administrative judgments about the grading categories most suitable for clear application and effective enforcement.

(c) A third consideration is whether a negligence standard will succeed in producing the desired results for women. This problem can be brought out by returning to the facts of Sherry. Will the choice between negligence and a subjective standard make a difference to the outcome of a case like this one? How could the defendants possibly qualify for acquittal under either approach? Given the victim's isolation, her intimidation by three naked men and her explicit protests, any belief in consent seems most unreasonable. But for the same reasons, it is hard to see how a belief in consent could be honestly held at all. Is there any reason that might lead a jury to acquit under a subjective recklessness standard?

There might be one way (p. 360, 1st indented quote). What if "no" does not really mean "no"? Any juror who holds this (possibly outmoded) view could easily believe that the defendants sincerely thought the woman was consenting. *But*, under a negligence standard, such a juror might also conclude that the defendants' belief was reasonable. Again, the choice between negligence and a subjective standard may make little or no difference, but differing substantive conceptions of what "consent" means can make a great deal of difference. See pp. 343-46, Note 3. Nonconsent, like many offense elements, is not a tangible fact but a social and legal construct. In part the argument for a negligence standard seems to be an argument for a stricter, more "woman-centered" conception of what should count as consent. But the move to a negligence standard produces this result only if juries share a "modern" or "feminist" conception of what is reasonable.

Why sweep this issue under the rug of jury findings about reasonableness? Compare the MacKinnon excerpt, p. 363, and the various efforts to define consent by statute, Cal. Penal Code §261.5 [p. 320]; NY Penal Law §§130.25(2),(3) [p. 321, a very restrictive definition]; Wis. Stat. §940.225(4) [p. 322]; and the proposed Model Statute §§202(b),(c) [pp. 364-65].

F. The Marital Exemption, pp. 366-371

The marital exemption is by no means a thing of the past. Some states still afford immunity from rape prosecution when the parties are living together; in some states, even after the wife has moved out, the husband retains his immunity until formal legal separation or divorce. The continued application of the marital rape exemption in cases of rape committed by life threatening attacks or other physical brutality (such as the facts in Liberta, p. 366) is difficult to defend. (But see the MPC comment at pp. 369-70.)

-92-

Should the marital rape exemption be abolished completely? The preceding materials have considered a number of directions from which the elements of rape are being redefined - - often, resistance by the woman or physical violence by the man are no longer required; nonconsent alone may be sufficient to make the defendant's conduct rape; some statutes treat silence or ambivalence as equivalent to nonconsent and require an affirmative manifestation of positive consent (e.g., the Wisconsin statute, p. 322, and M.T.S., p. 338). Where rape or other sexual offenses have been extended in these ways, should the same standards apply to married couples who are living together?

G. Problems of Proof, pp. 371-386

If time constraints require, exploration of the proof problems can be left for independent study by students who wish to pursue the issues.

When the course schedule permits, however, this practical side of rape law administration is worth at least part of a class hour. Credibility judgments are critical to society's ability to enforce rape laws effectively. They also provide a telling window into problematic gender role expectations, racial stereotypes and narrow standards of "proper" behavior that pervade the culture. See the Estrich excerpt, p. 375.

Consider Colbath, p. 380, Note 4. Should the challenged evidence be admitted? Does Justice Souter's approach in effect mean that the complainant's prior behavior in the bar makes her "unrapeable"? Of course, such evidence in no way "proves" that she consented, but admissibility ordinarily requires only that testimony cross the very low threshold necessary to establish evidentiary relevance (recall Chapter 1, p. 20). Is the evidence concerning the complainant's prior behavior relevant in that sense or not? If it is relevant, is there a legitimate reason to exclude it nonetheless? What if only a small number of people had been present at a private party? Would the complainant's heightened privacy interest then trump the defendant's need to use the evidence in his defense? Does Davis v. Alaska (pp. 378-79) permit such trade-offs?

Compare Wood, p. 381. Here the court upholds the exclusion of the evidence. Is the result justified? Is this approach necessary to protect the sexual autonomy of women like M.G. whose conduct does not conform to traditional middle class expectations? Or does the court's approach create a significant risk of convicting an innocent man? (Or both?)

Discussion of these cases should help bring out two basic problems that are posed by cases in this section. First, what kinds of facts about a rape complainant's personality, dress or prior behavior are truly relevant to her credibility and the likelihood that she consented? Second, when, if ever, should the victim's rights to dignity and privacy protect her from cross-examination (or other public consideration) concerning facts that may be relevant (perhaps only marginally) to a defendant's claims of innocence? Conversely, when must a defendant's constitutional right to confront and cross-examine witnesses take precedence over a victim's legitimate privacy concerns?

Rape-shield statutes attempt to address these competing concerns by identifying in advance the types of evidence that will be admissible. See p. 377, Note 3. But the categories often prove inapt (consider Neeley, p. 380, Note 3). What standards should be used to determine the relevance and admissibility of facts about the complainant's dress, behavior and prior sexual history?

Chapter Five
Homicide

Introduction, pp. 387-395

This chapter considers an offense that is of obvious importance, both for its own sake and as a vehicle for examining more general issues, including the precise delineation of the mental state sufficient for culpability, and the appropriate grading of conduct that is clearly criminal. The introductory material (pp. 387-95) should be assigned as background, and students should be encouraged to consult the specific statutory formulations in thinking about the problems posed throughout the chapter. This Manual assumes that the instructor will choose to spend three or four classes on intentional killings (one class on premeditation, pp. 395-405, and two or three classes on provocation, pp. 405-25); two classes on negligent and reckless homicide (pp. 425-439 and 439-448); and three classes on felony murder (pp. 448-59, 459-71, and 471-83). In addition, if time permits, the instructor has the option of spending one or two classes on the death penalty (483-93 and 493-515).

Intended Killing -- Premeditation, pp. 395-405.

This class should develop familiarity with different statutory schemes for identifying the most serious types of homicide. At the outset it may be helpful to note the difference between relatively modern statutes with specific definitions of operative language (e.g. New York), and those using older common-law language that is defined awkwardly (e.g. Cal. Penal Code §188, especially the third sentence) or not at all (e.g. Pa. Stat. §2502(c)). The first group of cases deals with the prevailing interpretation of the older common law language. In particular, since "malice aforethought" is clearly present in all the cases, the problem is to determine whether the killing is "deliberate" and "premeditated."

Carroll, p. 396. Where is the evidence of deliberation and premeditation? The court says the defendant's own testimony provides it (p. 399, last full ¶). But where in his testimony is there any hint of deliberation? The court's quote from Earnest, p. 398, 4th full ¶, implies that premeditation and deliberation can occur no matter how brief the space of time; in fact, that quote appears to equate "intent to kill" with "premeditation." Doesn't this simply read premeditation and deliberation out of the statute? The problem is that intent implies a choice, and if the defendant chose, then his

act can be considered deliberate and premeditated. See p. 400, Note 1.
Thus under the Pennsylvania interpretation, the adjectives "willful,
deliberate and premeditated" become essentially synonymous. See O'Searo,
p. 400, Note 2. Is there anything to be said for this interpretation? Why
would society be "almost completely unprotected" (Tyrrell, bottom of p.
399) by the sanctions provided for second-degree murder? Why shouldn't
premeditation be given its natural meaning?

At first glance, Carroll's dilution of the premeditation requirement
seems odd and hard to defend. See Guthrie, p. 400, where the court
overruled its prior precedent analogous to Carroll and chose instead to give
premeditation its natural meaning, requiring some "prior calculation and
design," with "some appreciable time elapse[d]" (p. 402, 3d full ¶). Does this
approach produce more satisfactory results in practice? Compare Carroll
and Guthrie (spontaneous killings that may not seem among the worst of
homicides) with Anderson, p. 403, Note 2 (a spontaneous but nonetheless
extremely aggravated killing).

Even by the stricter California/West Virginia test for premeditation,
why isn't the Anderson killing first degree? The evidence apparently isn't
sufficient to exclude the possibility of an impulsive killing in an "explosion
of violence"; in effect the multiplicity of brutal wounds becomes a
mitigating factor! Does this make more sense than the Carroll result, or is
there something wrong with both?

Consider how Guthrie would have been decided in Pennsylvania.
Presumably there would be adequate evidence for first degree. But
depending on the location of the wounds, could it still be argued, on an
"explosion of violence" theory, that there was insufficient evidence of
specific intent to kill? How would Carroll be decided in West Virginia?
Would the conviction be reduced to second degree? Perhaps, but not
necessarily. Apply the evidentiary guidelines (p. 403, Note 1, indented
quote). Arguably, motive and manner are both satisfied in Guthrie. Thus,
even under the Anderson-Guthrie tests, there could be adequate evidence
to sustain a first-degree conviction on appeal. Nonetheless, there is an
important substantive difference between the findings that a jury must
make under the Carroll and Guthrie approaches - - the latter requires that
some appreciable period of time must elapse between the decision to kill
and the execution of that intent.

Which substantive standard for premeditation is preferable? The
Pennsylvania approach produces a first-degree conviction in Carroll,
whether or not there is planning or deliberation in any real sense. But does

<u>Carroll</u> belong among the most heinous murders? If not, the Pennsylvania definition does not seem to select out the most truly aggravated cases. Compare the West Virginia approach. If a case like <u>Forrest</u> (p. 404, after the 1st indented quote) is first degree in West Virginia, while a case like <u>Anderson</u> is not, what does that say about the validity of the West Virginia interpretation? Arguably, neither the West Virginia nor the Pennsylvania interpretation works well in identifying the most heinous murders. Does the problem flow from the premeditation concept itself? Absence of premeditation can sometimes be an aggravating rather than a mitigating factor. See MPC comments, p. 404. Aren't the factors that render one killing more serious than another too diverse for any single factor (like premeditation) to serve as the sole distinguishing criterion? Consider the comment by Prof. Pillsbury (p. 404, 1st indented quote. Note that the MPC abandons the premeditation formula entirely. See § 210.2.

Where the statutory formula includes premeditation, how should it be interpreted? If you were representing Carroll, in a state not yet committed to either the Pennsylvania or West Virginia interpretations, how would argue for the latter? Note the argument that the Pennsylvania approach "completely eliminates" any distinction between the degrees of murder (p. 402, 2d full ¶. But is this accurate? (The Note at the beginning of p. 403 makes a similar point, though in more qualified terms. Under the <u>Carroll</u> approach, is there any kind of murder that would <u>not</u> be eligible for first degree? Note that the second-degree category includes various kinds of unintentional killing (essentially reckless killings). See pp. 389, ¶ 76. Against this background, what is the distinction between first and second degree in the two states? Note that the Pennsylvania approach produces the following division: intentional killing = first degree; reckless killing = second degree. In California the division is: intent + reflection = first degree; other intentional or reckless killing = second degree.

Consider which of the two grading schemes is the more workable. Is the distinction between adequate and inadequate reflection sufficiently clear? How much reflection is enough?

Discussion should help indicate that part of the objective in grading is to tailor the seriousness of the offense to the defendant's actual culpability under all the circumstances. The Swedish approach (p. 395) illustrates one way to achieve perfect accuracy in this substantive sense. Why not simply adopt the Swedish grading scheme? Obviously, a competing concern is to control discretion over the vast range of punishments available for homicide. To do this, the grading categories should be separable from one another on something other than a vague or purely subjective basis. From this perspective isn't the Pennsylvania approach preferable? Discussion can bring out two conflicting instincts: (1) emphasis on the most accurate determination of seriousness requires open-ended criteria and hence relatively little control of discretion; but (2) control of discretion requires clear, workable categories which inevitably fail to produce substantively satisfactory results in some individual cases. The grading process for homicide (and other crimes) reflects a constant tension between these two objectives.

Provocation, pp. 405-424.

Having discussed the distinction between first- and second-degree murder, we turn to the distinction between first- and second-degree murder on the one hand and manslaughter on the other.

Organization and allotment of time. The casebook is designed so that the provocation material may be taught straight through in two classes. The first class, pp. 405-15, should introduce the formulation and rationale of the defense, together with the two central problems in applying it: determining which situations should qualify as provocation and the relative roles of judge and jury in making that determination. The second class, pp. 415-24, should explore two problems: the MPC approach and the degree of individualization that should apply in the concept of the reasonable person.

An alternative approach is to allot three classes to this material. We find that the material intensely engages student attention and that it can be used to raise a variety of important issues. These include traditional concerns about the role of culpability in grading, the relative scope for rules versus discretion and judge versus jury, and tough questions about the meaning of a reasonableness standard (descriptive versus normative and general versus individualized). In addition, the typical "heat of passion" situation raises controversial questions about sexual roles and gender stereotypes, in a context of changing social mores and changing normative expectations. Teachers who find it profitable to allot three full hours to the provocation material may wish to split the material into three smaller segments: pp. 405-15, 415-20, and 420-24. If time permits the 2d and 3d classes could be supplemented by discussion of two controversial cases not included in this edition - - People v. Thornton, 730 SW2d 309 (Tenn. 1987), and DPP v. Camplin, [1978] 2 All E.R. 168 (H.L.)

<u>Introduction and statutory interpretation.</u> Under common-law formulations, the key defining criterion of murder is "malice aforethought." But what does this mean? Consider these cases:

> <u>Case 1</u>. Note the facts of People v. Roberts, 211 Mich. 187, 178 N.W. 680 (1920). The defendant's wife, who suffered from a painful, incurable illness, begged him to obtain a poison for her. Out of love for his wife and a desire to end her misery, he did she requested. (In <u>Roberts</u> the wife drank the poison herself; to clarify the example and eliminate any possible causation issue, it is helpful to assume that Roberts administered the poison.) Presumably, premeditation is easy to show here, but how can Roberts be guilty of murder? Where is the "malice"? Under the technical common-law definition (see p. 389, ¶ 76), Roberts clearly has malice aforethought; the absence of ill will or spite is irrelevant, so long as there is an intent to kill. Recall <u>Cunningham</u> at p. 204.) The result is the same under Cal. Penal Code § 188 [p. 390] and under Pa. Stat. § 2502(c) [p. 392] where "other murder," since undefined, must be given its common law meaning.

> <u>Case 2</u>. <u>Anderson</u>, p. 403, Note 2. We saw above that under California law, Anderson was not guilty of first-degree murder. Is he guilty of second degree, or is this manslaughter? Students will naturally want to begin examination of this issue by considering the statutory language. The case arguably meets the literal requirements for either murder (malice = intent to kill or a "malignant heart") or manslaughter ("sudden quarrel or heat of passion"). Does "heat of passion" negate malice, or is second-degree murder possible on the ground that the case fits both?

Common law language about "sudden quarrel" or "heat of passion" cannot be taken without qualification, as <u>Maher</u>, p. 407, makes clear. Although all recognized definitions of malice aforethought seemingly exclude killings committed when "reason [is] clouded or obscured by passion" (p. 407, 3d full ¶), the court indicates that actions in a sudden heat will qualify only if the passion or "heat of blood" is "produced by an adequate or reasonable provocation" (p. 407, 4th full ¶). Similarly, in California, the qualification in § 188 ("when no considerable provocation appears") must be read into § 192(1) as limiting the kinds of "heat of passion" that negate malice. This is true under all the common law formulations. Therefore to separate murder from manslaughter one must determine whether there was the right kind of provocation.

The test for provocation and its rationale

Maher, p. 407. Was the court right to reverse the conviction here? Is it really true that *reasonable* people ("ordinary men, of fair and average disposition," p. 407 last full ¶) would have lost control and responded violently? Some students assume that sexual jealousy was a mitigating factor only in the minds of 19th Century courts, and that this factor no longer carries (or should carry) weight in light of modern sexual mores. The facts and outcome in Thornton (730 SW2d 309) can be mentioned here to help some students to see the problem in its modern context.

Is it plausible today for a juror to view the defendant's actions in a situation like Maher's as the result of an understandable heat of passion? Should the manslaughter issue here be presented to the jury at all? The court viewed the facts as suggesting that the defendant was highly distraught and that such an emotional state was understandable ("reasonable"). Thornton indicates that even in contemporary culture, manslaughter in many states will be viewed as a possible verdict that must be submitted to the jury in killings resulting from the discovery of sexual infidelity. (Compare the 1997 Maryland statute, p. 406 n.a, which remains, to date, very much a minority position.)

What is the basis for the majority view? How can such a killing ever be seen as "reasonable"? One frequent source of resistance to the idea of a lesser, manslaughter verdict on facts like Maher is the student's assumption that mitigation should be granted only when the "reasonable" person would kill. (See Prof. Morse's comments, p. 410, last indented quote). Is this the rationale of the provocation defense? If the reasonable person would kill, how can we justify imposing any punishment on her at all? (See Maher, p. 408, 1st 5 lines). Students should see that the purpose of the defense is not to identify cases in which the reasonable person would kill, but merely to identify cases in which the reasonable person might be rendered highly upset and liable to act rashly. See the formulation by Judge Boochever (p. 410, 1st indented quote) and in Maher, p. 407, last full ¶.

What about deterrence? If the temptation to commit the crime is greater, doesn't deterrence theory call for a higher penalty? The notion of keeping punishment proportional to moral fault seems to provide a better explanation for why provocation is a mitigating factor.

Return to Maher with this test in mind. Applying this test, the result may still seem controversial to some students, but it should be easier to see why manslaughter is at least a possible verdict and why the court thought it so clear that the requirements were met.

The nature of the required provocation

Given the prevailing test for provocation and its underlying objective (that of identifying cases in which the defendant was understandably led to act rashly), is the result in Girouard, p. 405, correct? Note the graphic character of the verbal provocation. Is it clear as a matter of law that those circumstances could not be extremely upsetting to the reasonable person, or does the result reflect limits on the provocation defense adopted for additional policy reasons? If unexpectedly discovering a spouse in an act of adultery qualifies as sufficient provocation to go to the jury, why shouldn't a spouse's unexpected revelation of past adultery also qualify, especially if it is accompanied by vivid comments praising the lover and disparaging the other spouse.

Even if Girouard is right in its treatment of the sexual infidelity problem, why should courts hold that no sort of verbal provocation should ever be sufficient? Consider:

> Case 1. Smith meets Jones in a bar and reveals that he has just come from Jones's house, where he forcibly raped Jones's wife (or daughter). If Jones loses his self-control and kills Smith, should manslaughter instructions be given to the jury? Should evidence about the words Smith spoke to Jones just before the killing be held inadmissible?

The Girouard court (p. 406, 3d full ¶) and apparently most modern American courts would hold the evidence inadmissible and deny manslaughter instructions in Case 1. Why shouldn't judges simply leave all these kinds of questions to the common sense of the jury, as the court concluded in Maher, especially at p. 408, 2d full ¶?

Maher, p. 416, raises an additional wrinkle. Note the concern of the dissenting judge on appeal: The defendant must actually see the adultery; otherwise "the innocent as well as the guilty ... might be the sufferers" (p. 409, last 7 lines). But why should this be a relevant concern? The answer presumably depends on the reason why provocation mitigates punishment in the first place. Is it because the victim is partly at fault, or because the defendant is less deserving of punishment? Consider the following:

Case 2. Maher actually saw the adultery before confronting Hunt in the bar. His bullet, after going "in and through the left ear" of Hunt, hits and kills an innocent bystander. Should Maher be guilty of murder or manslaughter? Under the view of the dissent, the provocation defense arguably should not be available. Would this make sense?

What is the rationale of the provocation defense? Why does the defendant deserve a lesser punishment -- (a) because she is less blameworthy? (b) because her victim is <u>more</u> blameworthy? or (c) because her act is less deterrable? Each theory can be considered. With regard to the blameworthiness of the victim, see pp. 411, Note 2(b). The Dressler excerpt (p. 411, 3d indented quote) makes a powerful argument for why provocation should be considered a partial excuse, not a partial <u>justification</u>. But compare the cases at p. 414, Note 6(c). In those cases can a court plausibly find as a matter of law that no reasonable person could have been provoked to act rashly? On an excuse theory, it seems to follow that those cases necessarily were wrongly decided.

Discussion should make clear that focusing on the innocence of the victim would make liability turn on fortuitous factors irrelevant to culpability. Although some early common law decisions did hold that provocation must come from the actual victim, the cases now reject this view. See <u>Mauricio</u>, p. 414, Note 6(b); see also Pa. Stat. §2503(a)(2), p. 392. [But note the divergent instinct when the non-provoker is killed deliberately rather than accidentally, p. 414, Note 4(c).]

California, Pennsylvania, England and several other jurisdictions have followed <u>Maher</u> in rejecting arbitrary limits on the <u>kind</u> of provocation allowed. For related reasons, many jurisdictions (in this case, probably the majority of common law jurisdictions) reject arbitrary limits on the <u>period</u> sufficient for "cooling time" (p. 413, Note 5). Instead, the jury, who are "much better qualified" (<u>Maher</u>, p. 408, 2d full ¶), are normally entitled to hear the provocation evidence and to judge its sufficiency.

Does the <u>Maher</u> approach mean that the trial judge should never hold provocation evidence inadmissible as a matter of law? Note that the court in <u>Maher</u> still assumes some trial judge control. See p. 408, last full ¶. But why should the trial judge ever intervene, if jurors are "much better qualified" to decide such matters? Consider:

Case 3. B shoots A. Two years before, A seduced B's 15-year-old daughter, then behaved rudely toward B and his family, and abandoned the daughter after she became pregnant. B had no further contact with A until two years later when B, seeing A, immediately drew a gun and shot him. Should the evidence of A's earlier behavior be admissible? What are the costs of letting it in? If the possibility that a reasonable person might lose self control seems remote, then doesn't the prejudicial effect ("putting the victim on trial") greatly outweigh the probative value? Note that even after Maher, the prosecution can still argue, on this basis, that provocation should be deemed insufficient as a matter of law.

Case 4. Consider a defendant who claims that he was enraged and prompted to kill when another man sexually propositioned him. See p. 412, Note 4. These circumstances presumably would not lead an ordinary or "reasonable" person to lose self control. But why not let the "much better qualified" jury make that judgment? Note again the danger when allegedly provoking circumstances have little legitimate probative value (i.e., little likelihood of severely upsetting the reasonable person) but substantial prejudicial effect: The jury may mitigate punishment not because they conclude that the defendant was reasonably provoked but instead because they conclude that the victim did not deserve the normal degree of social protection.

Discussion of Cases 3 and 4 can be used to indicate the tension between the value of respecting the jury's competence (as Maher stresses) and the need to keep the trial focussed on issues that are legitimately relevant to culpability, rather than permitting defendants to "put the victim on trial."

The Model Penal Code Approach, pp. 415-20

Casassa, p. 415. What was the "provocation" here? (Basically, none.) Would defendant have a "heat of passion" defense to murder under the common law approach? (Clearly not.) Applying the MPC approach the court here also holds manslaughter inapplicable. Then how are the two standards different? Note that here the trial judge was trier of fact. In a jury trial, could the judge have ruled out manslaughter *as a matter of law* and refused to instruct the jury to consider it? Under the common law approach, yes (see Maher, p. 408, last full ¶). But applying the MPC, the court here holds that once there is proof of subjective emotional disturbance (regardless of its source), the question of its reasonableness becomes a jury issue. (See p. 417, last full ¶). As a result, defendants can get to the jury on the manslaughter issue even when there are no external provoking circumstances at all. (See, e.g., <u>Elliot</u>, p. 418, Note 2.) On this basis, isn't the defendant entitled to a jury instruction even in <u>Walker</u>, p. 419, Note 3? The lack of boundaries on the "EED" defense and the lack of a framework for jury control probably accounts for some of the discomfort with the MPC formulation (p. 418, Note 1).

<u>The Objectivity of the Standard</u>, pp. 420-24

This section deals with the question whether the ostensibly "objective" standard of reasonableness should ever be individualized to take account of a defendant's unusual personal characteristics. To start off discussion of this conceptually elusive issue a concrete factual situation like <u>Camplin</u>, p. 423, Note 3© is a good place to start. Students should note the specific provoking circumstances: the older man subjected Camplin to forcible sodomy and then taunted him about it. The question examined so far is whether such evidence should be admissible at all. This evidence clearly meets the test for admissibility. But what is the standard by which such evidence should be evaluated?

Class discussion should seek to develop familiarity with the concepts of subjective and objective standards (more accurately described as individualized or invariant standards, see Hart, p. 437, Note 6), and to determine which of these is appropriate for the provocation defense. Note the test adopted by the trial judge (p. 423, 2d indented quote). Should the "reasonable person" be viewed in terms of the attributes of the typical person or those of the defendant himself? Consider the following problems:

> Case 1. Note the situation in <u>Bedder</u> (top of p. 423). Does the court's approach there make sense? Given the purposes of the provocation defense, isn't it pointless to consider the effect of the taunts on a person who did not suffer from impotence? Doesn't the provocation have to be judged in terms of its impact on someone in the defendant's actual circumstances?

> Case 2. Suppose that D is drinking heavily in a bar when V, another patron, insults him and taunts him about his wife's sexual infidelity. D, enraged, grabs an ashtray and batters V over the head, killing him. Should the jury be instructed to consider the effect of this provocation on the reasonable sober man, or on the reasonable heavily intoxicated man?

The approach adopted by the House of Lords in Camplin is helpful in making clear the necessary distinction between Case 1 and Case 2. Normally personal characteristics are relevant only in assessing the gravity of the provocation, not in assessing the degree of self-control expected. In effect, the standard is subjective with respect to the former issue and objective with respect to the latter; the goal of the law is to uphold an external, normative standard with respect to self-control.

Now return to Camplin. Since the defendant was not taunted for his youth, why should his age be relevant? The court here holds that the defendant's personal characteristics should be considered, not only in assessing the gravity of the provocation addressed to him, but also in determining the degree of self-control to be expected. Is this sound? The problem is that the defendant cannot be expected to exercise the self-control of an adult. In Case 2, D can be blamed for being drunk. (Would this still be so if D was an alcoholic?) but Camplin cannot be blamed for being young. Thus, personal circumstances must be considered in Camplin in order to determine how much self-control can fairly be expected. But how far should subjectivity with respect to the self-control issue be extended? Consider the following:

Case 3. Suppose that the victim in Camplin had been a twenty-one year old, sober woman. Is the provocation to be judged by its effect on a reasonable person who is in the defendant's circumstances (a woman), or should the focus be on the reaction of a reasonable "person" generally? The court in Camplin says that the standard should focus on the self-control to be expected of a reasonable person of the age and sex of the accused (p. 423, last line). Why should the standard be different for men than for women? Is the court assuming that the "reasonable" woman reacts differently from the "reasonable" man? If so, in what way? Would a "reasonable woman" standard be more favorable to a woman defendant than a generalized "reasonable person" standard? Does the court have in mind a stereotype of women as more excitable than men? Or is the court assuming that a violent reaction to insult is a more legitimate reaction for a man than for a woman? Is there any good reason why the standard should be different for women than for men? See the articles cited at p. 421, Note 2(a).

Case 4. B, a man of Brazilian origin, kills another person who had publicly questioned the fidelity and morality of B's wife. Suppose that B offers to prove that in Brazilian society, an insult of this kind would immediately elicit a violent response. Should B be judged according to the self-control to be expected of a reasonable, law-abiding person of Brazilian background, or should he be judged according to the self-control expected from the reasonable person generally? If the latter, are we applying to the defendant a standard that he himself could not meet? (See arguments of the dissenting judge in Masciantonio (p. 421, Note 2(b)). On the other hand, wouldn't the former standard defeat the ability of the criminal law to establish a general norm of nonviolence?

Under current law, Brazilian background presumably would not be entitled to any special consideration in Case 4; society expects all citizens, regardless of cultural background, to conform to a general norm of nonviolent behavior. But doesn't this concern apply equally in Case 3. If in fact there is a different behavior pattern for men than for women, is this largely a hormonal phenomenon (as perhaps the immaturity of the teenager in Camplin) or is it largely acculturated? If the latter, shouldn't men and women both be held to the same normative standard? Even if men's greater propensity for violence is to some extent biologically explained, shouldn't the law still hold both men and women to the same high standard of nonviolence? Discussion of these problems can help suggest why the external, "objective" standard is only partly descriptive, and remains heavily normative. Camplin is the rare case in which a personal characteristic (age) can legitimately justify a different standard for self-control.

With respect to all of the above cases, how would they be decided under the MPC test? The MPC formulation (p. 420, Note 1) does not explicitly distinguish between assessing the gravity of the provocation and assessing the self-control to be expected. (The commentary even suggests that the vagueness of the MPC standard is deliberate.) Is this a helpful solution to the problem? Arguably, the Camplin distinction between characteristics that affect the gravity of the provocation and those that affect the expected degree of self-control is overly analytic and too difficulty for a jury to apply. But is it better to drop all reference to reasonableness, as Eblish law now requires [Smith (Morgan), p. 424, Note 3(d)] and simply ask the jury to decide whether the defendant's loss of self-control is excusable? Is this a standard at all? Isn't it dangerous to leave the jury with so much discretion in determining whether the situation is one that will "arouse sympathy" (p. 420, next to last sentence of the MPC Commentary)?

<u>Unintended killing -- Risk creation</u>, pp. 425-47

This material normally requires two classes. Pp. 425-39, dealing with involuntary manslaughter, develop familiarity with different concepts of criminal negligence and consider what factors should distinguish behavior that incurs no liability (or only civil liability) from behavior that is subject to criminal sanctions. Pp. 439-47 consider the circumstances under which risk creation should lead to liability for murder. At the outset it may be helpful to note four possibilities in the legal treatment of risk creation: (1) no liability, (2) civil liability, (3) manslaughter, (4) murder. Locating the line between (1) and (2) is a problem for tort law; locating the line between (2) and (3) -- or making (2) coextensive with (3) -- is the problem of criminalization on which pp. 425-39 focus; and locating the line between (3) and (4) is a problem of grading, which is the focus of pp. 439-47.

<u>Involuntary Manslaughter</u>, pp. 425-39

> <u>Case 1</u>. Suppose that the defendant was driving at 35 mph in a 30 mph zone and that while he was glancing to his left, he failed to notice a little child who ran into the street from the right, chasing a ball. The defendant hits and kills the child. Was this a criminal homicide?

Note the standard that applies to Case 1. (P. 428, Note 2) Both <u>Barnett</u> (p. 428) and Andrews (p. 428) acknowledge that the general common law position requires "something more" than ordinary negligence even under statutes that criminalize a killing "without due caution and circumspection" (e.g., Cal. Penal Code §192(b), p. 391). In Case 1 the defendant presumably would be considered negligent and therefore liable in damages, but without more facts, a jury would be unlikely to find that "something more" which is necessary for criminal liability under the prevailing view.

Which standard is preferable? Should the defendant be liable in Case 1? In favor of criminal liability, it can be noted that the conduct involves, by hypothesis, an undue risk, and therefore should be deterred. Also, fault is arguably involved in the failure to exercise due care. Then why has there been traditional resistance (see <u>Barnett</u> and <u>Andrews</u>) to criminal liability for negligence? If civil liability is appropriate, does it follow that criminal liability is also? Holmes apparently thought that the propriety of criminal liability followed <u>a fortiori</u>. See p. 435, 2d full indented quote. But shouldn't the answer depend on the purposes of liability? Both civil and criminal liability share deterrent objectives. But the primary purpose of civil liability is to apportion losses that arise from legitimate activity. If loss shifting makes sense, does it follow that criminal condemnation and stringent deterrence of the activity is warranted?

Consider some examples: Suppose that a doctor, because of a negligent (but relatively minor) error causes a death of a patient. Are criminal sanctions called for? What if a lawyer makes a negligent mistake leading to conviction in a capital case? What impact would criminal liability have on the willingness of law-abiding citizens to engage in potentially dangerous activities? The common law decisions reflect the view that criminal punishment in such cases risks overdeterrence and is disproportionate to whatever fault may exist. Normally imprisonment (or any <u>criminal</u> condemnation) requires behavior viewed as seriously antisocial. Something more than ordinary negligence is therefore typically required.

When something more than ordinary negligence is required, what is that something? What is the test? Note the various formulations: <u>Welansky</u>, p. 425 ("wanton or reckless conduct"); <u>Bateman</u>, from p. 428, bottom, to p. 429, line 3 ("mens rea"). Do these formulations provide a definition? <u>Andrews</u>, p. 428, makes clear the ambiguity and latent circularity of many common formulations. What factors should be controlling? Consider:

> <u>Case 2.</u> <u>Welansky</u>, p. 425. Why did the defendant's conduct go beyond ordinary negligence? The court stresses that there must be "a <u>high</u> degree of likelihood [of] <u>substantial</u> harm" (p. 427, 2d full ¶). But was this actually the case in <u>Welansky</u>? The trial judge's instruction, approved by the court, introduces another element: "grave danger . . . must have been <u>apparent</u>" (p. 427 1st full ¶). But was it apparent to the defendant here? (Would any sane nightclub owner consciously choose to run such a risk?) (It should be noted that the defendant himself usually was present in the club. P. 425, 2d ¶ of the opinion.) In any event, does the court really require actual awareness? Note the language at p. 427, last two sentences of the 1st full ¶. To similar effect, see <u>Pierce</u>, p. 434, Note 2, and especially p. 435, 1st full indented quote. In MPC terms, isn't this the language of negligence, rather than recklessness?

Discussion of <u>Welansky</u> can suggest three possible points of comparison between "criminal" negligence and ordinary negligence: the former often involves (1) a higher likelihood of harm, (2) the risk of a particularly serious harm, and (3) an actual awareness, or a greater likelihood of awareness, of that risk. But as <u>Welansky</u> indicates, the difference with respect to elements (1) and (3) may be very slight or non-existent.

Case 3. Consider a variation on Parrish, p. 430, Note 2(a). If the wife had survived and another driver had been killed, could the wife be convicted of manslaughter? Doesn't her conduct satisfy all three of the elements just considered? How can her case be distinguished from that of her husband in the actual Parrish case? Plainly, the magnitude of the risk created must be weighed against the justification for creating that risk. The husband had no justification, but the wife's action in creating the same risk was reasonable under the circumstances. The MPC definition of negligence, § 2.02(2)(d) makes plain that the risk must be both substantial and unjustifiable.

When, if ever, is it justifiable to create a high risk of death? Do the MPC definitions of recklessness and negligence really help? Is there criminal negligence if a death is caused by:

a. A driver hurrying away from a robber who has demanded the driver's wallet.

b. A driver hurrying to a meeting.

c. The railway companies referred to by Salmond, p. 430, 2d indented quote.

d. A motorist who drives at 65 mph, in violation of a posted 55 mph speed limit, so that he can arrive home before dark. (See p. 431, Note 2(b).

Discussion of such cases can bring out the vagueness of the standard upon which criminal liability for negligence depends, and the important substantive policy judgments reflected in the decision, together with the difficulty of formulating precise rules to deal with such cases in advance.

Williams, p. 431, permits exploration of a question raised in Welansky -- whether actual awareness of the risk is or should be required. Students often feel that the conviction was upheld only because the Washington statute in effect at the time permitted punishment for ordinary negligence. Under the revised statute that brought Washington law into line with the prevailing common law position (p. 433, Note 1), *criminal* negligence must now be shown. But given the nature of the baby's symptoms, if there was negligence here at all, wasn't it clearly *criminal* negligence? Would defendants escape liability for criminal negligence because they were not actually aware of the risk? Is it true that defendants were not aware of the risk?

Two interpretations are possible: either they did not realize the risk, or they were aware of some danger but chose to run the risk because of fear that the welfare department would take the baby away. Does the latter interpretation make their case stronger or weaker? Should their legitimate fear of overreaching by the welfare department constitute a justification for choosing (if they did) to run the risk? This issue recalls the above discussion of the difficulty of balancing risk against justification. Who should make the substantive policy judgment?

Now consider the former interpretation. The trial judge proceeded expressly on this basis (see p. 431, the indented quote). If the defendants were not aware of the risk, why should they be punished? Can punishment ever deter a defendant in a situation like theirs? In what sense can they be *blamed*? Were the defendants in Williams punished for a morally inappropriate choice, or were they punished simply for having had a limited education? To explore such problems, consider first whether punishment for inadvertent negligence serves any useful purpose. Can it deter? Compare G. Williams, p. 435, note 3 (no) with the MPC view, p. 436, Note 4 & the indented quote (yes).

Even if punishment can deter, is it just to punish when the defendant was unaware of the risk and therefore had no notion that he was doing wrong? Is it morally blameworthy to be ignorant? Compare G. Williams, p. 435 (no) with Holmes, who appears to argue at pp. 434-35 that blameworthiness should be irrelevant. Is there any sense in which a person can fairly be blamed for not knowing something? Note Prof. Pillsbury's argument, p. 436, note 5. If the defendant could have thought about the danger, then there is an element of fault in his failure to do so (and also a potential for deterrence). But does this approach lead to a totally subjective standard? Not necessarily, because most defendants, having ordinary capacities, are held to the precautions that the ordinary person would take. But, as Hart argues (p. 437, Note 6) this "objective" standard can individualized (made subjective) in the sense that it can consider whether the defendant did have ordinary capabilities and then hold him responsible only tot he extent that he failed to exercise the capabilities he in fact had.

How would Williams be decided under Hart's approach? The key issue presumably would be whether the defendants had the capacity to realize the risk; their education and intelligence would have to be considered. But note that capacity is a matter of degree. Is Hart's individualized approach workable?

Note that the court explicitly mentions the defendants' racial background. Why is this relevant? The court appears to apply to them a standard of white middle-class behavior. Is this a racist approach? Would it be more appropriate to test their behavior by the standard of the reasonable person in their own culture? Or would a differential standard of that kind be even more offensive? The problem appears analogous to that discussed in connection with Camplin. Just as the law ignores different cultural attitudes in that context, so here it ordinarily ignores different cultural attitudes toward risk-taking and appropriate standards of prudence. Nonetheless, if the defendants could not have been expected to realize the danger to the baby (as the facts suggest), then how can punishment be justified?

How would Williams be decided under the MPC? As with respect to the Camplin problem, the Code is deliberately ambiguous. But note the Comment at p. 438, note 7: differences in intelligence "could not" be considered. Does this mean that the Williams couple should be convicted even if, due to limited intelligence, they did not have the capacity to appreciate the risk? Can this be sound?

Discussion of the involuntary manslaughter material should bring out the three elements involved in the assessment of criminal negligence: the degree of the risk, the justification for the risk, and the defendant's awareness of the risk. With respect to the last point, students should see that the law often moves in the direction favored by Holmes, under which criminal punishment can be imposed (as in Williams) in the absence of identifiable moral fault. But inadvertent negligence can entail blame, at least when Hart's conditions are satisfied.

If time permits, the problem at pp. 438-39 provides a challenging and controversial setting in which to apply the doctrines relating to involuntary manslaughter. Consider the facts of Walker, p. 438. Is the case for liability stronger or weaker than in Williams. Note that in both cases the parents failed to get medical attention for a child facing a serious risk of death. How are the cases different? In Walker, the parents seem, in anything, much more explicitly aware of the risk. Is it "unreasonable" for them to believe that prayer can cure the illness? Should their religious beliefs provide a justification for running a risk that others would not run (i.e., they did not choose to run a "substantial *and unjustifiable*" risk)? Or should we say that their actions have to be judged from the viewpoint of a reasonable person in their situation, i.e., a reasonable person who shares their religious commitments and beliefs? Under the MPC should the defendants' situation be individualized to this extent? Applying Hart's framework, did they have the capacity to do otherwise, or (given their religious faith) was it impossible for them to do otherwise?

Unintended Killing -- Murder, pp. 439-47

Malone, p. 439. Why is the defendant guilty of murder rather than manslaughter? Three factors might be mentioned: the magnitude of the risk, the lack of any justification and the defendant's awareness of the risk. Note that these are the same three elements that sometimes distinguish criminal negligence from ordinary negligence. Consider carefully whether a murder conviction does in fact require one or more of these three:

1. The magnitude of the risk. Was the risk of death really 60%? Consider p. 441, Note 1. If it was 60% in Malone, what result if the gun had gone off on the first shot? Would the court have reversed a murder conviction because the probability of death then was only 20%? The language about a death "likely" to result (p. 440, last ¶) might suggest an affirmative answer, but would it make sense for the court to insist on a 50% probability? Note the facts of Commonwealth v. Ashburn, 331 A. 2d 167 (1975), another "Russian Roulette" case where a 20% probability was held sufficient. In practice "likely" may simply mean "possible."

2. Lack of justification. Is the reason for the defendant's behavior in Malone (amusement or thrills) sufficiently different from the reasons that lead to dangerous driving in cases prosecuted as involuntary manslaughter?

3. Awareness. Was Malone subjectively aware of the risk? Yes, if he twirled the chamber before shooting. But what if he didn't do so? (See p. 441, last full ¶) Perhaps then he was not aware. Under the latter assumption, would a murder conviction still be possible? From Malone itself, it is unclear whether subjective awareness is required in Pennsylvania. What result under the standards articulated in Fleming, p. 443? Note that the court ostensibly requires recklessness: the jury must be able to infer "that defendant was aware" (p. 444, 9 lines from the bottom). But a drunk defendant is deemed to have the awareness he would have if he were sober. P. 444 n.3. In effect, liability is based on what the defendant "should have known." Is this sound? Note that the question here is one of grading. Under Fleming and Dufield (p. 447, 1st full ¶), what is the

difference between murder and manslaughter? The prevailing common law position, in contrast, presumably would be that involuntary manslaughter ("without due caution and circumspection") implies gross negligence (see Andrews, p. 428), while murder ("malice") implies recklessness. Compare the MPC position, p. 446, note 4: both manslaughter and murder require subjective awareness, while negligence can be the basis only of the separate offense of negligent homicide. Is this a more coherent solution? Note that the MPC's treatment of intoxication reintroduces an objective standard (i.e. negligent murder) in the one area (drunkenness) where there is likely to be a significant practical difference between subjective and objective standards.

So far we have seen the malice for murder defined in terms of the reckless (or possibly negligent) creation of a risk of death. Does the risk have to be one of death? As indicated at p. 447, Note 5, a murder conviction can result from reckless or negligent creation of a risk of "great bodily harm." (And the latter concept may in turn be very loosely defined, see, e.g. Dorazio, 74 A.2d 125, 130 (any injury that will "seriously interfere with health and comfort.") What is the justification for this rule? Does it flow from recognition that great bodily harm usually is threatening to life? If so, why convert this relationship into an irrebuttable presumption?

Discussion should make clear that the question here is not one of criminality but solely one of grading. Thus "malice" presumably should be interpreted to require actual awareness of a risk of death; the culpability of the person who intends or consciously risks serious injury should not be equated with that of the person who intends or consciously risks death.

The Felony-Murder Rule, pp. 448-482

This material normally requires about three classes. The first class can consider both the basic doctrine and its rationale (along with the parallel misdemeanor-manslaughter rule), pp. 448-59. The second class can focus on the limitations to inherently dangerous and independent felonies, pp. 459-71, and the third class can be devoted to the problems relating to the identity of the actual killer, pp. 471-82.

Overview of the Felony-Murder Doctrine, pp. 448-59

This class introduces the basic structure and practical significance of the and felony-murder doctrine, and the debate about its rationale.

The structure of the felony-murder doctrine. Consider first the way that the rule fits into the principles of liability and grading examined so far. Suppose that a defendant escaping from prison drives through a stop sign and collides with another car, killing the driver. He might be convicted of manslaughter on a culpable negligence theory. But can he be convicted of murder? A Malone theory (extreme recklessness) theory seems weak. But note that escape from prison is normally a felony. Can this be the basis for a conviction of murder?

Note the various statutory approaches. Under N.Y. § 125.25(3), which does not use the traditional common law language (see p. 394), the prison escapee can be convicted of second-degree murder without regard to intent, recklessness or even negligence. What about a common law approach like that of California? Note that the felony of escape is not enumerated in §189, p. 390. Does this mean that the felony-murder rule is not available? Not necessarily, because § 189 also provides that "all other kinds of murders" are second degree. Can the case be brought within that language? Because the defendant committed a dangerous felony, there is "malice" (see Serné, p. 448, at p. 449, last full ¶); therefore in California this would be second-degree murder. By parallel reasoning, the act is probably third-degree murder in Pennsylvania (though query the effect of the restrictive definition of felony in § 2502(d), p. 392).

Students should see that the felony-murder rule does not depend on the statutory enumerations and has only an indirect connection to them. Non-enumerated felonies can trigger the rule, and enumerated felonies sometimes do not (e.g. Wilson, p. 467, last full ¶, to be discussed below). As Serné makes clear, the rule serves to establish malice as a matter of law; statutory enumerations may then determine the degree of murder that applies.

Practical effects. Does the felony-murder rule make any difference in practice. Consider:

> Case 1. Defendant perpetrates an elaborate securities fraud, thus committing a felony. A defrauded investor, who lost his life's savings, commits suicide. Is defendant guilty of murder on a felony-murder theory? Presumably not, because the underlying felony is not "known to be dangerous to life," as required by Serné at p. 449, middle of the last full ¶. But if the Serné requirement is met, why do you need a felony-murder theory at all? Won't the defendants always be guilty of murder anyway on a Malone theory?

Case 2. Return to the prison escape example above. What result under Serné? Case 2 obviously involves less danger than the Clerkenwell example (p. 450, 1st full ¶). But isn't escape still sufficiently dangerous to support a felony-murder theory? Consider Stephen's analysis of his rape example (top of p. 449, last full ¶). Does the example fit his own definition of an act "likely in itself to cause death"? Stephen's own analysis shows that he applies his test of dangerousness rather loosely: the felony-murder rule can be invoked with respect to such offenses as rape and prison escape, even when they involve a relatively low likelihood of death. In contrast, a murder conviction would seem unlikely under a Malone theory.

Case 3. Consider Stamp, p. 450. Without a felony-murder rule, what degree of homicide could the defendant be convicted of? Arguably, not even involuntary manslaughter since the court assumes that the death was not reasonably "foreseeable." But note that the felony-murder rule here produces a conviction for first-degree murder.

While a murder conviction often is possible even without the felony-murder rule, Cases 1-3 should help students to see that the practical effect of the rule is to extend murder liability to cases where recklessness did not exist, or cannot be proved. But liability cannot be extended indefinitely. Is there felony-murder liability if a pilot smuggling marijuana crashes and kills a passenger in the plane? See King, p. 451, 1st full ¶. The felony-murder rule eliminates the mens rea requirement but ordinary causation requirements must still be met. In Stamp they are, because the felony was the but-for cause of death, but in King causation requirements are not met. Causation principles, of course, will be examined in detail in Chapter 6.

Policy considerations. What justification is there for the felony-murder rule? Does strict liability have any deterrence value? See the arguments of Macaulay (p. 452, Note 2) and Tomkovicz, p. 453, Note 4.

Note the low frequency of death even in the most dangerous felonies (p. 454 n.5). Will the behavior of felons be influenced by probabilities that are so remote? On the other hand, doesn't even a 0.14% fatality rate for robbery imply that the conduct is extremely dangerous? See Prof. Cole's discussion, at p. 454 n.5, the indented quote.

Even if felony-murder liability (like other instances of strict liability) can have some crime prevention value, isn't it nonetheless fundamentally unfair? The defendant has by hypothesis committed a very serious crime. But is that any reason to punish him for something else *in addition*? Or is a defendant who commits a very serious crime less entitled to a careful determination of fault or to properly proportional punishment? Recall the <u>Cunningham</u> principle (p. 204) of maintaining liability proportionate to fault. And see Macaulay, p. 452, 1st ¶ of the excerpt, noting that the felony-murder approach "confound[s] all the boundaries of crime."

To make the grading impact of the felony-murder rule concrete, it may be helpful to ask students what the normal punishment should be for an offender (e.g., a first offender) who commits burglary or robbery. Students may suggest 10 years, 20 years, or even life imprisonment. In fact, the punishment typically imposed is very much lower. In 1990 in state courts, only 75% of convicted burglars were sentenced to prison or jail, and the average maximum sentence for those incarcerated was 61 months. (The comparable figures for robbery: 90% sentenced to prison or jail; average maximum sentence: 97 months.) Of course first offenders would tend to be at the lower end of the distribution. See U.S. Dept. of Justice, Bureau of Justice Statistics, Sourcebook of Criminal Justice Statistics - 1993, p. 537.

The pattern under the federal sentencing guidelines (often criticized as too harsh) is similar. The sentence range for a first offender's armed residential burglary is 30-37 months, and only 21-27 months after a guilty plea (technically "acceptance of responsibility"). For armed robbery the range is 57-71 months, or only 41-51 months after a guilty plea. [A further detail: for offenders charged with the weapons offense under 18 USC §924(c), there is a 60 month mandatory consecutive sentence, but the guideline sentence range *drops* 2 levels for burglary and 5 levels for robbery because the weapon enhancement can't be counted twice; the net effect is an increase of about 4-1/2 years for burglary, and about 3 years for robbery.]

Whatever the qualifications, the burglar or robber whose crime does not cause death gets a far lower sentence than that applicable to first-degree murder. Does it make sense to impose an automatic sentence of life imprisonment on such an offender in the rare case in which a victim is (perhaps accidentally) killed. What does such a penalty accomplish? Is it worth its dollar costs to the state? Is it disproportionate to fault (as measured by the sentence that the defendant's conduct would otherwise warrant)?

<u>The misdemeanor-manslaughter rule</u>. The parallel misdemeanor-manslaughter rule (pp. 455-57) can be mentioned briefly here but should

not require extended discussion in class. The Powell case, p. 456, last ¶, is a vivid recent example. Students should review pp. 455-57 as background, to be aware of the continued survival of this rule in some jurisdictions and the debate, similar to that for the felony-murder rule, concerning its policy justification and proper limits. [An added source of unfairness in misdemeanor-manslaughter cases is that the "unlawful act" may not involve any criminal negligence, either because the risk was very low, or because there was a strong justification for taking the risk - - e.g. a case where a defendant runs a stop sign because he is taking a bleeding friend to the hospital. The misdemeanor manslaughter rule obviates the need for any proof of fault other than the potentially very minor or purely technical fault entailed in the commission of the unlawful act.]

Reform, pp. 457-59. Where the felony-murder rule exists through the common law definition of malice, are courts free to abrogate it? Or do statutes like Cal. Penal Code § 189 codify the felony-murder rule by implication? Compare Aaron, p. 457, last line, and Ortega, bottom of p. 458, with Dillon, p. 458, last full ¶. If the governing statute does not leave the court free to reinterpret "malice," there are a few other routes to a similar result. See p. 459, Note 3. Discussion can indicate that courts face a dilemma in trying to elaborate coherent principles of just punishment, at the same time that they must interpret and apply a statutory scheme inconsistent with such principles.

Limitations on the Felony-Murder Doctrine, pp. 459-82

Phillips, p. 459. Why didn't this offense satisfy Stephen's requirement that the underlying felony be inherently dangerous? Note the court's insistence that dangerousness be assessed in the abstract. Does the abstract approach make sense? The answer may depend in part on the specific purpose of the felony-murder rule. What is it? If the purpose is to deter the underlying felony, it is arguably sound to consider only on those felonies that are perceived as especially dangerous. But then why not just increase the punishment for all such felonies? More likely, the main purpose is to provide an extra incentive for felons to minimize the danger associated with their felonious acts. But then isn't the case for strict liability the same whether the felony is inherently dangerous in the abstract, or only dangerous under the circumstances of the particular case?

What other considerations may explain the court's deliberate preference for a highly formalistic inquiry? Which test of dangerousness (abstract or concrete) will result in broader scope for the felony-murder rule? Note the court's concern that any offense which proximately caused death would almost always be found dangerous if assessed under the concrete circumstances (p. 461, 2d full ¶). Since the court considers that the felony-murder rule is itself highly artificial (see p. 460, last full ¶), the choice of the abstract approach may simply reflect a desire to keep the felony-murder rule within the narrowest possible bounds. But if the rule is a required part of the statutory scheme (see <u>Dillon</u>, p. 458, Note 2), is it legitimate for the court to restrict the rule in this way? Note that some courts have rejected the abstract approach. See <u>Stewart</u>, p. 464.

Assuming that the abstract approach is the proper one, how should it be applied? Consider:

> <u>Case 1</u>. <u>Satchell</u>, p. 462. Isn't this felony inherently dangerous *even* in the abstract? Should it be enough that the felony is usually (or often) dangerous, or should the courts require that the felony <u>always</u> be dangerous? If the crime must *necessarily* involve danger to life (see <u>Henderson</u>, p. 463, Note 2), what will the felony-murder rule add to the other ways of establishing murder? In this connection it is interesting to mention the result in <u>Burroughs</u>, 678 P.2d 894: the California Supreme Court held that the offense of "felonious unlicensed practice of medicine [under] conditions which cause or create a risk of great bodily harm, serious physical or mental illness, or death" was *not* inherently dangerous because a "serious physical *or* mental illness" need not be life threatening.

> <u>Case 2</u>. Note the facts in <u>Jenkins</u>, 230 A.2d 262 (Del. 1967) (two burglars independently tried to break into an abandoned warehouse; they collided when one tried to leave as the other was arriving, and one burglar was killed in the collision). Does the felony-murder rule apply on these facts? Compare the approaches in California and Rhode Island.
> > Under the California court's approach, even burglary might not qualify as *necessarily* dangerous to human life. The abstract approach, if taken seriously, could lead to complete abolition of the felony-murder rule. [Cf. <u>Moran</u>, 442 N.E.2d 399 (Mass. 1982), holding that unarmed robbery is not inherently dangerous.] So courts usually assume that burglary qualifies as inherently dangerous in the abstract. But then the abstract approach may produce a *wider* felony murder rule in a case like <u>Jenkins</u>.
> > What result under Stewart. Now it could be argued under the opstensibly broader, non-abstract approach that this felony was not "inherently dangerous in the manner . . . in which it was

committed" (p. 464, last line, to p. 465, 1st line). In Jenkins, the Delaware court, applying a non-abstract test, concluded that burglary was *not* dangerous. But again, does the felony-murder rule, so interpreted, add anything to the other ways of establishing murder?

Smith, p. 466. Before examining the court's reasoning, it may be best to present a problem. Recall the facts of Maher, p. 407. If the provoker in that case (Hunt) had died, could Maher be convicted of murder on a felony-murder theory? Note the assault with a deadly weapon. Isn't the inherent dangerousness requirement clearly satisfied? Then why isn't the offense murder? Students should see that to permit use of the felony-murder rule here would render all the law of provocation irrelevant. Therefore an additional limitation emerges -- even when the felony is inherently dangerous, it cannot trigger the felony-murder rule unless it is independent of the homicide. See Ireland, p. 467, 1st ¶.

Note the paradoxical effect of this independence or "merger" doctrine: the "inherent dangerousness" requirement removes the non-dangerous felonies from the operation of the felony-murder rule, but the merger doctrine removes the most dangerous felonies (assaults with deadly weapons). Thus the felony-murder rule applies only to a middle ground of somewhat dangerous felonies. Does it really make sense to invoke strict liability only with respect to crimes in this middle category?

Consider some applications of the independence requirement:

> Case 1. Wilson, p. 467, last full ¶ & n.a. Shouldn't the burglary be considered independent of the homicide? Note the differences between the elements of burglary (p. 467 n.a) and homicide. But if assault outdoors will not trigger the felony-murder rule, why any difference for an assault indoors?

Since the court considered it anomalous to treat assault without an entry differently from an assault with an entry, the result was that the burglary in Wilson did not trigger the felony-murder rule even though it was an offense specifically enumerated in §189. Compare the reasoning in Miller, p. 469, Note 1 especially at p. 470, the indented quote: assaults indoors differ because they are more likely to culminate in homicide. Which result is correct -- Wilson or Miller? Does it just depend on whether we want to see the felony-murder rule restricted (Wilson) or enforced (Miller)?

The Miller reasoning should be examined closely to see whether it succeeds on its own terms. Is there really a significant difference in dangerousness between indoor and outdoor assaults? Even if there is, is dangerousness the relevant issue here? Presumably the answer should depend on the reasons for the merger exception to the felony-murder rule. Are outdoor assaults excluded because they are considered less dangerous? Outdoors, even an assault *with specific intent to kill* will merge. Obviously the merger doctrine is not designed to identify (and exclude from felony-murder) those felonies considered non-dangerous. Rather, its purpose is to preserve the integrity of the normal homicide grading structure with respect to personal assaults not linked to some independent criminal objective. Thus, the reasoning in Miller is analytically unsound even if assaults are in fact more dangerous indoors than out.

> Case 2. Burton, p. 468, 2d full ¶. If the burglary in Wilson is not independent of the homicide, then can't the same argument be made about robbery? The elements of the two offenses need to be analyzed. Both involve one element included in the homicide (the assault) and one independent element (the entry in burglary and the taking in robbery). Apply the Ireland test: If the burglary is "included in fact" in the homicide, isn't the robbery also? But what would be the effect of accepting this argument? How much of the felony-murder rule would survive?

Note the Burton court's solution: the "included in fact" test is discarded in favor of looking for an "independent felonious purpose" (p. 468, last full ¶), which is present in Burton but not in Wilson. Does this represent a coherent solution? Consider Sears, 2 Cal.3d 180: the defendant entered a cottage, intending to kill his estranged wife, and in the ensuing struggle, he killed his daughter, who had come to her mother's assistance. Isn't there an "independent felonious purpose" here? Yes: the intent to assault the wife. Since a defendant X who enters with the intent to kill A -- and does so -- may be guilty only of manslaughter (because of provocation, for example), the California Supreme Court found it "anomalous" to hold that if the same defendant accidentally kills B instead, the crime is first-degree murder. But does the Sears approach avoid the anomalies? Suppose that Y enters a home, intending to steal a TV set and accidentally kills C. If it is anomalous for X to be guilty of murder when he accidentally kills B, isn't it even more anomalous to hold Y (who never planned to kill anyone) guilty of first-degree murder when he accidentally kills C?

How should "merger" principles be applied in the context of the felony child abuse offense involved in Smith, p. 466? Note the elements, p. 468 n.4

The statute reaches only conduct that is intentionally life-threatening. Obviously, this is a classic situation in which the merger doctrine must apply and felony-murder therefore should be unavailable. But is there really any difference between assaultive child abuse (Smith) and abuse by willful neglect (Shockley, p. 469, 3d full ¶). If the neglect is intentional, with knowledge that it endangers the child, shouldn't the same principles apply? The distinction between the two situations is clearly fragile; as implied at p. 469 n.7, the court may ultimately reexamine Shockley and apply the merger doctrine there too. But why can't the prosecution claim an "independent felonious purpose" - - i.e. disciplining the child). Won't this argument be available in *every* child abuse case? In any event, why should defenses like provocation and diminished capacity be available to parents who beat their children *with* intent to kill, while parents who beat their children without intent to kill are *always* guilty of murder? The Hanson decision, p. 470, Note 2, responds to these anomalies by abandoning both the Ireland and Burton tests. After Hanson, how would Smith be decided? How would Sears be decided? (Under the "great majority of all homicides" test (p. 471, 1st line), it looks like merger would still apply in Sears but would no longer apply in Smith. Then again, how can we be sure?) Which felonies now merge in California?

Discussion of these problems can help show why anomalies are inherent in the felony-murder rule, which assumes that a finely calibrated grading of culpability is appropriate for some categories of defendants but seeks to deny that fine calibration to other categories of defendants. Yet some defendants in the latter group will inevitably be less culpable than some of those in the former.

Killings by Persons other than the Felons, pp. 471-82

Canola, p. 471. Students should be clear on the underlying felony (robbery: meets the inherently dangerous test and does not merge; on who started the shooting (one of the robbers); on who was killed (the store owner (O) and Lloredo, one of the robbers); and on who shot whom (O presumably was shot by a felon (F); Lloredo was shot by O).

Consider first whether there is any problem holding Canola (C) for the killing of O. This is a classic felony-murder situation. But does it make any difference what C's personal role was? Suppose, for example, that C was outside in the getaway car and never fired a shot. Careful analysis of C's liability in that context will help make clear the theories of liability upon which the more complex variations depend. (a) Note the possibility of vicarious responsibility. C and F are co-conspirators who agreed to help each other commit a crime. Therefore (under rules to be examined in detail in Chapter 7) each is responsible for the foreseeable crimes committed by the other in furtherance of the joint plan. Since F shot O in furtherance of the robbery and is therefore himself liable for felony-murder, C is vicariously responsible for the felony-murder committed by F. (b) Alternatively, consider C's liability under normal felony-murder doctrine. C himself is guilty of robbery. Under principles of proximate cause (considered in detail in Chapter 6), the death of O was a direct result of the robbery. Therefore, under <u>Stamp</u>, p. 450, C is liable for the death proximately caused by <u>his</u> <u>own</u> felony.

Now apply these principles to the killing of Lloredo by O. Can C be held liable under a vicarious responsibility (agency) analysis? O is not a co-conspirator acting in furtherance of the felony. Therefore, C cannot be held vicariously responsible for O's act and would not be liable under an agency analysis. But what about the proximate cause approach? Isn't the analysis of C's liability for the death of Lloredo identical to the analysis of his liability for the death of O? <u>Stamp</u> does not even require foreseeability, though the lethal reaction of O is presumably foreseeable anyway. Therefore C could easily be held liable under a proximate cause approach.

Since the agency and proximate cause approaches produce different results with respect to the killing by O, we have to decide which line of analysis is the proper one. Would it make sense to hold C responsible if the requirements of <u>either</u> theory are satisfied, or should felony-murder liability require meeting the elements of <u>both</u>? As a matter of policy, is there any good reason why C should not be held liable? Consider the following arguments:

a. Felony-murder liability should always require that the act of killing be done by the defendant or an accomplice. This is the essence of the holding in <u>Redline</u> (p. 472, italics in the middle of the 1st full ¶) which is followed in <u>Canola</u>. But <u>why</u> should the act of killing have to be committed by someone acting in concert with the defendant? Consider the "shield" situation. In that context all courts are willing to hold the defendant responsible for a foreseeable killing by a party acting in opposition to the crime. See p. 473, 1st full ¶. In other words, the proximate cause approach governs. Then why can't the proximate cause approach be invoked in felony-murder cases? In <u>Redline</u>, the court distinguishes the shield cases on the ground that there the malice is express. Is this an adequate answer? Is the issue here one of establishing mens rea? Note that the problem is to decide whether the defendant can be held responsible for the *act* of killing.

If he can be (as the shield cases establish), why can't we then prove mens rea in the appropriate way (expressly in the shield cases and automatically in the felony-murder cases)?

b. Canola cannot be liable for the killing of Lloredo because this killing was a justifiable homicide. See Redline, p. 476, Note 3(b). Is this sound? If so, what result in the hypothetical at the top of p. 477. Students should see that in the hypothetical, the immunity of the officer should be irrelevant to the possible liability of A, who commits an act knowing that it will send B to his death.

c. Assumption of risk. Some courts consider the felony murder rule inapplicable, when a felon is killed, on the ground that in this situation, the victim has assumed the risk. Is this convincing? Aren't the lives of felons also entitled to legal protection? (See again the hypothetical at the top of p. 477; see also Judge Posner's comment in Martinez, p. 477, last indented quote). Should assumption of risk or contributory negligence ever be a defense in a criminal prosecution? If the objective is not to allocate a loss between parties, but rather to prevent the underlying behavior by both, why should assumption of risk ever be relevant? See p. 429, Note 1, and p, 477, Note 3(c), p. 477.

d. In terms of deterrence, is felony-murder liability unnecessary? Arguably, the doctrine was not intended to protect felons. See Williams, p. 477, Note 3(c). But compare Judge Posner's arguments in Martinez, p. 477, suggesting the broader deterrence effects on dangerous behavior in general. Can felony-murder liability for the death of co-felons actually endanger such felons, by giving victims an extra incentive, at the margin, to inflict a fatal wound (thus "killing two birds with one stone")? As a practical matter, does the prospect of felony-murder liability have any realistic effect on a felon's decision (as in the vivid facts of Martinez, p. 477) to heedlessly endanger his own life?

Discussion here may indicate that deterrence reasoning gives little firm guidance for this kind of a problem. Within the kinds of assumptions that underlie any strict liability approach, it may follow that defendants should be held liable for the widest possible consequences. The opposing view is that deviations from the culpability principle, as in felony murder and other strict liability doctrines, reflect a judgment that important social-protection needs warrant an exception to the usual requirement of keeping liability in proportion to fault. Where the deterrence pay-off is tenuous or quite speculative (as in the case of liability for killings committed by third parties) normal fault principles presumably should be permitted to govern.

e. What about the particular statutory language in New Jersey (p. 473 n.a)? Is the court's restrictive interpretation persuasive? Note that the court admits its reading is supported by a desire to limit the effect of the felony-murder rule (p. 473, last full ¶).

Discussion of the various theories can help show why, within the assumptions of the felony-murder rule itself, liability may logically be appropriate regardless of the identity of the killer or victim. Thus, the prevailing agency limitation may not be sound on its own terms but may instead be based primarily on hostility to the felony-murder rule itself.

To clarify the arguments, and to test student understanding of the various theories of liability, consider several variations on the Canola facts. Would C be guilty of felony-murder in each of the following situations:

Case 1. Suppose that Lloredo had been killed by a bullet from the gun of another felon F. Students should see the need for showing that the act of shooting was in furtherance of the felony. See Heinlein, p. 476, Note 2. If F shot at O and hit Lloredo by mistake, felony-murder should apply; the fortuity of who is hit should be irrelevant. But if F had shot at Lloredo in anger (as in Cabaltero, p. 476, Note 2(a)), then the killing probably would not be "in furtherance" and the felony-murder rule would not apply.

Case 2. Suppose O is hit by a police officer shooting at the felons. What result on an agency theory? (C is not liable). What result on an assumption of risk analysis? Note that under that approach C would be liable for a killing by a third party in Case 2, even though he would not be liable under that approach for the killing by his own co-conspirator in Case 1.

Case 3. Suppose O is hit by bullets from both the police officer and F. What result under agency theory? Note that C is liable only if F's bullet is the proximate cause of death. But in the context of a general shootout, why should liability depend on identifying the particular bullet that caused the more serious wound? What if it could not be proved beyond a reasonable doubt which bullet was the fatal one? This was the factual setting of Almeida, p. 472, 1st full ¶, where the Pennsylvania court decided that identifying the actual trigger person should be irrelevant. Wasn't the original Almeida approach the correct one? But under Almeida, wouldn't C be liable in Case 2 as well? Students should see that the only way to restrict felony-murder without abolishing it is to make the rarefied distinction required in Case 3, so that liability turns on identifying which bullet is the proximate cause of death .

Taylor, p. 477. Again, students should be clear on the identity of killer and victim. Here a co-felon (Smith) was shot by one or both of the victims (Mr. & Mrs. West). Can defendant be convicted of murder? Note that California had adopted the agency theory in Washington, pp. 478-79. But here the court upholds the murder indictment. Does this overrule Washington? Note that the court purports to reaffirm Washington, at the top of p. 479, but upholds the murder indictment on a vicarious liability theory. On that approach what elements are required for conviction? The act of the co-felon must satisfy the requirements for murder. What are those requirements? Consider the formulation in Gilbert, p. 479, 1st full ¶. This is essentially the conscious recklessness formulation of Malone, p. 439. But what degree of murder do you get on a Malone theory? (2d degree only.) How does it get to be first-degree murder?

Students should understand the analytic move reflected in footnote 2 at p. 480. But in what sense is such a killing "in the perpetration" of the robbery? Verbally, either result seems defensible. Doesn't this issue simply replay the considerations at stake in Canola and in Washington? If so, then if the California court was correct in Washington, isn't it necessarily incorrect in upholding the *first-degree* murder possibility in Taylor?

Since the California court holds that its grading provision (§ 189) applies regardless of the identity of the actual killer, is there any practical difference between the approach approved in Taylor and the approach ruled out in Washington? Note the interpretation in the Taylor dissent. Judge Peters assumes that the difference is factual: In Washington, the defendant "merely" pointed a gun without using threatening language; in Taylor the threat was made explicit. It is hard to see why anything should turn on whether the threat is implicit or explicit. On the other hand, if Washington was correct, then isn't some factual line-drawing crucial? How would Judge Peters decide a shield case? Logically, to reject all line-drawing requires either no liability in a shield case, or reversing Washington and upholding felony-murder liability even for the killing of Lloredo in Canola. Both results seem unacceptable

Presumably there is a different kind of distinction between the liability that Taylor permits and the liability that Washington bars. Suppose that two unarmed burglars X and Y break into a store at night and unexpectedly encounter the store owner, who shoots and kills Y. If these facts arose in California, would there be murder liability? Without Washington there could be felony-murder, even though the lethal shot was fired by the homeowner under unexpected circumstances. Washington bars this. But does Taylor simply lead to liability by a different route? Note that under the vicarious liability approach, neither of the two felons would meet the test for malice established by such cases as Gilbert (p. 579, 2d indented quote) or Malone (p. 439). Thus, even under the Taylor analysis, there is no murder liability.

Students should see that the difference between felony-murder liability and Taylor liability is procedural: under Taylor mens rea must be litigated and the jury must find actual malice. In Washington itself the jury might have found the act of pointing a gun sufficiently reckless to establish malice under a Malone standard. Washington holds only that such conduct does not automatically establish malice by operation of the felony-murder rule.

Given Taylor, what result if the person killed is F, the very felon who provokes the lethal attack. Note Antick, p. 482, Note2. Logically, under a vicarious responsibility approach, there is no crime to attribute to the co-felon. But what if an innocent third party is killed by a bullet aimed at F? Now under Taylor, the co-felon can be held liable. The difference in outcome seems purely fortuitous, but these anomalous results flow from the logic of vicarious responsibility, under which - by hypothesis - the defendant is not punished for his own conduct, but solely for whatever crimes may (or may not) be committed by a co-conspirator for whom he is legally accountable.

In winding up the felony-murder material, it may be helpful to summarize the limitations that have been imposed upon the doctrine [inherent danger, felony not included in the homicide, killing in furtherance of the felony, identity of the killer and victim], and to note the stresses and strains that have emerged in the process of attempting to give these limitations coherent shape. An overview of the problem can help students to see that some of the complexities of felony-murder doctrine may be the result of judicial ambivalence and unwillingness to accept the basic doctrine. But some of the problems (especially the inherent danger and merger limitations) seem inherent in the rule and presumably would cause problems even for courts enthusiastically committed to the basic felony-murder concept. Is it possible to impose responsibility for the most serious of crimes on a strict-liability basis, while maintaining finely calibrated principles of fault that are supposed to coexist with the strict-liability regime?

<u>The Death Penalty</u>, pp. 483-515

Detailed discussion of this material normally requires two full classes. Where time requires more abbreviated treatment, we recommend devoting one class to either the current context and policy questions (pp. 483-93) or the current legal issues (pp. 493-515), with the instructor providing a brief summary of the pertinent problems in the area not discussed. Both topics serve well to develop and extend the overall themes of the course. (a) The policy issues can complement and enrich the analytic and philosophical themes of the course, especially when presented in a way that builds from the standard pro and con arguments (with which most students will be familar) to the issues that pervade criminal law doctrine as a whole, namely whether utilitarian gains can justify punishment without regard to desert, the interdependence of judgments about just outcome and judgments about workable procedure, and finally the general interdependence of facts and values. (b) The specific legal and constitutional issues provide an excellent vehicle for working through the complexity of doctrine that tries to reconcile the competing demands of rule (predictability and evenhandedness) and discretion (individualization) when momentous interests are at stake. The legal materials also provide an important context for focusing (through a discussion of <u>McCleskey</u>, p. 506) on the issue of racial bias in criminal justice administration and in the wider society.

<u>Policy Considerations</u>, pp. 484-93.

The case for or against the death penalty has of course been a subject of widespread attention; many of the arguments are familiar to a broad public. Class discussion can help marshal the relevant facts, but more important, it should serve to bring the facts and issues into the kind of focus permitted by professional study of the subject of punishment. In particular, class discussion can show how the debate turns on three issues of general importance throughout the course: (1) the question whether utilitarian gains can justify punishment without regard to desert, (2) the interdependence of judgments about just outcome and about administratively workable procedure, and finally (3) the more general interdependence of facts and values.

For launching class discussion, it may be useful to encourage student debate to unfold naturally, without attempting to impose a preconceived framework at the outset. But the instructor can provide structure and content by raising, throughout the discussion, the kinds of themes (such as the three mentioned above) that pervade the criminal law course.

It may be useful to begin with brief discussion of one special case: the killing committed by a prisoner already serving a sentence of life imprisonment without possibility of parole. Do the abolitionist arguments apply even in this extreme situation? If so, what incentive is there for such a prisoner to comply with the law? Would withdrawal of collateral prison privileges (if any remain) provide a sufficient incentive for conformity? Would withdrawal of such privileges provide sufficient condemnation for the deliberate taking of human life?

Next, turn to the more usual case, in which the defendant is not already serving a life sentence. Why isn't life imprisonment a sufficient punishment?

a. <u>Deterrence</u>. Intuitively, isn't it clear that death is bound to be more effective as a deterrent, at the margin, than life imprisonment? Note van den Haag's argument, pp. 485-86. But compare the countertendencies noted intuitively by Bedau, p. 486. If there are plausible tendencies working in both directions, how do we determine how they balance out? Is the answer intuitively obvious? What does the evidence suggest? Compare the Sellin study (p. 485) with that of Ehrlich (pp. 486-87). With respect to the Ehrlich study, note that one of the variables held constant is the <u>certainty</u> of punishment. But we know that increases in severity (especially in the area of death penalty policy) tend to reduce the certainty of punishment, through jury nullification for example. If certainty effects are considered, couldn't the deterrence effect disappear or even become negative (i.e. an increase in homicides), even under Ehrlich's own findings? On this and related points, the Lempert article, p. 487, is especially helpful.

Whatever the technical problems in the data, do the empirical studies leave us in the end with a sufficiently clear indication of which way the countervailing deterrence tendencies balance out? If not, what do we do? Is this just a matter of the burden of proof? If so, who has it? Is the moral that the deterrence issue is not really decisive (for <u>either</u> retentionists or abolitionists)? But how could a death penalty opponent continue to favor abolition if it were clearly demonstrated that the death penalty did save a significant number of innocent lives? Likewise, how could a retentionist want to keep the death penalty if it caused a net loss of innocent lives?

b. <u>Error</u>. Note the data collected by Bedau, pp. 488-89, and the dramatic exonerations that have resulted from recent DNA testing (p. 490, Note 2. Do these exonerations show that the system "works"? Or is there reason to think that scrutiny of more cases would have exposed erroneous convictions in the case of some convicted defendants who were actually executed?

Relative to the total number of death sentences is the error rate too low to worry about? Or could there be large numbers of errors in cases that do not afford possibilities for confirmation of guilt by forensic tests? Compare van den Haag's approach at p. 489. Van den Haag argues that even if the death penalty is <u>known</u> entail the execution of innocent people, it is still justified by its benefits. To what extent would the public share his willingness to support a death penalty under these assumptions? Is there something wrong with his analogy to deaths in surgery or in auto accidents? Haven't those who die in such activities usually assumed the risks? Perhaps more fundamentally, do we think of people killed in such activities as having been <u>punished</u>? Note that there is no implication that what happens to such people is <u>deserved</u>. Is van den Haag arguing that the death penalty can be justified by social benefits even if the person executed does not deserve that treatment? Conversely, if desert is crucial, what degree of reliability must be obtained before an irrevocable punishment can be inflicted?

c. <u>The sanctity of human life</u>. Does respect for life <u>require</u> the death penalty? Even for accidental or negligent killings? Or is the death penalty required for <u>all</u> intentional killings? If desert requires consideration of the circumstances of the offender and the offense, what kind of death penalty procedure is implied? Does the need to consider offense and offender characteristics defeat the need, also generated by desert principles, to achieve accuracy and equality in the distribution of the death penalty? What happens to deterrence, if the death penalty is structured to permit careful <u>ad hoc</u> evaluations of desert? Note in particular the implications for the deterrence goal of preserving the swiftness and certainty of punishment.

Discussion should bring out the interdependence of pragmatic objectives (deterrence) and moral principles (accuracy, equality and desert) in the death penalty debate, and the elusive nature of the knowledge on which both depend. Much may turn on how the death penalty is actually administered in practice. How much is the debate influenced by assumptions about the way that the guilt-determining procedures work in the American adversary system? By assumptions about the reliability and accuracy of the institutions of justice in our own society?

<u>Constitutional Limitations</u>, pp. 493-515

The doctrinal tests for application of the cruel and unusual punishment clause (p. 495, 2d & 3d ¶'s of the Stewart opinion) can be mentioned, but the specific formulation is less important for present purposes than the fact that under all versions, it incorporates notions of both utility and desert. See especially the 3d ¶. Discussion of the constitutional cases can show how the effort to translate these notions into a concrete legal framework raises the kinds of tensions between rule and discretion that pervade the formulation of substantive criminal law doctrine.

<u>Gregg</u>, p. 494. Students should understand the two distinct issues -- whether the death penalty may ever be imposed, and if so, pursuant to what procedure. Does the procedure approved in <u>Gregg</u> avoid the capriciousness condemned in <u>Furman</u>? Consider especially the Court's discussion at pp. 498, 2d & 3d full ¶'s. Are the Court's arguments persuasive? Why should it make any difference whether the standardless discretion to withhold the death penalty is exercised by the jury (as under <u>Furman</u>) or before trial (as under <u>Gregg</u>)? Even with respect to the jury's decision, does the procedure approved in <u>Gregg</u> really avoid capriciousness?

Isn't the real solution to the problem of capriciousness a more rule-like approach, making the death penalty mandatory under certain circumstances? Why did the Court rule this solution unconstitutional? See p. 499, Note 1. Is Justice Stewart's rationale in <u>Woodson</u> convincing? If a mandatory death penalty "paper[s] over" the problem of capriciousness [p. 499, Note 1 (ii)], isn't this true of the guided discretion scheme in <u>Gregg</u> as well? If the concern for dignity requires careful individualization [see pp. 499-500, Note 1 (iii) and pp. 501-02, Notes 2(b) & (c), isn't this goal inconsistent with the need to avoid unguided and unchecked jury discretion? If so, isn't <u>Lockett</u> (p. 501, 1st full ¶) inconsistent with <u>Furman</u> and with <u>Gregg</u>?

In <u>Callins v. Collins</u>, p. 504, Note 4, Justices Scalia and Blackmun agree that the Court's demands for guidance (<u>Gregg</u>) and individualization (<u>Lockett</u>) are incompatible. Are they right about that? Compare Prof. Sunby's argument, p. 505, Note 5 (b). If they are right, what follows? Should one of the requirements be abandoned, as Justice Scalia suggests (if so, which one?), or is the death penalty incapable of being fairly administered in contemporary American society?

Discussion of the death penalty cases can help bring the tensions of the rule-discretion debate into sharper focus. In particular contexts throughout the course, it may seem appropriate to sacrifice either the desire for careful individualization (discretion) or the desire for clarity, predictability and evenhandedness (rule). In such contexts the choice between rule and discretion may not seem to pose an inescapable dilemma. But which desire should be compromised in capital cases? When the ultimate punishment is at stake, evenhandedness and careful individualization both seem essential; cases like Woodson and Gregg coexist. Can an appropriate balance between rule and discretion be struck? Or is acceptable administration of the death penalty inherently unattainable?

The proportionality problem can also be explored if time permits. What is the test adopted in Coker (p. 502, Note 3(a))? Would it preclude the death penalty for a hijacker who does not take life? Or even for a hijacker who does take life? Carried to its logical conclusion, Coker could rule out the death penalty except for intentional or reckless killings.

Enmund (p. 502, 3 lines from the bottom) seems to permit the death penalty for a getaway driver only if he knew that his accomplice intended to kill (see p. 503, end of the carry-over ¶). What if the getaway driver did not expect a killing but knew that lethal force would be employed to frighten away pursuers? Students should see that this fact would satisfy the recklessness standard approved in Tison, p. 503, 1st full ¶.

Since recklessness is required for an accomplice like the getaway driver, what result if the actual shooter did not employ deadly force, and death occurred accidently or negligently? Consider, for example, the facts of Stamp, p. 450. Can the death penalty be imposed in such a case? The narrow wording of the Enmund and Tison holdings implies an affirmative answer (p. 503, line 4; p. 504, lines 2-3); the California Supreme Court has so held (Anderson, p. 504, line 4). But doesn't the principle that underlies Coker, Enmund and Tison require the opposite answer - - that as a matter of punishing in proportion to fault, intent or at least recklessness is a prerequisite to imposition of the death penalty? See, again, the H.L.A. Hart quotation in Enmund, p. 503, end of the carry-over.

A different aspect of the proportionality and standards-of-decency requirement is presented in McCarver v. North Carolina, No. 00-8727, cert. granted, March 26, 2001. The Court is expected to decide during the 2001-02 Term whether the Eighth Amendment categorically forbids execution of the mentally retarded. (As discussed in Ch. 8, p. 877, Note 2(b), the Court ruled in 1986 that execution of the mentally ill violates the Eighth Amendment.)

McCleskey, p. 506, can be summarized briefly if time limitations require. Otherwise the case will repay careful attention for part of the class hour. Either way, students need to understand the nature of the racially disparate impact of the death penalty and the Court's reluctance to use constitutional doctrine to mitigate this problem. Racial disparities may therefore be (at least in many jurisdictions) a given in death penalty administration, so long as the death penalty is retained at all.

Students should be sure to understand precisely what the racially disparate impact is. Do black defendants get a disproportionate share of the death sentences? Actually not, see p. 506, last sentence of the last full ¶.) Why is this? Are Georgia juries prejudiced against white defendants? Students who have read carefully presumably will understand that white defendants are more likely to have killed white victims, and that the pattern reflects a greater tendency to exact the death penalty when the victim is white. Blacks, in short, are not being equally protected by the death penalty.

Students should also be sure to understand exactly what the extent of this victim-disparity is. Note the data at p. 506, next to last sentence of the last full ¶ - - defendants who kill whites are 11 times more likely to get death than defendants who have killed blacks. Is this the right measure of disparity? No, because this raw measure does not control for non-racial differences between the two groups of cases. See p. 507, first full ¶. Only after controlling for such variables do we arrive at a plausible estimate of the disparity - - it proves to be much lower than the 11 to 1 ratio but is still a substantial 4.3 to 1. Race of the victim is almost as important as a prior conviction for a life-threatening crime (p. 512 n.10) and almost two times more important than being the prime mover of the crime (p. 512 n.9).

Against this factual background, the equal protection and eighth amendment issues need to be analyzed separately in McCleskey. As to equal protection, discrimination has to be purposeful. (p. 507, last full ¶). Why does the Baldus study fail to satisfy this requirement? Note that in constitutional litigation the complaining party usually has to prove his case by a preponderance of the evidence. Does the Court find that McCleskey hasn't met the usual standard? At places the Court implies that the racial disparities are "unexplained." See, e.g., p. 509, text at n.b. Is it true that we cannot tell whether the death sentences are "more likely than not" imposed solely because of race? Alternatively, is the Court imposing on McCleskey a much higher burden of proof? (The Court appears to acknowledge as much, see p. 507, last ¶.) Is that higher burden justified?

On the eighth amendment issue, Furman and Gregg rule out statutory schemes that pose a "substantial risk" of arbitrariness in decisions to impose the death penalty. (See Gregg, p. 496, last full ¶) Is the risk shown by McCleskey *less* substantial than the risk under the statute in Furman? Is it more speculative? From most perspectives, McCleskey's case seems more substantial than Furman's. Then why does the Court reject McCleskey's claim? Note the concern about analogous complaints of inequality in other criminal sentencing, and on bases other than race (p. 509, last full ¶). Is it sound to reject any distinction between death and short prison sentences? Or between discrimination based on "facial characteristics" and discrimination based on race? It seems difficult to accept at face value the concerns expressed at p. 509, last full ¶.

More plausibly, is the Court concerned about the difficulty of designing a workable statutory (or administrative) remedy for the problems that the Baldus study identifies? If so, is the Court right about the inability to eliminate death sentence disparities? Compare p. 512 (last ¶ of the Blackmun dissent) and pp. 512-13 (last ¶ of the Stevens dissent). Even if the Court is right about the lack of workable statutory or administrative remedies, does this justify a conclusion that the problem McCleskey alleges does not exist? If we cannot have a racially neutral death penalty, is the proper outcome to accept a discriminatory death penalty or to rule that there cannot be a death penalty at all? Compare p. 512 (first paragraph of the Stevens dissent).

Chapter 6
The Significance of Resulting Harm

A. <u>Causation</u>, pp. 517-54

There is an infinite variety of possible situations. The examples on pp. 517-18 illustrate the range of problems. The goal of class discussion should be to provide a framework for organizing the different types of problems and for considering the variety of existing legal approaches. Students should come away with an appreciation of the underlying factors that make causation problems seem so metaphysical or intractable. Generally two classes will be required. In the first (pp. 517-30) the basic legal doctrines can be introduced and the policies that may explain these doctrines can be considered. The second class (pp. 530-54) can permit further exploration of the problem of the intervening human actor and the question of how to give statutory form to sensible principles of causation.

1. <u>Foreseeability</u>, pp. 517-30

<u>Acosta</u>, p. 518. The case is a useful introduction to the problems of causation. The conduct of the defendant was egregiously reckless as well as lawless and but for that conduct the three officers in the crashed helicopter would not have been killed. Why then should there be any problem in holding Acosta liable for the homicides? Both the majority and the dissent agree that this is not enough, and that in addition the result has to be foreseeable to constitute proximate (or legal) cause. They also agree that the result would not satisfy the foreseeability test if it was extraordinary or extremely remarkable and unusual.

Discussion might focus first on the question of the point of these requirements. If the defendant's conduct was culpable and if it led to the deaths of the officers, in the sense at least that if he hadn't acted as he did they would not have been killed, why isn't that enough? The majority at pp. 519-20 throws out some hints, suggesting it is partly a matter of policy, partly of expediency and partly a matter of fairness and justice. In-depth exploration of these issues would be premature at this point -- the issues run through all of the causation materials -- but it might be useful to get the students thinking about them. E.g.: "Fairness and justice? Why isn't it rather unfair and unjust to permit the defendant to escape liability for the regrettable upshot of his egregious conduct? Policy considerations? But what policy requires the defendant to be relieved of liability for the deaths? Is his conduct less reprehensible or his future dangerousness less because the accident happened in a remarkably unusual way?

Discussion might next turn to the issue that divided the court -- whether the helicopter crash was extremely remarkable and who should decide, court or jury? In the end, of course, the jury decides, as it does all issues of guilt in a criminal case, but subject to the determination of the court that the jury could "reasonably" conclude from the evidence that the deaths were sufficiently unremarkable to constitute legal cause. This was the issue before the court on appeal. The court says the decision is one based on common sense. What is the common sense of the matter? How often do police helicopters crash on the job? Virtually never, apparently. How did the crash happen -- through normal pursuit procedures? No, the Costa Mesa helicopter was found by the FAA to have been guilty of gross negligent misconduct in the way it was piloted. How then could the majority conclude as it did? Might its conclusion have been different if the defendant's conduct had been less egregious? If this is so what does it say about the test of foreseeability?

Arzon, p. 521. This case permits further exploration this and related issues. Students should be clear on the sequence of events, the existence of two fires, the evidence about who was responsible for each, and the evidence about how Fireman Celic died. To clarify the issues, it may be helpful to begin with some variations:

> Case 1. Suppose that Celic had died of a heart attack. Same result? If the heart attack resulted from the strain of fighting the fire, clearly yes, but assume that Celic was a supervisor not exposed to the most dangerous part of the fire and that the medical evidence showed his condition would have caused his death on that day, no matter what his activities had been. What result? What if the medical evidence showed that Celic's condition might have caused a heart attack regardless of what his activities had been? Is Arzon guilty of murder?

Note that both the actus reus and the mens rea of murder are satisfied and that a death has occurred. But is there the necessary connection between Arzon's act and the result? As seen from the Acosta case the first prerequisite is that the defendant's action be the factual (i.e. but-for) cause of death. (Consider, for example, hypotheticals 1 and 6(f), pp. 517-518.) And since but-for causation must, like any other element, be

-136-

proved beyond a reasonable doubt, the defendant is presumably not guilty under either version of Case 1.

> Case 2. A sailor falls overboard, and the captain refuses to turn the ship around in order to search and attempt a rescue. If there was a 50/50 chance that the sailor could have been saved (and if the captain knew this), is the captain guilty of involuntary manslaughter?

Note the need for careful analysis of each element. The actus reus is satisfied by the captain's omission, because he has an affirmative duty to protect the crew; the mens rea is presumably satisfied because the failure to intervene exposes the sailor to a substantial and unjustifiable risk of death. But is this culpable omission the cause of death? But-for the omission (i.e. if the captain had acted properly) there is still a 50% chance that the sailor would have died anyway. Since causation is not proved beyond a reasonable doubt, the captain is not liable for homicide. (See U.S. v. Knowles, 26 Fed. Cas. 800.)

The result in Case 2 seems paradoxical because the captain is clearly culpable; rescue was surely obligatory even if it was not clear beyond a reasonable doubt that the sailor could be saved. Case 2 helps make clear that but-for causation is an independent requirement. But is there any good reason why the captain should not be liable, given the actus reus and the mens rea? In other words, is there any good reason why causation (even basic but-for causation) should be an independent requirement? This fundamental problem will have to be considered with respect to all the materials in this section.

Return now to Arzon itself. Were defendant's acts the but-for cause of death? Clearly yes. Is this sufficient for liability? Suppose that Celic had been shot by a sniper while he was attempting to put out the fire. Wouldn't defendant's acts would still be the but-for cause of death? (Yes.) But would he be held responsible? (No; the court's discussion of Stewart and Kibbe indicates that the defendant's conduct must also be a "sufficiently direct" cause.) Is the result in Arzon consistent with the result in Stewart? Note that the defendant escaped liability in Stewart because the court concluded that the victim "would, in all likelihood, have survived except for" the independent intervening factor (p. 522, end of the 3d full ¶). But isn't that also true in Arzon? Wouldn't Celic in all likelihood have survived had it not been for the fire on the second floor?

Apparently, the possibility that the victim might have survived, but-for the independent intervening factor, is not crucial; the more relevant question is whether the victim would have died, but-for the defendant's conduct. In Stewart, it was not even clear that the defendant's conduct "was an actual cause of death" (p. 522); in other words, the victim might have died from his hernia problem, whether or not he had been stabbed by the defendant. In contrast, in Arzon, it is clear that Celic would not have died, but-for the fire on the fifth floor.

Given the various situations in which the defendant's conduct is the factual cause of death (i.e. most of the examples on pp. 517-518), what determines when the defendant's conduct will also be considered the proximate or "sufficiently direct" cause? Consider the test at p. 522, 4th full ¶: "the ultimate harm is something which should have been foreseen as reasonably related to" the defendant's conduct. If Celic had been killed by a sniper's bullet, presumably this would not be considered foreseeable. But by this approach, why should the fire on the second floor be considered foreseeable? Why does the court treat the actual Arzon facts differently from a case where a fireman might be killed by a stray bullet or by lightning?

Consider first whether the court is influenced by the physical similarity of the second floor fire to the danger the defendant himself created. But analytically, is there really any difference in terms of foreseeability between the intervening second floor fire and an intervening stroke of lightning? If not, what other factors distinguish the former from the latter? Is it important that a stroke of lightning would kill the fireman quickly without interacting with the fifth floor fire? Note the comment in Arzon that when the second floor fire erupted, the fifth floor fire continued to operate in exposing the fireman to danger (p. 522, last few sentences of opinion). Thus, it may be easier for the court to see the defendant's own act as actively contributing to the death.

Does this mean, by a similar analysis, that there should be a difference in treatment between hypotheticals 6(c) and 6(d) on p. 518? Although the result in Arzon seems intuitively plausible, students should see that the court's foreseeability test does not really solve any of the problems.

Warner-Lambert, p. 523. Why wasn't the harm here foreseeable? Note that in fact this harm was actually foreseen. (The defendants had been explicitly warned of the explosion hazard.) Then why does the court find insufficient evidence of proximate cause? Does the defendant have to foresee not only the harm in general but also the mechanism by which that harm occurs? Compare the variations on the <u>Kibbe</u> facts posed by the court (pp. 523-24, last sentence of the opinion). But on this analysis, what would be the result in <u>Arzon</u>? Are the two decisions reconcilable? By the <u>Warner-Lambert</u> standard, wouldn't the second <u>Arzon</u> fire have to be considered unforeseeable. Conversely, by the <u>Arzon</u> analysis, wouldn't Warner-Lambert's allowing the high concentration of MS dust leave the employees "particularly vulnerable to the separate and independent force" (p. 522, 4th full ¶, last sentence) that triggered the actual explosion, whatever that force may have been? That approach is also followed in <u>Deitsch</u> p. 524, Note 1(b).

Which approach is the better one? Don't we need to know why the existence of a harmful result should ever affect the defendant's liability? Note how the vagueness of the foreseeability test leaves the courts free to impose liability upon unattractive defendants (<u>Acosta, Arzon</u>) and to insulate defendants with whom the court seems to feel more sympathy (<u>Warner-Lambert</u>). But analytically, isn't the underlying behavior clearly wrongful in both <u>Arzon</u> and <u>Warner-Lambert</u>?

To develop further familiarity with the content of the foreseeability test, consider the following:

> <u>Case 1</u>. Defendant hits the victim over the head, inflicting a wound that ordinarily would not be fatal if properly treated. But the doctor treats the wound incompetently, and the victim dies. Can the defendant be convicted of homicide? Apparently the cases permit this; medical malpractice is ordinarily not treated as an intervening force that breaks the causal "chain", unless the incompetent treatment is really extraordinary. See <u>Hall</u> at p. 526.

> <u>Case 2</u>. Same injury, but this time the doctor falls in love with the patient's wife, and deliberately kills the patient to get him out of the way. What result? Here the doctor's actions presumably would be considered unforeseeable, and the defendant would not be liable.

> <u>Case 3</u>. Same wound, but this time the doctor gives grossly improper treatment. What result? This situation falls somewhere between Case 1 and Case 2. The cases seem to treat grossly abnormal treatment as a factor that will break the chain. See <u>Cheshire</u>, at p. 526. In effect, ordinary medical malpractice

is deemed "foreseeable," but gross negligence is deemed "unforeseeable."

Case 4. Same wound, but this time, while in the hospital, the victim contracts Legionnaire's Disease and dies. How should this problem be analyzed? If the victim contracted the disease as the result of carelessness by the hospital staff (e.g. hypothetical 6(b)), the situation presumably would be like Case 1; defendant would still be liable. But assuming no negligence, isn't a very rare disease just as unforeseeable as the situations in Case 2 and Case 3?

Case 5. Same wound, but this time the victim is a hemophiliac; he dies from the wound despite receiving the best possible care. How should the causation question be analyzed? The cases usually find that the defendant is liable. But why should this be so? One answer is that the defendant must take his victim as he finds him. See p. 525, Note 2. But this just leads to another question -- why should the defendant have to take his victim as he finds him? Logically, what is the difference between Case 5 and Case 4?

Verbally and visually, courts may be more readily inclined to see the germs in Case 4 as "intervening." But is there really any reason to treat germs that "intervene" differently from a disease which is already latent? In terms of any of the purposes of the criminal law, is there any reason to distinguish Case 5 from Case 4? In other words, is there any good reason why the defendant in Case 5 should be held guilty of homicide? One can put this question the other way around, as well -- is any good reason not to hold the defendant guilty of homicide in Case 4? Obviously, all such problems present facets of the question of why liability should depend on the actual results of conduct, as distinguished from results intended or risked.

Consider two clear cases: (a) the defendant shoots with intent to kill, hits his victim in the head, and the victim dies instantly; and (b) the defendant shoots with intent to kill, the bullet misses, and the victim (who does not fall afoul of any law school hypotheticals) is unharmed. In effect the question in the bizarre causation cases is whether such cases are more like (a), where the victim dies immediately in the way intended, or more like (b), where the victim does not die at all. Is Case 5 closer to (a) or (b)? How can we tell? Presumably the answer depends on the reasons why we treat (a) differently from (b). But what are those reasons? (See pp. 528,

Note 2.) If different treatment of (a) and (b) is a vestige of retaliatory impulses or intuitive feelings, then is the foreseeability test just an effort to capture those intuitive feelings? If so, can we expect application of that test to reflect logical consistency or pragmatic policy analysis?

2. Subsequent Human Actions, pp. 530-54

Campbell, at 530, introduces a line of authority that gives special significance to whether the events subsequent to the action of the defendant took the form of actions by other persons. Sometimes the analysis in such cases is terms of the traditional search for foreseeability (compare Acosta or the medical maltreatment cases). But often the terms of analysis turn out not to be foreseeability at all, but other kinds of considerations. Campbell may serve as a rather clear and dramatic example of it. Campbell wanted Basnaw dead. He gave him his own gun and shells in the hope and expectation that Basnaw would kill himself. That Basnaw would do so was hardly unforeseeable; it was foreseen and intended. Likewise for the deaths of Ms. Miller and Ms. Wantz in the Kevorkian case, p. 531. But in these cases the courts concluded that foreseeability was not enough to conclude that Campbell and Kevorkian had "caused" the deaths.

Why not? The intervention of the informed and uncoerced action of the second person (Basnow, Miller and Wantz) was the cause of his or her own death. That action may have been influenced or helped by Campbell and Kevorkian (indeed, it's clear that this was the case), but the law nonetheless stops at saying that the defendant "caused" the deaths. The explanation for this doctrinal turn is developed in the Note on Intervening Human Action at p. 536. It is particularly evident in cases where the second actor intends to produce the result - - the casebook starts with those situations.

Stephenson, p. 537. The case can be used as a vehicle for careful analysis of a complex factual sequence. On which of defendant's specific actions can liability be grounded? Consider what mens rea accompanied each of defendant's acts; consider which acts most clearly "caused" the result. For example, if defendant had a duty to aid after his victim took the poison, and *if* he failed to discharge this duty (note that the facts may leave room for debate on the latter point), causation would be easy to show, since the victim died in precisely the way made more likely by the defendant's culpable omission.

The main issue in Stephenson can be brought into focus by putting aside all the defendant's acts after the initial attack and asking whether the jury could properly find that the rape and bite wounds alone "caused" death. What does the answer depend on? Does it depend on foreseeability of the subsequent events? Is this an adequate approach to the problem? Consider:

Case 1. Preslar, p. 538, last full ¶. Here the defendant is held not liable. Is the reason one of foreseeability? What result if, because of previous episodes of a similar nature, the wife's response *was* foreseeable?

Case 2. Suppose that immediately after Stephenson's attack in the train, the victim had jumped out a window to her death. Would the defendant be held liable here? Cases such as Valade, p. 538, last 3 lines, suggest an affirmative answer. But can it be said that such a response by the victim is "foreseeable"? Is it realistic to characterize such a response as a "natural and *probable* consequence" (p. 540, final sentence of opinion)?

Case 3. What if the victim had returned home after the rape, had brooded about it for two weeks, and then finally decided to commit suicide? Would Stephenson still be liable for the death? If so, why does the court stress that in the actual case "at the very moment Madge Oberholtzer swallowed the poison she was subject to the . . . will of appellant" (p. 539, 8-9 lines from the bottom)? Apparently, Stephenson would not be liable in Case 3. But why? Is it because of foreseeability? In terms of foreseeability, is there really a sharp distinction between Case 3 and Case 2?

Case 4. Suppose that H tells his wife W that if W files for divorce, H will kill himself. Because of a prior suicide attempt that was very serious and nearly successful, W has reason to believe H's threat. Nonetheless she goes ahead and files for divorce. The following day H commits suicide. Is W guilty of murder? Why not? How would the Stephenson court analyze this problem? Note that the court relies heavily on Bishop's test at p. 539, 1st 5 lines, suggesting an emphasis on the victim's irresponsibility rather than foreseeability.

The upshot of Cases 1 through 4 is that where the intervening factor is a human agent who intentionally acts to produce the result, the foreseeability test fails to work. Apparently, the courts use a different approach: The voluntary action of a responsible human actor will break the chain of causation even if that action is foreseeable (Case 1, 3 and 4); on the other hand, an involuntary or irresponsible action will not break the chain even when it is essentially unforeseeable (Case 2).

Why is mental irresponsibility so much more important than foreseeability in these situations? One reason may be that when the human actor is irresponsible, the action may appear analogous to the intervention of some inanimate thing. But then, shouldn't foreseeability be required? With respect to intervention by an irresponsible human actor, perhaps a defendant must take her victim as she finds him. But when the victim is a rational, self-determining actor (Cases 1, 3 and 4), why should a defendant escape liability for victim behavior that is foreseeable? Is it because courts have difficulty seeing the freely chosen human action as "caused" by someone else? Would such a deterministic view conflict with the assumption that human beings are responsible for their freely chosen actions? For discussion, see the Note at 536.

How should the voluntariness or responsibility test be applied in Stephenson itself? Was the case more like Case 2 or more like Case 3 above? Cases like Valade, p. 538, and those discussed in the Comment, pp. 541, 2d full ¶, indicate the range of responses that may be considered involuntary, whether because of instinctive self-preservation, performance of a legal duty, etc. Did the court correctly apply these principles to the facts of Stephenson? The court argues that the evidence was sufficient for a jury to find that the defendant's actions "rendered the deceased distracted and mentally irresponsible" (p. 540, last sentence of opinion). The Comment at p. 540-41 disagrees. Is it correct?

Root, p. 545. This case introduces situations where the action of the second actor is not intentional with respect to the result. In these situations the courts are more willing to hold the first actor as the cause of the result of the second actor's action. Root is a case of this kind, and though the majority denies that Root caused his partner's death, note the dissent. Why isn't the defendant liable in Root? Is it because the victim's reckless act was unforeseeable? Is the victim's act less foreseeable here than, say, in Case 2 above? Any claim of unforeseeability seems untenable (see dissent, p. 546, last full ¶). The court's rationale is the intervening human act doctrine we saw at work in Campbell and Stephenson -- the fatal act was "done by the deceased and by him alone" (p. 546, 2d full ¶). But is the pull of that doctrine as strong in Root?

The McFadden case at p. 548 rejects the Root approach and holds the surviving racer liable for causing the death of a passenger in another car, Faith Ellis, as well as the death of Sulgrove, his racing partner. Should McFadden's liability be different with respect to the two victims? Could it be argued that McFadden caused the death of Ellis but not the death of Sulgrove? Weren't the two deaths caused by precisely the same sequence of events? The defendant makes the argument at p. 576, 3d full ¶, that Sulgrove assumed the risk. Why did the court reject it?

One plausible ground for the court's result in McFadden is the settled doctrine that in criminal cases, unlike civil cases, the contributory negligence of the victim never constitutes a defense -- the victim's fault precludes his recovery of damages, but it does not render the defendant's actions less culpable or any the less subject to punishment. See Note on Contributory Negligence at p. 429. But the faulty actions of the victim may be a defense, not because of the doctrine of contributory negligence, but because they, rather than the actions of the defendant, were the cause of the harm. Note however the quotation from the Peak case (p. 549, indented quote) to the effect that separate contributory actions can both be the legal death of a result. Is this a satisfactory answer? What does "contribute" mean? That McFadden's actions contributed to the result? But that only makes his actions the but-for cause, not the legal cause.

Why does the result in McFadden differ from that in Root? Root took the view that broad *tort law* concepts of proximate causation are too harsh to be just for criminal cases. McFadden sees no policy differences that would lead to differing proximate cause conceptions in torts and criminal law. Are there any? How about the difference that the point of criminal liability is to find blame, impose punishment and deter crime, while the point of tort liability is to apportion losses? Should the law require more to do the former than to do the latter? Does it follow that because courts have enlarged the concept of proximate cause to permit victims to recover damages that the same enlargement is in order when determining the proper extent of criminal punishment? Note also, on this issue, that in one particular the scope of criminal liability is greater than the scope of civil liability: the victim's contributory negligence would preclude tort liability (barring comparative negligence statutes), but *not* criminal liability. Is this anomalous?

How would the McFadden court deal with Campbell at p. 530, the assisted suicide case? Would its reasoning require the court to hold that Campbell was the legal cause of Basnaw's suicide? If not, how can Campbell be distinguished from McFadden? In Campbell the second actor intentionally caused his own death, while in <u>McFadden</u> the victim risked his own death but did not *choose* to die. Is that difference important? Why should the intention of the second actor make so much of a difference?

<u>Atencio</u>, p. 550. Here the deceased shot himself. Yet the court finds this no barrier to liability. Is this case distinguishable from <u>Campbell</u>, p. 530, where defendant actually gave the suicide the gun and shells with the intention that he should use them to kill himself? Again the students should see the difference just pointed out in connection with <u>McFadden</u> -- deceased in <u>Campbell</u> intended to kill himself, while deceased in <u>Atencio</u> killed himself accidentally.

What about <u>Root</u>? Is <u>Atencio</u> really distinguishable from <u>Root</u>, as the former court says, p. 551, next to last ¶ of opinion? Why is the role of "luck" critical with respect to voluntariness, foreseeability, or anything else? Perhaps the force of the <u>Atencio</u> court's reasoning is something like this: In drag racing much depends on many driving decisions made by the competitor. In Roulette all deceased does is pull the trigger, so that whether the gun fires is a matter of luck, with no further choice to be made. The more choices the third party is called upon to make, the greater is his exercise of will and the greater is the impulse to settle causal responsibility on him alone.

If <u>Atencio</u> and <u>Root</u> are indistinguishable, which result makes more sense? What if each player in <u>Atencio</u> had aimed at another player when he pulled the trigger? Clearly, the victim's consent would not be a defense. <u>Malone</u>, p. 439. Is there any good reason why the result should turn on the way that the game is played?

If time permits, the statutory solutions to these problems (p. 553, Note 4) can be explored. How would <u>Stephenson</u> be decided under the MPC? Note the need to specify the theory of liability. If it is felony-murder based on rape, § 2.03(4) applies. Was the result a "probable consequence"? Does this section make inquiries about foreseeability and voluntariness both irrelevant? If the prosecution is based on a theory of recklessness or negligence, § 2.03(3)(b) would apply. What does this section mean? Does it require attention to foreseeability and/or voluntariness? As Hart and Honore suggest, p. 553, indented quote, the MPC seems to fudge these issues.

How would <u>Root</u> be decided under the MPC? Would §2.03(3)(b) be satisfied in <u>Root</u>, or is § 2.03(3) inapplicable because the result *is* within the risk? If the latter, does the Code mean that the causation element *is* established, or is the MPC silent on that question?

B. <u>Attempt</u>, pp. 554-601

For adequate coverage of this material, at least three classes should be allowed. The first class can introduce the questions of why attempts are punished at all and how they are defined and graded (pp. 554-56); can cover the mens rea issues (pp. 556-64) (with particular attention to the question of why the mens rea for attempt is often different from the mens rea required for the completed crime); and can introduce the problem of preparation (pp. 564-69). In the second class the preparation problem can be explored in depth and alternative tests for deciding the issue can be evaluated (pp. 569-81); solicitation (pp. 581-85) can be examined if time permits or can be assigned as background reading. The third class can focus on impossibility (pp. 585-601).

<u>Introduction</u>, pp. 554-56

Why do we punish attempts at all? Since no harm actually occurs, is there any basis for retribution? Probably not, if retribution means retaliation or some kind of paying back for harm done. But if retribution means condemnation for morally blameworthy behavior, isn't punishment equally appropriate? Does the threat of punishment for attempt deter? Note the MPC commentary at p. 556, next to last sentence, suggesting a negative answer. Is this persuasive? See the first paragraph of the Hart excerpt, p. 555.

Why should an attempt be punished <u>less severely</u> than the completed crime? Note that nearly all statutes provide a lower penalty for the attempt. See p. 554, 2d full ¶. But don't the reasons for punishing attempt call for the same punishment whether or not the attempt is successful? This question is closely related to those that underlie the rules of causation: for what reason should we distinguish between the treatment of cases in which a harmful result occurs and cases in which such a result does not occur.

One argument of particular relevance to attempt is the claim that lower punishment provides the defendant with an incentive to desist. Is this a sufficiently common situation to explain the automatic penalty reduction for unsuccessful attempts? Does the argument apply at all when the attempt miscarries after the defendant has done all that was necessary to carry out the crime? (Sometimes yes, if the defendant can take a second shot. In any event, can we promote a stronger incentive to desist by an automatic penalty reduction, or by a specific defense of abandonment?

Some statutory definitions of attempt are provided at p. 554, 1st ¶ of the Introduction. What are the elements of the offense? The New York and Illinois formulations give some guidance. Compare the California statute. What actus reus and mens rea are required? A "definition" like that of California obviously serves only to incorporate the common law tradition, which is examined in detail in the materials that follow.

2. Mens Rea, pp. 556-64

Smallwood, p. 556. What mens rea is the appellate court requiring? It's clear that the defendant was, at a minimum, extremely reckless. Why shouldn't this degree of culpability be sufficient for conviction? Smallwood accurately states the generally prevailing approach, under which "specific intent" (i.e. MPC purpose) is required. But what is the reason for this approach? Especially since punishment for attempt is lower than the punishment for the completed crime, why should the mens rea for the attempt be *more stringent*?

If Smallwood is not guilty of attempted murder, what crime (if any) did he commit? Students may raise the possibility of charging a lesser degree of assault. But note that assault is typically defined as an attempted battery - specific intent to injure is required for that charge as well.

The paradox of the stringent mens rea for attempt is illustrated by Thacker, p. 560, last full ¶. If the woman is killed, the defendant is guilty of murder; if the bullet luckily misses, the defendant is not guilty of any crime at all. (If a specific statutory offense of reckless endangerment exists, it might cover such a case, but with a rather low penalty.)

Why not have complete parity - - whatever mens rea is appropriate for the substantive offense should also apply to an attempt? See, e.g., the Colorado statute at p. 561, 1st indented quote. This looks like a coherent solution, but does it work? Consider:

> Case 1. Defendant enters a bank, pulls a gun and announces a stick-
> up. A teller hits the alarm button, guards rush in and the defendant

flees while firing in the air to scare off his pursuers. A bystander is grazed by a bullet but is not seriously wounded. What crimes has defendant committed?

Defendant is clearly guilty of attempted murder (and possibly weapons offenses) in Case 1. But if parity is the right standard (as under the Colo. statute), is he also guilty of attempted murder? That sounds silly, but note that the statute is met: the defendant is "acting with the kind of culpability otherwise required for commission of the offense [of felony-murder]" i.e., just the intent to commit the felony and no culpability at all with respect to the risk of death. Does a conviction for attempted murder make sense?

For an even more extreme possibility, what if the defendant enters the bank with only a toy gun, makes his threat but then flees, and is quickly caught. Is he guilty of attempted murder? No one is injured; the teller does not have a heart attack due to fright. But if such a victim had died, the defendant *would* be guilty of murder (as in Stamp, p. 450), and since the defendant has all the culpability required for the completed offense, it would seem he is guilty of the attempt under the Colorado approach.

Very few courts would accept that result. See p. 561, Note 4. Even with the specific language of the Colo. statute, that state's Supreme Court was unwilling to apply it literally; Thomas, pp. 560-61 read in a requirement of at least recklessness. Neither negligence nor strict liability with respect to the result are acceptable bases for attempt liability under the Colo. Statute (as interpreted), even when they are sufficient for conviction of the completed offense.

What mens rea is required under the MPC formulation? See §5.01(1) and Comment at pp. 563-64. Students should understand the effect of the Code provisions. The drafting is awkward and imprecise but the result the drafters intended is fairly clear - - with respect to attendant circumstance elements (a girl's age in statutory rape, an assault victim's status as a police officer), the parity principle governs; negligence or even strict liability are sufficient if they are sufficient for the completed offense. But what result under the MPC in a case like Thacker, p. 560? Note that §5.01(1)(b) and the Comment both contemplate acquittal in a Thacker situation. With respect to result elements negligence is insufficient and even recklessness is insufficient; the actor must have a purpose to produce the result. But why should recklessness as to attendant circumstances be treated differently from recklessness as to result?

Students should see that in terms of policy objectives, the requirement of a purpose with respect to results is anomalous. Part of the explanation (justification?) for the law's position on this matter may flow from the ordinary verbal meaning of an "attempt" as an effort to try to achieve a particular result. We can try getting around this problem by the verbal ploy of calling recklessness a kind of intent, but this does not work very well. In any event does this view suggest that we should not punish recklessness not resulting in harm, or only that in punishing such conduct, we should not call it an "attempt"?

3. Preparation, pp. 564-85

a. The traditional approach (physical proximity), pp. 565-67

Suppose a defendant does satisfy the mens rea of attempt, for example by making it his conscious purpose to kill V. Should this fact, by itself, be enough for criminal liability? If more is required, how much more?

Case 1. Suppose a defendant:
    a) buys a gun,
    b) searches for V,
    c) finds V,
    d) walks toward him,
    e) takes aim,
    f) and finally fires.

At what point in this sequence should the defendant be guilty of attempted murder? Note that buying the gun will satisfy the minimal requirement of some act. Why isn't this enough? Why does the common law tradition, as summarized in Barker, pp. 564-65, characterize some acts as mere "preparation" insufficient to trigger attempt liability? Consider the following concerns:

Concern (1). We can't be sure he really intended to do it. If that is the concern, when is it satisfied in the example above? Only when the defendant aims? Or earlier? What if we have other very clear evidence of intent when he buys the gun?

Concern (2). Even if the defendant clearly intended to commit the crime, he might have changed his mind and repented, i.e. "he still has a locus penitentiae" (p. 564, at fn. 16). If that is the concern, when is it satisfied in the example above? Only when the defendant shoots? Perhaps even then he can still repent by choosing not to shoot again.

Note that concern for preserving a locus penitentiae led the court in Eagleton, p. 564, top of the last full ¶, to hold that an attempt is not punishable until the defendant takes the very last step. Is this a workable approach? If we really take the "locus penitentiae" problem seriously, we would have to deny liability even in last-act cases, at least whenever the defendant has in effect lit a very long fuse.

The opposite problem with the last-act test is posed by step (e) of Case 1, above. The defendant is actually aiming at the victim but a further step is still required, so liability would be precluded under the Eagleton test. Is this a tolerable result? Clearly some situations will require the point of criminality to begin prior to the last act.

To address this line-drawing question, consider Rizzo, p. 565, and Duke, p. 567, 1st full ¶. Why is there insufficient evidence for an attempt? What is the *test* of sufficiency? In terms of concern (1), are we really uncertain that the intent is firm in Duke and Rizzo? Discussion should make clear that Duke and Rizzo reflect an essentially physical, spatial notion of proximity; In Rizzo, the defendants never got close to Rao at all. But didn't Duke get close to what he thought was his victim?

Is the physical proximity approach workable? An obvious problem is its vagueness. But in any case, why should physical proximity be relevant at all? Consider whether the acquittal in Rizzo really makes sense. If it does, what can the police do in a similar situation in the future? Note that the Rizzo court commends the police work in that case (p. 565, 1st sentence of the opinion), but hasn't the court just held that the arrest was illegal? Requiring physical proximity seems to deny the police the power to do anything more than temporarily stop a suspect, until the suspect actually finds the victim and gets close. Thus, Rizzo suggests a third concern relevant to placing the line between preparation and attempt: Concern (3) is that the police should have a power to intervene sufficiently early. See the Williams excerpt, p. 567, Note 2, 1st indented quote.

What approach to the preparation problem is suggested by concerns (1), (2) and (3)? How should the balance be struck? Students should see that the difficulty is that concern (3) suggests the desirability of placing the line as early as possible, while concern (2) suggests the need to place the line at the very last act or if not, then at least as late as possible. The physical proximity approach (which often appears dominant in the common law cases) may produce the worst of both worlds: the line is so close to the final act that proper police action may be hampered (<u>Rizzo</u>), but is not close enough to the final act to protect the defendant who really does have a change of heart and decides to turn back. Nonetheless many of the modern cases remain committed to the physical proximity approach. See, e.g., <u>Acosta</u>, p. 567, 3d line, and Duke, p. 567, 1st full ¶. Another vivid example is United States v. Schoof, 34 Mil.J.Rptr. 811 (subsequently reversed, 37 Mil.J.Rptr. 96), where the intermediate court reversed the conviction, despite clear evidence of intent and substantial acts actually done (a sailor stole secret documents and rode several hundred miles on his motorcycle, heading for the Soviet Embassy before he turned back), because "more than a hundred miles of locus penitentiae" remained.

Is there some way to avoid the dilemma? Why not have a very early line, but allow abandonment as a defense, *provided* that abandonment actually occurs? An abandonment defense seems to provide a way out of the dilemma, but courts committed to a formal analysis consider such a defense inconsistent with the principle that a crime, once complete, cannot be extinguished by remorse or restitution. See the note at pp. 567-69. The prevalent modern approach is to allow the abandonment defense and thus mitigate the tension between concerns (2) and (3). But in jurisdictions where there is no abandonment defense, courts remain under pressure to require close proximity to the final act.

The note at pp. 567-69 explores the abandonment defense in more detail. Students should be sure to note the prerequisites for invoking the abandonment defense: the abandonment must be both voluntary and complete.

Once we have an abandonment defense to satisfy concern (2), why not reject the proximity requirement entirely. Note Professor Williams' proposal to this effect (p. 567, Note 2). Is there any problem with this approach? Consider <u>McQuirter</u>, p. 569.

b. <u>Alternative approaches (especially equivocality)</u>, pp. 569-75

<u>McQuirter</u>, p. 569. Is the result correct? Students often feel that the evidence of intent is insufficient. They may want to argue that an unbiased appellate court should reverse on this ground. A close look at the record is warranted. Note the police chief's testimony (p. 569, last full ¶). Can a reasonable jury accept that testimony as true? (Imagine what criminal trials would be like if juries were required to credit defendants' retractions whenever they denied confessing to the police.) If the jury is permitted to

decide whether the police chief's testimony is credible, then is there enough evidence for the jury to find intent beyond a reasonable doubt? (Clearly yes.)

Part of the problem here is that the usual rules about credibility, the jury's role and the requirement of proof beyond a reasonable doubt are not enough by themselves to assure the reliability of findings that intent really existed or was a firm commitment that the defendant would actually act upon (Concern 1, above). The actus reus requirement functions in part to meet this concern about the problematical character of evidence about intent.

Do the McQuirter facts satisfy the actus reus requirements for an attempt? Under the proximity test, arguably not. But note how close the defendant actually got to the alleged victim; even a strict test of physical proximity might be satisfied here. How would McQuirter be decided under G. Williams' test? Presumably the only requirements are some act, plus proof beyond a reasonable doubt of intention (a jury question). Wouldn't Professor Williams have to uphold the conviction? What is the problem here? Can we trust confessions or rely on juries to find intent without the corroboration of some apparently dangerous action? Note the difficulties of finding facts about "intent" when the context is racially charged. But even if there were no racial dimension, could we then have adequate confidence in jury fact-finding about intent? See the concerns discussed at pp. 180-82.

If the Williams approach goes too far in departing from some proximity requirement, but if physical proximity is an unsatisfactory test, what are the alternatives? The Wisconsin statute, p. 571, last indented quote, is designed to address this problem. How would McQuirter be decided under this approach? Conviction is barred where the intent with which the acts were done is equivocal. On this approach the McQuirter conviction might be reversed. But how is unequivocality established? If a confession would be sufficient, then the equivocality test would add nothing to the ordinary requirement of proving intent beyond a reasonable doubt. Note how the equivocality test is formulated in Barker, bottom of p. 570, and Miller, p. 571. Under these approaches, a confession clearly cannot establish intent; McQuirter would be acquitted because the unequivocality must be established by an act which in effect "speaks for itself" -- the act must "show criminal intent on the face of it" (Barker, p. 570, 2d sentence of the quote).

Does the unequivocality requirement provide a workable approach? Is the intent in the haystack example (p. 571, 1st full ¶) really unequivocal?

What if the defendant had a pipe in his mouth when he struck the match? See the G. Williams hypo, p. 572, 1st indented quote. Does the intent remain equivocal even after the defendant tosses the match onto the haystack?

If the unequivocality requirement is taken seriously, it would pose a very inconvenient barrier to conviction in cases that seem to require some power of intervention. If that is too high a price to pay, we may be thrown back to some kind of proximity approach. Possibly such an approach, strictly applied, could permit reversal of convictions in cases like McQuirter. But is that too high a price to pay too. Students should be asked to consider a hypo like McQuirter but without the racial overtones:

> Case 2. A woman alone on an urban street at night is persistently followed and stared at by a strange man. If we arrest the defendant and obtain evidence of an intent to rob or rape, shouldn't that be enough to permit conviction for attempt?

Case 2 poses a situation that can surely be very frightening for most women. Shouldn't it be punishable as an attempt? If not, should some other offense be available? The concern has prompted support for stalking statutes, discussed in the note at 573-75.

Stalking statutes, pp. 573-75, were initially enacted in response to extreme situations like the murder of TV actress Rebecca Schaeffer. Do they help in a situation like Case 2? Is the defendant there guilty of stalking? What if there is no specific evidence that he intended to commit rape? Note the narrow coverage of the California statute, p. 574. Under the California statute, there appears no chance of conviction because the defendant never articulated a "credible threat." (Query whether the following itself should count as an implicit threat.) Even if there is an implicit threat, the California statute (and those of many other states are similar) requires that the defendant "repeatedly" follow. Thus, even the recent criminalization of "stalking" seems too restrictive to reach a situation like that in Case 2. Should such statutes be broadened still further?

An article in the ABA Journal, Sept. 1994, p. 68, discusses the expansion of "stalking" behavior that may be perceived as threatening from street following into other repetitive behaviors including contacts through telephone, fax, and even "on-line" electronic stalking. Several states have sought to enact new anti-stalking statutes to reach such conduct. Students should consider how the law should be drawn, through either attempt doctrine or specific statutes, in order to capture culpable and dangerous conduct preemptively, without sweeping in innocent conduct and risking

-153-

the abuses of over-criminalization that a McQuirter situation potentially poses.

c. The Model Penal Code approach, pp. 575-81

Jackson, p. 575, illustrates the MPC alternative to the various proximity tests. Note that the Code requires some element of both proximity (a "substantial" step) and unequivocality (the act must "strongly corroborate"). P. 612, indented quote, and MPC § 5.01(2). The Code approach *may* be a practical way to capture both proximity and unequivocality concerns without the disadvantages of either approach in isolation. How would McQuirter be decided under §§ 5.01(1)(c), 5.01(2)? Arguably, under §5.01(2)(a), McQuirter's acts could be considered a substantial step. But would they be enough under all the circumstances to "strongly corroborate" the alleged criminal purpose?

The Problems, pp. 578-81, can be used to test student understanding of the MPC approach and the arguments available to each side under it.

In Harper, p. 578, Note 1, are there "substantial steps"? The court thought not. Is it realistic to say that the defendants' conduct was not substantial just because they were not "walking toward" the bank, as in Moore. On this analysis wouldn't the attempt convictions have to be reversed in Jackson too? Under the court's view, at what point could police intervene and still be assured of getting a bank robbery conviction?

What should be the result in Mandujano, p. 579, Note 2? Under the MPC-Jackson approach, are the defendant's acts "strongly corroborative" of an intent to sell heroin? What if he had thought about stealing the $650 and then changed his mind? Note that the court here upheld the conviction. Is this extending the attempt notion too far? Students should see that the MPC approach, though a plausible compromise, cannot fully avoid the dangers of drawing a line that is either too late to meet concern (3) (as in Buffington and Joyce p. 579, Note 3) or too early to meet concern (1) (as in Mandujano).

d. Solicitation, pp. 581-85

The solicitation material presents interesting variations on the problem of distinguishing preparation from a punishable attempt. But if time constraints require, this section can be summarized quickly or skipped - - partly because under the MPC approach, solicitation of a human principal can constitute a punishable attempt whether or not the party solicited is innocent of the criminal intentions or instead is thought to be a co-participant in the criminal plan. See §§ 5.01(2)(g); 5.01(3).

Davis, p. 581. Why does the court find no attempt here? Didn't the defendant perform his very last act? Further acts are still necessary by Dill, but isn't Dill just another long fuse? To see whether there is a difference, consider the following variations:

> Case 1. Suppose that Dill had in fact killed Lourie. Could Davis be convicted of murder? Probably not on a theory of directly causing the death. See the discussion of the voluntary intervening human actor in the causation materials, pp. 563-64 above. If Davis is guilty of murder, it can only be on the theory that he is an accomplice responsible for the crime committed by Dill.

> Case 2. Suppose that Dill shoots at Lourie but misses. Is Davis guilty of an offense? By similar reasoning, Davis cannot be held to have "caused" Dill's actions, but Dill himself is guilty of an attempt, and Davis, as his accomplice, would also be.

> Case 3. Suppose that Dill buys a gun but is arrested before he tries to use it to kill Lourie. Has Dill himself committed any crime? Under a traditional attempt analysis, he would not have gone far enough. But then, how can Davis be convicted of anything? If Dill himself hasn't gotten close enough for an attempt, the courts would find it anomalous for Davis, who is even further removed from the victim, to be held guilty of an attempt.

> Case 4. Suppose that Davis had given a package, containing a concealed bomb, to a messenger who was unaware of its contents. If the messenger delivers the package, and the bomb explodes, killing Lourie, can Davis be convicted of murder? In this case, since the innocent agent is not himself morally (or criminally) responsible, and did not freely choose to commit the wrong, courts have no difficulty in seeing his action as "caused" by the defendant; the innocent agent is in effect simply a long fuse.

The upshot is that a defendant who attempts to commit an offense through an innocent or irresponsible human agent can be convicted of attempt even if the agent never gets close to carrying out the offense. But when the agent is responsible and aware of the plot, traditional conceptions permit holding the defendant only to the same extent as the agent himself. Therefore, in the actual Davis case, the defendant can't be convicted of attempt because Dill never went beyond "mere preparation." (If Dill *had* committed a substantive crime, Davis' liability would then turn on the question whether Dill in fact can be his accomplice. That problem is explored in connection with the <u>Hayes</u> case, p. 633.)

Note the reform efforts to produce a more coherent approach to this problem. Where a statutory offense of solicitation exists, p. 584, Note 2, a defendant in Davis' position can be convicted of this attempt-like crime, whether or not the person solicited ever gets close enough to be guilty of an attempt. See, e.g., MPC § 5.02. Are these provisions adequate to eliminate the arbitrariness of the traditional common law concepts? Consider the Note at p. 583, 3d ¶ of the indented quote: it still may make a great difference to punishment if the defendant cannot be convicted of attempt. One solution is to hold that the defendant has in effect lit the fuse or fired the missile and is therefore punishable for attempt. See <u>Church</u>, p. 582, especially at p. 583, last 2 lines before the Note. See also § 5.01(3). With respect to the innocent agent, attempt liability is made clear by § 5.01(2)(g).

4. <u>Impossibility</u>, pp. 585-601

<u>Jaffe</u>, p. 585. Students should note the original charge (receiving stolen goods) and the reason why the defendant can't be guilty of this completed substantive offense -- the element of actually receiving stolen goods is missing. Why isn't the defendant guilty of an attempt? Two partially distinguishable theories need to be considered: the "impossibility" of the attempt, and the statutory requirement of "knowledge" rather than "belief."

Is the court really relying on "impossibility"? The language at p. 586 (lines 1-3 of the 1st full ¶) and the repeated emphasis on the difference between knowledge and belief raise doubts. But what if the statutory language had made it a crime to receive stolen goods, knowing *or believing* them to be stolen -- would the court have reached a different result? Consider the court's statutory rape example (p. 586, last line). Why can't there be a conviction for attempt here? Is it because the statute requires "knowledge" of the victim's age? Clearly not, because statutory rape is presumably a strict liability offense. Discussion should make clear that the "impossibility" notion is what is crucial here, not the wording of the particular statute.

But when does "impossibility" prevent conviction for attempt? Consider the pickpocket cases, p. 585, last full¶. The court recognizes that here impossibility does not prevent conviction. How are these pickpocket cases different from Jaffe. The court's language draws a contrast between cases in which "the immediate act which the defendant had in contemplation was an act which, if it could have been carried out, would have been criminal" (p. 586, last sentence of the 1st full ¶), and cases in which "all which an accused person intends to do would, if done, constitute no crime" (p. 586, beginning of the last ¶). In the former cases (pickpocketing) the attempt is punishable, while in the latter cases (receiving stolen goods) it is not. The contrast corresponds to what most courts, as explained in Dlugash (p. 589, 2d full ¶), call factual and legal impossibility. Does the distinction make sense? Consider these applications of the factual impossibility/legal impossibility distinction:

> not constitute the crime" (p. 585, last 2 Case 1. The voting example, bottom of p. 586. Why is this a case of legal impossibility? The notion seems to be that what the defendant was trying to do was to vote. As in Jaffe, this effort, "if it had been completely effected, could lines). (The age, an attendant circumstance, may be viewed as irrelevant to what the defendant wanted to accomplish. The statutory rape example fits the same pattern.)

> Case 2. The pickpocket case, p. 585, last full ¶. Why is this a case of *factual* impossibility? Here the defendant's objective was to steal money. Thus the money in the pocket is not simply an attendant circumstance, but is part of the result the defendant is trying to achieve.

In effect, legal impossibility seems to arise when the defendant makes a mistake about attendant circumstances, while factual impossibility seems to arise when the defendant's mistake relates to his or her ability to achieve the result. But why should liability turn on which kind of a mistake the defendant makes? Is the rule about "legal" impossibility a product of the verbal connotations of "attempt" (effort, trying) or are there good policy reasons for not punishing legal impossibility under any verbal rubric? In this regard consider further applications of the distinction:

> Case 3. Guffey, p. 589, 2d ¶. Why is this considered *legal* impossibility. In terms of the defendant's desire and objective, it is presumably to take home an edible deer, not a bag of straw. Here the nature of the target can be considered part of the "result" just as easily as it can be characterized as an attendant circumstance. But the court treats this as legal impossibility, even though (unlike Case 1) the mistake is not at all irrelevant to what the defendant was trying to accomplish.

Case 3 makes clear that the <u>Jaffe</u> test requires characterization of what is included in "all which an accused person *intends* to do" (p. 586, last ¶). Does it make sense to say that all Guffey intended to do was just to hit the target in front of him and not to shoot a *deer*?

Is the formulation in <u>Berrigan</u> (p. 592) more helpful? The court explicitly separates the defendant's desire or objective from his "intent." (p. 592 n.35). Does this solve the <u>Guffey</u> problem? For that matter does it solve <u>Berrigan</u> itself? Why can't we say even in Berrigan that success was prevented by "extraneous circumstances unknown to the actor," and therefore that this was a case of *factual* impossibility? Consider whether other examples help give content to the factual/legal impossibility distinction:

> <u>Case 4</u>. Suppose a pickpocket's victim does have money in her pocket, but the money, unknown to the defendant, turns out to be his own. What result? This case presumably has to be treated like <u>Jaffe</u>, and defendant would be acquitted. But is there any possible policy reason for treating this case differently from Case 2.

> <u>Case 5</u>. See <u>Mitchell</u>, p. 589, 3d full ¶. Defendant shot into a room expecting his victim to be there, but luckily the victim was elsewhere at the time. In what sense is this *factual* impossibility? How is it different from <u>Guffey</u>? But if <u>Mitchell</u> should have been held a case of "legal" impossibility, then what if the victim had been in the bed, lying one foot to the left of the spot that the bullet struck? Would that be legal impossibility too, on the ground that the defendant's intent was to shoot at the spot he actually hit, even if his "motive, desire and expectation" had been to hit a spot one foot to the left? If so, aren't we forced to say that a defendant's "intent" is never different from what he actually does, which by hypothesis does not constitute a crime? Doesn't the analysis at p. 592 n.35 in effect prevent conviction whenever the attempt misfires? Doesn't that analysis force us to say that there would be "legal" impossibility even in Case 2.

Discussion should make clear that the distinction between factual and legal impossibility is at best difficult to apply. Part of the reason is that courts fail to consider what policy reasons might justify acquittal in the context of an impossibility problem. The MPC concludes that generally there are no such reasons; therefore neither factual nor legal impossibility should be a defense. See <u>Dlugash</u>, at p. 689, last ¶. Is the MPC analysis satisfactory? Or are there cases in which conviction for an impossible attempt would raise serious problems of fairness? Consider the following situations:

1. Note the facts in <u>Ovieto</u>, p. 593. Would a conviction here involve any serious dangers? Note the court's concern that eliminating the objective element will "increase the risk of mistaken conclusions" about the defendant's subjective intent or belief (p. 594, 1st 2 lines). The court's comment recalls concerns about the "equivocality" of intent that arise when the defendant is prosecuted for preliminary steps of preparation. See <u>McQuirter</u>, p. 569. As <u>Ovieto</u> suggests, the same concerns can arise even when the defendant has completed the last act. (For an illustration, consider the umbrella case, at p. 600, 2d full ¶.)

But are doubts about the equivocality of intent a relevant concern in <u>Jaffe</u>? In <u>Berrigan</u>? Often the very decoy operations that raise questions about "legal impossibility" serve to <u>strengthen</u> the evidence of intent. Does the <u>Ovieto</u> opinion suggest the value of a legal impossibility defense, or only the value of an unequivocality requirement for <u>both</u> legally and factually impossible attempts? Note the court's formula requiring that (presumably for both kinds of attempts) the objective acts "mark the defendant's conduct as criminal" (p. 594, 1st full ¶). For a similar, but less extreme suggestion, see the proposed revision of MPC § 5.01, at p. 600, and the indented quote on p. 601.

2. Does an impossibility defense make sense in the context of the voodoo problem at the bottom of p. 598? Wasn't the conviction of the Ivy brothers plainly inappropriate? Consider whether the voodoo practitioner is dangerous. Presumably not, but how do we know that such a person won't choose a more effective weapon next time?

In any event, if punishment of such a person seems inappropriate or even absurd, is a defense of legal impossibility the solution? Was their lawyer correct to advise them to plead guilty, or did they have a defense under <u>Jaffe</u> and <u>Berrigan</u>? Presumably they did not have a defense, because inadequate means are uniformly held to involve a problem of *factual* impossibility. Like the equivocality problem, the problem of the harmless crank may (or may not) arise with respect to *both* legal and factual impossibility. Students should see that to the extent that the voodoo case raises a genuine problem, it calls for a separate kind of defense. See, e.g., the Minnesota formulation and Prof. Robbins' proposal, both at p. 599, 1st full ¶.

3. Does an attempt conviction make sense in the case of the self-described money smuggler who thought his conduct was illegal (p. 597 n.8). Again, wouldn't punishment of this behavior be absurd? But how can such cases of "true" legal impossibility be distinguished from the cases in which legal impossibility is *not* a defense? Is there really any significant difference between the original Lady Eldon hypothetical and the variation at p. 597, 1st full ¶, or between Mr. Fact and Mr. Law on p. 599, last ¶?

To examine such questions, consider first how the sugar case would be analyzed under the MPC. Can we argue for conviction of attempt under §5.01(1)(a)? The defendants can respond that everything they did would not amount to a crime. But how is this response different from the argument for acquittal in Jaffe? Can't we argue, as we would argue there, that the conduct would constitute the crime "if the attendant circumstances were as [the defendants believed] them to be" (i.e. if smuggling sugar did constitute a crime as the defendants believed, then they would be guilty of it). Analytically, the question is whether the criminality of sugar smuggling can be considered (like the stolen status of the goods) an "attendant circumstance," as that term of art is used in the MPC. Given §§ 1.13(9), 2.02(9) the answer has to be no. Thus the MPC acquits the sugar smugglers and Mr. Law, but not Jaffe or Mr. Fact.

Nonetheless, as a matter of policy, is there any reason to distinguish between these two groups of cases, or to distinguish the original Lady Eldon hypothetical from the variation? The argument against drawing the distinction is developed at p. 599, last ¶. But consider Taaffe, p. 597 n.8. The court reversed a conviction for the completed offense of knowing importation. Defendant claimed that he thought he was smuggling currency, and smuggling currency was not a crime. What if the defendant had been prosecuted for attempt? Under the foregoing MPC principles, the defendant is like Mr. Law and would be acquitted: he can take advantage of his mistake of fact for exculpation, but the prosecution can't take advantage of his mistake of law for inculpation. Is this fair? Isn't there a lack of reciprocity here?

To examine that question, consider the situation if Taaffe knew he was carrying marijuana and had thought (erroneously) that this conduct <u>was</u> legal. Of course, this mistake as to penal law would not be a defense. In this sense the law is consistent -- just as a mistake about the legality of conduct can't exculpate, a mistake about the illegality of conduct can't inculpate.

But isn't the defendant in <u>Taaffe</u> dangerous and deserving of punishment? Note the response of Dutile & Moore, p. 599 n.11 Dangerousness is not really relevant, if the acts the defendants intended to carry out (viewed from their own perspective) have not been declared illegal. Their own (erroneous) opinion about the illegality of their conduct can't inculpate them because society has not chosen to condemn or deter the acts that they have tried to commit.

One might argue that the defendant who was willing to break a law he (erroneously) thought existed might be willing to violate another law that he (this time correctly) thought existed. If Taaffe is willing to smuggle currency, on his next trip he may try to smuggle marijuana, which *is* illegal. But what basis do we have for making this kind of prediction? Lady Eldon evidently would be willing to break a law against smuggling French lace, if there were such a law. Can we therefore infer that she would be willing to break the law against smuggling goods which *are* on the duty list? Do we worry that on her next trip, Lady Eldon may choose to smuggle heroin or hashish? There seems no coherent way to make such judgments, and thus it makes little sense to impose attempt liability unless the thing the defendant thought she did was (judged entirely from her own perspective) something that society had chosen to make illegal.

The impossibility discussion can be used to bring out the continuing hold of traditional concepts, as well as the need for tailoring each defense as precisely as possible to the specific concerns that prompt it.

Chapter 7
Group Criminality

A. <u>Accountability for the Acts of Others</u>, pp. 603-44.

This material normally warrants between two or three full classes. The first class can provide an overview (pp. 603-06) and begin to examine the mens rea problems (pp. 606-621). The second class can be used to complete the mens rea problems (pp.621-28) and to begin the problems of actus reus (pp. 628-33). The third class may be used to cover the specific problems arising from discrepancies between the liability of the parties (pp. 633-44-683).

The material at pp. 603-03 reviews the common law background and provides examples of the contemporary statutory framework. Consider the California and U.S. provisions. Note the kinds of actions that can make a secondary party punishable as a principal -- aiding, abetting, counseling, encouraging, etc. Do the California or U.S. provisions require any mens rea to make one who aids punishable as a principal? At this point in the course, students should see that such a question can be answered only after considering the common law tradition, which is presented in the next section.

The theoretical points in the Kadish extract, p. 606, are designed to suggest the relationships between complicity doctrine and other doctrines of the criminal law, such as actus reus, mens rea, causation, which the student has already encountered. As usual there are two ways to raise these issues: either as a whole right here at the outset, or piece by piece as they become relevant to specific points of doctrine.

1. <u>Mens Rea</u>, 606-28.

This section covers a number of distinguishable mens rea problems identified as subsections. Subsection a. deals with the required mens rea as to the criminal action of the principal, the primary party, focusing mainly on whether knowledge is enough or whether a genuine purpose to aid is required; Subsection b. deals with the required mens rea as to attendant circumstances; Subsection c. considers the mens rea required for results of the conduct aided.

a. <u>Mens Rea as the Actions of the Principal</u>

This section focuses on the required mens rea with respect to the actions of the primary party. The conventional requirement (which has been challenged in recent years, as we shall see in <u>Luparello</u>, p. 615) is that the secondary party must have intended to aid or encourage the primary party to perform the criminal action.

<u>Hicks</u>, p. 607. Students should be clear on the precise nature of the defendant's conduct. Why didn't Hicks's actions (his laughing and his words to Colvard) meet the requirement that the defendant have encouraged Rowe? Note that the court adds a requirement that the words of encouragement be used with the *intention* of encouraging the principal (p. 608, 4th full ¶). Should the same result be reached if liability is based on aid rather than encouragement? Suppose that Hicks had positioned his horse so that it blocked Colvard's escape route. Would this aid be sufficient to convict under the U.S. statute (bottom of p. 604)? Again the question would remain whether Hicks <u>intended</u> that this effect be produced; he might (perhaps negligently) have failed to realize the effect.

What is wrong with the second quoted portion of the trial judge's instructions? Here the trial judge does require a *purpose* of aiding or encouraging, so why was the instruction erroneous? Students should see that the problem now is that the necessary mens rea would be satisfied, but there would be no contribution by the secondary party -- i.e. no actus reus. Why does the court say that a previous conspiracy or arrangement could render the instruction correct? Presumably the pre-arrangement, combined with Hicks's presence, would encourage Rowe, so that there would then be an actus reus as well as the mens rea.

To develop familiarity with this analytic framework, consider the four variations on <u>Hicks</u> (p. 609, Note 1). How should each one be analyzed? In (a) there is neither the required mens rea nor actual aid. In (b) there is actual aid, but without the required mens rea. In (c), unlike (a), then is the required mens rea, but no actual aid. In (d) there is finally both the required mens rea and actual encouragement (or aid) in the assurance Hicks gives to Rowe. Actus reus problems are explored below, but students need to bear in mind that absence of <u>either</u> actus reus or mens rea will defeat liability.

To explore further the traditional requirement of intention to aid, students could be asked to work with the following examples:

Case 1. Wilson, p. 609, Note 2. Is the result correct? Didn't Wilson intend to aid Pierce (i.e. by helping him enter)? (Yes.) Didn't Wilson also intend that Pierce should commit the crime (i.e. taking the liquor with intent to steal)? (Yes.) If so, why isn't Wilson guilty as an accomplice? Compare:

Case 2. What if Wilson had handed Pierce an axe with which to break open the door, all with the same purpose of having him arrested for burglary. If Pierce breaks down the door, would Wilson have a defense to a charge of malicious destruction of property charge? Presumably not. Then why is Wilson acquitted in Case 1?

Analysis of these examples requires careful attention to the crimes involved. In one sense, Wilson clearly wanted Pierce to commit an offense; otherwise his plan to get Pierce in trouble would fail. But larceny is a taking with intent to deprive the owner *permanently* of possession. Did Wilson intend this to occur? Since he didn't, he lacks the mens rea of theft. How about burglary? Wilson did intend for Pierce to enter with intent to commit theft, so in a sense he may be said to have intended to help Pierce commit burglary and therefore to have been guilty of burglary as an accomplice. On the other hand, Wilson himself lacked the mens rea for the theft and therefore of burglary, which is breaking in with intent to steal: he did not intend that Pierce should permanently deprive the owner of the whiskey, only that he should be caught in the attempt. Students may be asked to compare this hypothetical: S gives P a gun to shoot V. S knows the gun to be unloaded but P does not. P points the gun at V and pulls the trigger. P is guilty of attempted murder. Is S? If not, then how can Wilson be liable for burglary?

The point here is that in Case 2 and the attempted murder variation, the secondary party fully satisfies the mens rea requirements and is therefore guilty unless an affirmative defense (e.g., a law enforcement officer's privilege) is available. But in Case 1, the principal and the secondary party do not share an intention that the object crime be committed.

Gladstone, p. 611, raises the question whether the mens rea of complicity requires a genuine purpose to promote commission of the object crime, or whether knowledge that one's actions will aid the principal in committing the crime is enough. Why isn't the defendant liable in Gladstone? What elements of accomplice liability are missing here? The court stresses the lack of a "nexus" (p. 611, 4th full ¶). Where does this fit into the analysis of actus reus and mens rea? Why *should* a nexus be required? Suppose that bystander S, seeing a robber P flee from a holdup, drives into the intersection so that police cars can't pursue P. Assuming that there was no previous contact between S and P, and that P was not aware of S's act, would S escape liability because of the lack of a "nexus"? Conversely, suppose that there *had been* a clear nexus in Gladstone (i.e. if Gladstone had been charged with aiding and abetting Thompson's purchase rather than with aiding Kent's sale). Would the presence of a clear nexus have changed the result? Students should see that the "nexus" notion is a red herring. S would be liable without a nexus (as the court appears to concede at p. 611, last ¶). Conversely, Gladstone would escape liability even with a nexus, because of the nature of his mens rea (same ¶, last three lines).

Why *should* Gladstone's mens rea be insufficient? What if Thompson had been looking for a hired gun to carry out a contract killing and Gladstone had referred him to Kent. Is there any good reason not to hold Gladstone liable? The materials following Gladstone explore the policy questions. Consider these variations:

Case 3. A farm boy F clears land for a still. Is F's contribution too incidental to justify liability without a true purpose? What result under the MPC draft proposal (p. 613, 2d indented quote)? Presumably, F does not "substantially" facilitate. Compare the New York solution (p. 614, Note 3). Apparently, under the New York approach the aid need not be "substantial," but F might still escape liability if the offense is not a felony.

Case 4. Gladstone itself. Would G's contribution be considered "substantial"? Does the proposed MPC formulation give any concrete criterion for resolving this question? Should it be relevant that G's aid was not given "in the ordinary course of business" (Williams, at the bottom of p. 613). Compare the N.Y. statute, which presumably would acquit G even if G's help was essential, provided that the object crime is a misdemeanor. But why should the result turn on whether sale of marijuana is classified as a felony or a misdemeanor?

Case 5. What result in the Gladstone variation, in which Thompson is looking for a hired gun, Gladstone refers him to Kent, and Kent kills the victim? Under the N.Y. formulation, conviction seems clear, but what is the degree of the offense? Note that G is not guilty of murder, but only of the separate misdemeanor offense of criminal facilitation. What result under the MPC proposal? Since the aid would presumably be considered substantial, G can be convicted of murder. But if the aid is substantial here, wouldn't it have to be considered substantial in Case 4 also? If, as Professor Fletcher argues (top of p. 614), the problem involves in effect the extent of the duty to intervene to prevent harm, isn't it essential to consider the seriousness of the object crime?

What result in Cases 3-5 under the MPC provision as finally adopted? Students should see that under the Code, the secondary party escapes liability in all three cases, even in Case 5. Does it make sense to require a true purpose even when the defendant substantially facilitates the most serious crimes? Discussion can help indicate the difficulty of formulating a compromise position that assures liability (and appropriate grading) for Case 5 without raising the problems of vagueness or overbroad duties that were thought to impair the MPC draft proposal. Consider the solution reached by Judge Posner in the Fountain case, p. 615, indented quote.

Luparello, p. 615, introduces an important qualification to the traditional view that the crucial actions of the principal must be intended (either in the strict sense of purpose or in the looser sense of knowledge).

Did Luparello intend his henchman to kill Martin? Students should see that the killing did not occur while the accomplices were trying to extract information from Martin under duress. Since L wanted information from Martin, the killing totally defeated L's plans. Wasn't this a "departure from the common design"? (Obviously, yes.) Yet the court concludes that L. is liable anyway, since "liability is extended to reach the actual crime committed, rather than the planned or 'intended' crime, on the policy that aiders and abettors should be responsible for criminal harms they have naturally, probably and foreseeably put in motion" (p. 656, end of the 2d full ¶).

Under Luparello, what is the mens rea required for complicity? Luparello, contrary to the traditional view reflected in the MPC, in effect permits liability based merely on negligence.

What is the court's justification for this dilution of the traditional mens rea requirement? Does Judge Wiener in his dissent mount a convincing case against it? Given L's intentions, is liability unfair? Note that L is not a sympathetic character. But did he have the culpability normally required for first-degree murder? If not, should he be convicted of that offense just because one of his accomplices *was* that culpable? What result if L had encouraged the others simply to threaten Martin with a simple assault and the others had then (foreseeably) killed Martin? Could L still be convicted of first-degree murder? (Under Luparello, yes.) Is this a justified result?

Note that Judge Wiener analogizes the Luparello doctrine to the felony-murder rule. Is that right? What are the similarities and differences? The Luparello rule, *like* the felony-murder rule, may offer some deterrence benefits, but the key problem (as with the felony-murder rule) is that it permits liability greatly disproportionate to fault.

Arguably, felony-murder liability is worse, in that it extends even to deaths that are not foreseeable (though causation requirements must be established). But felony-murder liability is also narrower: Is the accomplice guilty on a felony-murder theory when the principal deliberately kills after an accomplice agrees to help the principal commit a simple assault? (No, because of the merger doctrine.) Similarly, only felonies inherently dangerous to human life can bring the felony-murder rule into play.

In sum, there are the stringent limitations on the predicate felonies that can trigger the felony-murder rule. In contrast, under Luparello, *any* predicate crime can trigger liability for foreseeable crimes committed by the accomplice. As a result, the deviation from the principle that liability should remain proportionate to fault is far greater under the Luparello doctrine than it is under the felony-murder rule.

b. Mens Rea as to Circumstances

Take a case in which S purposely helps P to perform some action, but is innocently unaware of some fact which makes P's action a crime. Can it be said that S is guilty of P's crime because she purposely helped him do the action? Or must we conclude that the action of P she actually aided was not the action she intended to aid, so that she is not liable as an accomplice? Consider this hypothetical:

> Case 6. A customer C asks pharmacist P for a certain drug. Clerk S passes the drug to P and P sells it to C. The drug turns out to be contaminated. Since the applicable drug law imposes strict liability, P can be convicted (recall Balint, p. 235). Can S be convicted as an accomplice? Note that S aided, and intended to aid the sale. Should we say that S not only must intend to aid, but also must have the mens rea for the offense charged? Yes, but that does not help S, considering that the crime charged is a strict liability offense. So is S

guilty as an accomplice? Why not? Is he less at fault that P, who is made liable under the strict liability statute?

United States v. Xavier, p. 621, suggests that S would not be liable, on the theory, apparently, that accomplice liability carries its own mens rea of intentionality, so that if S is unaware of some circumstances which materially affects the character of the action he helps P to do, he can not be said to have intentionally helped P do the action. Is this an enslavement to doctrine, or does it make sense? Note how the Model Penal Code "passes" on this one. P. 622, Note 2. How should the hypothetical, p. 622, last 2 lines, be resolved? If one policy pulls in favor of liability, another policy of not extending strict criminal liability any further than legislation requires pulls the other way. Recall that the analogous problem arises in connection with the law of attempt. See pp. 562-64, Note 7. It arises again in connection with the crime of conspiracy. See p. 713, Note 4(c).

d. Mens Rea as to Result

If A intentionally helps P do an action which is criminal only if it causes some result (e.g., death), but A does not intend that P's action should produce that result, can A be held as an accessory if the result occurs? How can she be, if the law of accomplices requires an intention? This is the issue presented in McVay, p. 623. The court's conclusion that McVay could be convicted as an accessory to manslaughter undoubtedly states the law. But is the law consistent with sound policy? And how can that result be made consistent with the rule that accomplice liability requires intentional aiding or encouraging?

The Model Penal Code seems to put the rule as an ad hoc exception to the requirement of intentionality. See Section 2.06(4) at p. 626, Note 1. One can also see the rule as consistent with the fault principle, in that S is as culpable as P insofar as he intentionally helped him to do an act which negligently or recklessly caused the deaths. We can say in these situations that S intentionally aided P to do the act, and therefore joined in causing the deaths; while he did not intend the result, he was negligent or reckless as to that result, which is all the mens rea that is required (for manslaughter, for example, as in McVay). On the other hand, students who find this explanation persuasive may be asked why the same reasoning should not apply to allow a person to be convicted as an accomplice to a strict liability crime, the issue we considered just above.

People v. Russell, p. 624, provides a further test of this reasoning. The defendants' gun battle is analogous in some ways to the road race situation once again (the <u>Abbott</u> case discussed at p. 625, 3d full ¶), but here the issue is whether the co-player can be held liable for the death of an innocent person, on the theory that he was the accomplice of the surviving fellow player.

Consider the following hypothetical:

> <u>Case 6</u>. S, rushing to catch a plane, orders his cab driver P to drive to the airport at 100 mph. P collides with another car and kills its driver. If S must intend the result, then he is an accomplice in the speeding offense, but not in manslaughter. But under <u>McVay</u>, S can be convicted of manslaughter because he intends the underlying act of recklessness which causes the death.

Can this analysis be applied if an innocent bystander is killed in a case like Root, p. 545? In Case 6 the defendant intended that the driver do the reckless act that caused death (i.e., driving at 100 mph). In <u>McVay</u> Kelley intended that his crew fire the boiler. But did Root intend that the deceased should pass in a no-passing zone? Even if Root knew that D would drive very fast and might do such a thing as pass in a no-passing zone, did Root *intend* these actions? Some students say no, since Root wanted to win. On the other hand, victory is empty unless the competitor drives fast too. Realistically, all the drag racers "intend" the reckless driving of the others.

How are these problems handled under the MPC? See Section 2.06(4), at p. 626, Note 1. Would this provision permit conviction in <u>McVay</u> and Case 6? Presumably yes, because the defendant is an accomplice in the underlying action that caused the death. Would it permit conviction in <u>Root</u>? That depends on whether the defendant is "an accomplice in the conduct." What does that mean? The MPC never says. (Accomplice in "an offense" is defined in § 2.06(3), but that definition is not satisfied here). Apparently, we are back to the problems of determining what aspect of the other driver's conduct Root actually intended.

   2. <u>Actus Reus</u>, pp. 628-33.

<u>Wilcox</u>, p. 628. How, precisely, did the defendant aid or abet the offense? How significant was his encouragement? Would the offense have occurred even without the defendant's aid? Probably, or perhaps certainly. If it is clear that the prosecution can't prove causation beyond a reasonable doubt, how can the defendant be liable? Students should see that accomplice liability does not require proof of a but-for relationship

between the aid or encouragement and the result. (See the last paragraph of Talley, pp. 629-30, and p. 630, Problem 1.)

Why is causation not required to be proven in accomplice cases? Is it fair to convict Wilcox without any showing that his encouragement made a difference? Consider these cases:

Case 1. Hicks, together with one hundred others, encourages Rowe to shoot (p. 609, Note 1). Does Hicks's encouragement affect the result? (Clearly not.) But is liability therefore inappropriate?

Case 2. Hicks alone accompanies Rowe and urges him to shoot. Now his encouragement may have made a difference. But can the prosecution prove beyond a reasonable doubt that Rowe would not have shot, but for Hicks's intervention? Students should see that part of the reason for abandoning causation is the difficulty of establishing it. But is this a good reason? If we are serious about the principle of proof beyond a reasonable doubt, shouldn't we accept acquittal in Case 2? To see why not, consider another variation:

Case 3. Rowe wants to kill Colvard but can't find a gun. Hicks loans him one, and Rowe immediately uses it. Now can we prove causation? Even if Rowe could have obtained a gun from another standing nearby, Hicks' aid certainly shortens Colvard's life, and the but-for effect is therefore clear. But can we meet the requirements of proximate causation? Can we say that Hicks "caused" Rowe to kill? Even in Case 3, proximate cause cannot be established, because of prevailing attitudes about the notion of the intervening volitional human act.

Students should see that the rejection of causation requirements does not flow simply from sloppiness about the burden of proof, but flows more fundamentally from the inappropriateness of causation analysis in situations involving human action. But-for causation is the most we could possibly show, but even this element is elusive where human action is concerned.

Finally what result if it is wholly clear that there was no but-for connection, as in Case 1 and probably in Wilcox itself. Then is liability inappropriate? Consider:

Case 4. W enters a bar to make a phone call. P decides to grab her, throw her to the floor and rape her. While P is tearing off her clothes, X and Y applaud. In such a case isn't it likely (or virtually certain) that P would have gone through with the rape even without actual encouragement? Yet is there any good reason not to hold X and Y accountable? Morally, X and Y are clearly blameworthy, and deterring their acts of approval can, in the long run, deter conduct like P's. (Conversely, what would be the effect on behavior, and on prevailing moral standards, of *failing* to condemn the acts of X and Y?) Discussion should bring out that here, as in Case 1, the accomplice is held responsible not because he has in any sense "caused" the crime, but rather because he has, by his behavior, adopted or ratified the crime, in effect made it his own.

If the accomplice need not cause the crime, does he at least have to cause some actual aid or encouragement? Did Hawkins actually derive any perceptible encouragement from Wilcox? What if Wilcox's applause was drowned out by that of the rest of the audience? Arguably, Wilcox's encouragement still contributed, since each spectator drowned out the applause of the others. But consider the problems at p. 630, Note 2:

> Case 5. What if Rowe were deaf and unable to hear Hicks' encouragement? Here there is only an unsuccessful attempt to encourage. Under common law principles, the actus reus would not be satisfied and there would presumably be no liability.

> Case 6. Talley variation (a) at p. 630, Note 2. Here there is only an attempt to aid. Talley does not succeed in facilitating the result or putting the decedent at any possible disadvantage. Again, no liability.

> Case 7. Talley variation (b). Assuming that, as in the real case, actual aid was rendered, Talley would be an accomplice in any crime committed by the Skelton brothers upon Ross. But what crime did the principals commit? At common law, probably none because they committed no acts proximately close to success (recall Rizzo, p. 564).

> Case 8. Talley variation (c). Now Talley presumably can be charged with attempted murder.

Note that where Talley's aid misfires (Case 6), Talley is guilty of nothing, even if the victim is in fact killed. Where his own attempt is successful, he may nonetheless be guilty of nothing (Case 7) or of a mere attempt (Case 8). These are the traditional answers at the common law.

But note the different, more coherent approach taken by the MPC. See p. 631. Note the MPC result in Case 6. Talley's unsuccessful attempt leads to liability for a successful murder. Does this make sense? In § 2.06(3)(a)(ii) the MPC equates liability for successful and unsuccessful attempts. But with respect to the most serious crimes, is this approach inconsistent with the grading of attempts in § 5.05(1)?

3. The Relationship between the Liability of the Parties, pp. 633-44

Hayes, p. 633. Why isn't Hayes guilty of burglary? Clearly Hayes is an accomplice of Hill. But what crime did Hill commit? Since Hill did not enter with intent to commit a crime, he is not guilty of burglary; analytically, therefore, there is no crime to attribute to Hayes. But does the result make sense? In terms of penal policy, is there any good reason why Hayes should not be guilty? Consider in this connection the Vaden case at p. 634. Does the dissent in that case state a good reason why the acts of a feigned principal may not be imputed to the targeted defendant in order to convict him as an accomplice? Perhaps that policy would support the decision in Hayes. But does it support the dissent's opinion in Vaden? Was it the case that Snell was a *feigned* principal, or was he not an actual principal? He did, after, illegally kill the foxes. See the other questions at p. 636, Note 1.

Consider the following variations of Hayes:

> Case 1. Suppose Hill had opened the window and Hayes had climbed through. Isn't it clear that Hayes would be guilty here? Is there any good reason for the result to depend on who is standing where?

> Case 2. Suppose that Hill had been forced at gunpoint by Hayes to go into the building. Here, as in the main case, Hill would not be guilty of the crime (this time because he would have the defense of duress). But would it not be absurd for Hayes to be acquitted when his own conduct is the source of Hill's defense?

If it seems clear that Hayes should be convicted in Cases 1 and 2, how can we support such a result analytically? In both cases, isn't it still true that conviction of Hayes is inconsistent with the logic of accomplice liability? Note the answer for Case 1. We don't have to convict Hayes as an accomplice, because he is guilty as a principal based upon his own conduct. Can we apply the same analysis to Case 2? Hayes has not actually done the acts of burglary himself, but in this case he has used Hill as an innocent instrument of his own will. Under common law principles, we can still say that Hayes is guilty as a principal. Note that the Code reaches the same result under §2.06(2)(a).

Can we apply the same analysis to the actual <u>Hayes</u> case? Note how <u>Hayes</u> is different from Case 2: In the actual case Hill's acts are fully volitional. Under common law principles, we cannot say that Hayes "caused" Hill's acts. Note that the same result follows under MPC §2.06(2)(a). Is there, then, any other theory of liability on which we can hold Hayes in the actual case?

(1) How about attempted burglary? But is Hayes' conduct sufficient to constitute this offense? Arguably, his opening the window goes beyond "mere preparation." But note that Hayes did not open the window with the intent to climb through it himself.

(2) Will broader accomplice liability do the trick? Note MPC § 2.06(3)(a)(ii): Hayes's mere attempt to aid Hill is sufficient to make him an accomplice. But does this solve the problem? Students should see that this is no help because it only renders Hayes guilty of whatever crime Hill in fact commits.

(3) Broader attempt liability may be the only answer. Under MPC § 5.01(3) Hayes's conduct is sufficient to render him guilty of an attempt.

The Notes and Problems at pp. 639-42 discuss the problems created by the traditional axiom that the liability of the accomplice is derivative, so that the accomplice cannot be convicted if the principal has committed no crime. If time is short, it may be sufficient to refer the student to the Notes.

The problem of the *excused* principal is sometimes solved through the innocent-agent doctrine (Note 2). Does that approach work in <u>Taylor</u>, p. 636? It seems implausible to say that Taylor used Moore as an innocent instrumentality of her own will. Moore is an independent actor, but should his act be considered criminal at all? If his act is genuinely justified (as argued by the dissent), then it would be improper to convict Taylor of a crime for assisting in that permissible conduct. Is that the right way to classify Moore's defense? The concepts of justification and excuse become important here. If Moore's conduct is properly viewed as wrong-but-excusable, then it makes sense to convict Taylor, who commits the same wrong but is not eligible for the same excuse. The cases involving a wrong-doing but unconvictable principle (p. 641, Note 4) have essentially the same character.

The innocent-agent doctrine also fails when the crime is so defined that it can be committed only by the personal hand of the defendant and not through the hand of another. Note 3 attempts to lay out the difficulty. The problems of the culpable but non-convictable principal and the principal who was acquitted in a previous trial have been solved without the aid of any statutory change, as indicated in Notes 4 & 5: in both cases the guilt of the principal is demonstrated in the trial of the accomplice, even though the principal cannot be convicted of the offense.

Another problem flowing from the derivative theory of accomplice liability is whether the secondary party be convicted of a greater crime than the principal. Consider Richards, p. 642, Note 1(a). Is the reversal here correct? On an ordinary accomplice analysis, the result seems inevitable, since the secondary party cannot be convicted of a crime that the principals did not commit. Can we convict Mrs. Richards as a *principal?* Note the prosecutor's argument to this effect, attributing to Mrs. Richards the *actions* of the two assailants rather than their "crime." What is wrong with this argument? Students should note that Mrs. Richards cannot be convicted as an accomplice to unlawful wounding with intent, because the assailants did not commit that offense. And presumably she cannot be convicted as a principal because she cannot be said to have "caused" the actions of the assailants. Their actions are still volitional, rather than those of an innocent or irresponsible agent. Compare:

> Case 5. The Othello situation, p. 643, Note 1(b). Can Iago be convicted of first-degree murder? On what analysis? As an accomplice, he can be convicted of the crime committed by Othello, but that crime is only manslaughter, let's assume. As a principal, he cannot be said to have caused Othello's acts since Othello was not innocent or irresponsible. But isn't it absurd under these circumstances to (in effect) permit Iago to use his own provocation as a defense, reducing the grade of his offense to manslaughter?

Note Prof. Williams' solution, p. 643, last ¶. In effect, Othello is only a partially responsible agent. To the extent that Othello's actions were partially irresponsible, Iago can be convicted of the higher offense as a principal who *to that extent* used an innocent instrumentality to commit the offense. Or perhaps we should say simply that the secondary party can "cause" the action of the primary party whenever the latter is either wholly or *partially* irresponsible. This suggestion is made at the top of p. 644. What are the difficulties with this solution?

B. Liability Within the Corporate Framework, pp. 644-671

In a three-credit course this material ordinarily should be skipped, in order to allow adequate time for less readily severable material. Where time permits, two classes can usefully be spent on this section, in order to complement the ordinary emphasis on violent crime, and to draw attention to the important issues that arise in the area of business activity and "white collar" offenses. The first class should cover the question of criminal liability for the corporate entity itself (pp. 645-58). The second class should consider the liability of individuals who commit crimes while acting on behalf of the corporation (pp. 658-71).

1. Liability of the Corporate Entity, pp. 645-58

Hilton Hotels, p. 647, is a useful place to start. Why should the corporation be liable here? Note especially the agent's testimony that he cut off the supplier out of personal pique. Why isn't this sufficient to insulate the corporation from liability? Presumably it would be, if the jury believed it; the action would no longer occur within the scope of the agent's employment. Here the instructions required the jury to find that the acts *were* within the scope (p. 647, indented quote), so presumably the jury disbelieved the agent's testimony.

Note next the corporate manager's testimony that participation in the boycott was contrary to corporate policy. Why doesn't this afford a good defense? Again, students may find the testimony implausible. But if the jury did believe it, would it afford a defense? This time the answer is no. The instructions told the jury to convict even if they believed that the conduct was contrary to instructions (p. 647, indented quote).

What if the purchasing agent bought goods illegally (in violation of export-import laws, for example) from a corporation controlled by his sister, in order the provide her with profits that she would share with him. Can Hilton be convicted of the crime? Here the purchasing agent's act of placing the order is within the scope of his employment (see the definition at p. 650-51, carryover ¶): placing orders is his job. But the act is not done with intent to benefit the corporation, so Hilton would not be liable.

The upshot of Hilton is that corporate criminal liability has three requirements, but only three: the crime must be committed (1) by an employee or agent; (2) within the scope of employment; and (3) with intent to benefit the corporation (p. 650, 1st ¶ of the indented quote). The instructions approved in Hilton list only the 1st two requirements (p. 647, indented quote), but their effect is identical, since the court includes the third element as part of its definition of when conduct is within the scope. See p. 648, n.4. In any case, these are the *only* requirements under the traditional approach, which is still followed in the important domain of federal criminal law. It is not a defense that the agent acted contrary to instructions or contrary to stated policy, even if the jury finds that those policies were genuine.

Is corporate criminal liability sensible? Fair? Consider:

Case 1. Jack is a bouncer at the Hilton Hotel nightclub. When an unruly patron refuses to leave, Jack forcefully throws the customer out into the street, using unnecessary force and inflicting severe injuries. Hilton explicitly instructs its bouncers not to use excessive force and tries hard to hire responsible employees. Is Hilton liable for aggravated assault? Is this case distinguishable from the actual Hilton case?

Intuitively, corporate criminal liability may seem inappropriate in Case 1. But on what basis can we distinguish Hilton? Some students may want to limit corporate liability to regulatory offenses. But then would there be no criminal liability if a corporate officer bribes a police officer to overlook Jack's conduct? No criminal liability if the manager locks most of the nightclub's exit doors (to prevent patrons from leaving before they pay their bills) and dozens of customers are killed in a fire?

It seems unacceptable to exclude all possibility of corporate liability for non-regulatory crimes, but the scope-of-employment test alone seems too sweeping to produce fair results. What underlying considerations account for these conflicting intuitions? What are the arguments for and against corporate liability?

(1) Can corporate liability deter? (Presumably it can to some extent.) But why is it needed? The employee himself can be punished directly and much more effectively, and the corporation is in any case liable for civil damages that may be much greater than the applicable criminal fine. So what can criminal fines add in terms of deterrence? In Case 1, it is hard to see that corporate liability can add much to the other applicable sanctions. But often it is hard to identify the individual culprit, and even if he or she is caught, the jury may be reluctant to punish for some kinds of crimes committed to benefit the corporation. See the MPC Comment, p. 649, Note 1. In these contexts, corporate liability may be critical to create strong enough disincentives for criminal conduct.

(2) Is corporate criminal liability fair? Who, in fact, is punished? The fine, presumably falls on the shareholders. Is this a form of vicarious liability? The shareholders cannot be imprisoned, of course, and they do not even bear the

stigma of criminality. But there may be a degree of unfairness in punishing shareholders, or at least in inflicting stigma on the corporation itself, in the absence of showing some kind of fault on the part of the owners or their top management.

The MPC approach (§2.07) can be understood as a way of limiting corporate liability to the situations where its justifications are strongest and the potential for unfairness is weakest.

How would <u>Hilton</u> and Case 1 be resolved under the MPC approach? Students often see the broad "scope of employment" test under §2.07(1)(a) as adopting the same test as <u>Hilton Hotels</u>; they may therefore argue that there is liability in both <u>Hilton</u> and Case 1 under this sub-section. The key point here is that the coverage of offenses described in the 1st line of §2.07(1)(a) is not as broad as it may at first appear. A "violation" covers only minor, no-jail offenses (see §1.04(5)); offenses defined by statutes other than the Code are essentially regulatory offenses (like the Sherman Act) but not traditional crimes like the physical assault in Case 1, or other staples of penal law like theft, bribery, etc.

Results:
(1) In <u>Hilton Hotels</u> itself, the MPC would probably impose liability because §2.07(1)(a) applies and the traditional three elements (employee within the scope and for the benefit of the corp.) are sufficient. But for crimes not based on strict liability (the Sherman Act offense requires specific intent) the MPC would afford a due diligence defense under §2.07(5); Hilton might be able to successfully claim this defense if additional facts were available.
(2) In contrast, in Case 1, §2.07(1)(a) cannot apply, because the offense is defined by the Code. Now only §2.07(1)(c) applies, and corporate liability requires the involvement of a high managerial agent (HMA). The bouncer obviously is not one, so this time Hilton is not liable, *whether or not* it can prove due diligence in the sense required for a defense under §2.07(5).

The MPC scheme can be understood as a way of permitting liability in regulatory situations (§2.07(1)(a)), where the stigma of corporate criminality is least and where the need for corporate liability as a deterrent is strongest because the human perpetrators of regulatory offenses are typically hard to identify and convict. The Code also permits liability in non-regulatory situations if HMA's are involved (§2.07(1)(c)), because in such situations it seems fair to stigmatize the corporate entity, and deterrence benefits can be substantial. Conversely, the Code prevents liability in situations like Case 1, because in the absence of involvement of HMA's, stigma seems unfair and adequate deterrence benefits can be obtained by prosecuting the individual perpetrator.

Beneficial Finance, p. 652, serves to illustrate the importance of the corporate liability option in the context of a traditional crime (bribery). The case also helps illustrate the differences between the Hilton Hotels and MPC tests. What result under the former approach? Obviously the three prerequisites of liability are easily met. What result under the MPC? Because §2.07(1)(c) applies, the key question is whether the individuals (principally Farrell and Glynn) were HMA's.

The HMA issue will be hard for many first-year students to appreciate or analyze on their own, but the BFC case helps make the meaning of this key concept more concrete. The court's opinion indicates some of the difficulty of treating the individual offenders as top officials in the usual sense. Farrell was an officer, but only of a subsidiary, not of BFC itself. Glynn was even lower down. The court expands the HMA concept to include those who exercise de facto responsibility for setting corporate policy. See p. 655, end of the last full ¶. This seems to make practical sense, while preserving the essence of the MPC effort to confine liability to situations in which it is both necessary and fair. Other alternatives to the Hilton Hotels and MPC tests are described at p. 657, Note 2.

2. Liability of Corporate Agents, pp. 658-71

Gordon, p. 659. Before discussing the facts of Gordon, it may be helpful to consider a hypothetical:

Case 1. Assume that federal price control regulations prohibit selling sewing machines at prices greater than $100 each. George, a salesman for Singer Sewing Machines Inc., tells customers that supplies are short and that he can't arrange delivery unless the customer pays $110 per machine. A customer agrees: he orders 11 machines, pays $1100 to Singer Inc., and tacitly agrees that he will accept a shipment of 10 machines as full delivery on his order. The Feds discover the scheme. George pleads guilty. Is Singer guilty of a crime under the Price Control Act?

Analyzing this case under the principles considered in the preceding section, it is apparent that Singer is liable. The Hilton test is easily met (the employee's act is within the scope of employment and for the benefit of the employer), and likewise there would be liability under MPC §2.07(1)(a) (unless there was evidence to support a due diligence defense).

What result in Case 1 if (call this Case 2) Singer Sewing Machines is organized as a partnership rather than as a corporation? Can the owners of the business, Alan, Bill and Charles Singer, be convicted? What result under Gordon? The 10th Cir. opinion upholds liability of the individual owners: the statute in Gordon punished only intentional violations, but the court held the owners responsible for intentional acts that were committed by their employees to benefit the company (p. 660, last ¶ of the majority opinion). Under the 10th Cir. approach, the owners obviously would be liable in Case 2. But the Supreme Court reversed that opinion and held that the individual owners could *not* be held liable (p. 661, indented quote).

Given the end result in Gordon, the owners could not be held liable in Case 2. But why shouldn't they be? (The Supreme Court never actually gives a reason, except the government's confession of error.) Was the government right to confess error? What was wrong with the 10th Cir.'s approach?

Several arguments might be made in favor of the 10th Circuit's result: Why should the owners be able to escape liability by choosing to do business as a partnership rather than organizing in corporate form? Note that the sales staff's actions are designed for the benefit of the owners, not for the immediate benefit of the sales people themselves. In this situation a corporation clearly would be liable. If the reasons for holding the corporation itself liable are sound (e.g., difficulty of identifying and convicting the individuals, added deterrence, equity of liability's resting on the party for whose benefit the crime was committed), don't those reasons apply with equal force when the owner is an individual?

Of course, the key distinction is that in Case 1, the owners suffer at most only the financial penalty of the criminal fine. Because liability falls only on the corp. as an entity, the owners themselves do not suffer any personal stigma, and they obviously cannot be imprisoned. So Case 1 does not involve any vicarious liability for the owners as individuals. But liability in Case 2 (the 10th Cir.'s approach) would mean vicarious personal liability for crimes committed by others. Whatever the pragmatic advantages of such a doctrine, it represents too great an incursion on the principle of fault. Thus, the criminal law almost invariably rejects vicarious liability for individuals. Recall Guminga, p. 244. The force of this tradition is so strong that in the Supreme Court the government did not even try to argue for the 10th Cir.'s result, and the Supreme Court reversed in a short opinion, apparently assuming that the 10th Cir.'s error was too obvious to require any explanation.

Do the complicity doctrines of aiding and abetting undercut this line of reasoning (and undercut the Supreme Court's approach to Gordon)? Aiding and abetting principles do sometimes permit individuals to be held liable for crimes committed by others. But could the owners in Gordon be convicted under an aiding and abetting theory? Surely yes, *provided* that there was proof the owners had the necessary mens rea (if they know what the salesmen are doing, that part would be easy since the owners have an obvious stake in the venture), and *provided* that the owners aided or encouraged the salesmen's actions. In such a situation, the owners liability is in a sense derivative (it is based on the crimes committed by the salesmen), but it is not truly vicarious, because it is based on their personal actions of aid or encouragement and their personal mens rea.

The upshot is that aiding and abetting liability is not an exception to the criminal law's rejection of vicarious personal liability. The critical point in the 10th Cir.'s approach to Gordon is that the court upheld liability based solely on respondeat superior notions (within the scope and for the benefit) without any proof of the personal acts and mental state necessary for liability as an accomplice. Liability on the former basis is truly vicarious and thus impermissible.

Park, p. 661. Here the Court holds the corporate president personally liability for crimes committed by subordinates. Is the result consistent with Gordon? How is Park distinguishable? One point many students are likely to bring up is that the offense in Park is a strict liability offense; no mens rea is required.

If that difference is critical, the implication is that the result in Gordon itself would have been different if the Price Control Act had imposed strict liability. But is that correct? Could the owners have been convicted if the Price Control Act had imposed strict liability? No: Recall Guminga (p. 244). Even under a strict liability statute, business owners cannot be held on a respondeat superior type of theory for crimes committed by their employees, because the owners would still lack a personal actus reus. Given cases like Guminga, the result in Gordon would have been the same even under a strict liability statute.

Then how is Park distinguishable from Gordon? The key difference is that the Park statute imposes liability for an omission. In a case like Park the the rule against vicarious liability remains valid *in theory*, but all personal mens rea requirements are met (there are none because it is a strict liability statute), and all personal actus reus requirements are met (there are none because the statute imposes liability for inaction, at least whenever there is a "responsible relationship," p. 663, last ¶ of n.9). In effect, the rule against vicarious liability remains valid in theory, but all practical differences between personal and vicarious liability disappear.

Is it true that the Park result really holds the corp.'s chief executive without any personal culpability at all? Note Justice Stewart's claim that the Court in effect imposes liability only for negligence (p. 666, 2d ¶ of the dissent). But is Stewart correct? Could Park defend by showing he had exercised due care to prevent further rodent infestation? No: Under the trial judge's instructions which the Court approves (p. 663 n.9), once the duty to prevent adulteration exists, there is no need for the prosecution to prove negligence. Nor would an affirmative defense of due care be permitted: the Supreme Court is explicit in holding that only an objective impossibility of performing the duty would be a defense (p. 665, last full ¶). (This exception is consistent with the traditional view that an omission cannot be considered voluntary when the required act is impossible to perform. See MPC §2.01(1)). Thus, Stewart's interpretation appears to be wishful thinking; Park is truly a case of strict liability.

Nonetheless, is the result in Park really unfair? Doesn't criminal liability at least give Park some incentive to start taking the rodent problem more seriously? And note the mild sentence, only a total $250 fine for the five counts (p. 664, line 2). But if the fine was so small, why did Park fight the case? (Imagine what his attorney fees totaled for the Supreme Court appeal.) Consider why Park might have had a large stake in trying to win the appeal. What happens to him next? What if, despite all his best efforts, the rodents still keep getting into the Baltimore warehouse? What sanction will Park face for his next strict liability violation? Under 21 USC §333(b) (not reproduced in the casebook) a second conviction carries a possible prison sentence of up to 3 years. And note the sentence imposed in Hanousek, p. 670, 3d ¶ of the indented quote. If you were Park, would you stay in the grocery business?

Despite the lenient sentence actually imposed, Park clearly paves the way for liability based almost exclusively on the corporate officer's hierarchical position, in situations where penalties potentially could be quite severe. What statutory standards could be drafted to avoid such results without unduly weakening deterrence?

C. Conspiracy, pp. 671-48

Organization and allocation of time

In a four-credit course, this section warrants roughly five classes: (1) the procedures and consequences associated with conspiracy (pp. 671-84); (2) the vicarious liability feature of conspiracy (pp. 684-94) and the actus reus of conspiracy (pp. 694-703); (3) the mens rea (pp. 704-14); (4) the scope of the agreement (pp. 714-23) together with (if time permits) parties (pp. 723-30); and (5) RICO (pp. 730-48).

In a shorter course, the material can be completed in three classes by (a) trimming the case and Problem at pp. 699-701 and pp. 710-14, Notes 3 & 4, so that the essentials of the actus reus and mens rea can be covered in one class; (b) skipping the material on parties (pp. 723-30); and (c) omitting pp. 735-48, so that the problems of scope of the agreement can be covered in depth, along with a brief introduction to RICO, in one class. Even in the more abbreviated treatment, we believe it useful to take up the material on procedures and consequences (subsections 1 and 2) at the outset, in order to provide students with the background they will need to assess the implications of the issues that arise with respect to mens rea and the scope of the agreement. On this approach, the three class assignments would be as follows:

(1) pp. 671-78 and pp. 684-94, with pp. 678-84 as optional or background reading.

(2) pp. 694-99; 701-03; and 704-10 or 704-14.

(3) pp. 714-23 and 730-35.

1. <u>Overview</u>, pp. 671-84

<u>Krulewitch</u>, p. 671, introduces the evidentiary significance of a conspiracy charge and provides, through Jackson's concurrence, an overview of other procedural implications. The specific hearsay issues warrant close attention. Students should note the specific statement the admissibility of which was challenged (p, 672, indented quote) and should understand why it was incriminating (because the statement that Kay couldn't stand to take the blame in effect indicated that the witness believed Kay to be guilty.). Why was the statement hearsay? See p, 676, Note 1. Why is hearsay evidence generally ruled inadmissible? (The reliability problem and rights to confrontation and cross-examination should be explained at this point.)

Given the hearsay rule, why did the trial judge admit the statement? Note the "co-conspirator" exception. What is the rationale for this exception? See especially p. 677, Note 3. Is the asserted rationale convincing? Consider:

Case 1. Suppose that in <u>Krulewitch</u> the complaining witness had testified that K's co-conspirator W had said, "It's all K's fault." Assume that the conspiracy was clearly still in existence at the time W's statement is made. Is W's statement admissible against K?

Legally the answer for Case 1 is that the statement is admissible, but why should it be? Under the "agency" theory, is it plausible that K actually authorized W's statement? Isn't the agency concept just a fiction? In terms of the policies underlying the hearsay rule, shouldn't the overriding concern be reliability? Note that if W had said, "It's all my fault," that statement would have some inherent reliability as an admission against interest. But why is W's statement in Case 1 reliable?

Discussion should indicate the difficulty of arguing that the conspiratorial relationship provides any guarantees of reliability sufficient to overcome the usual concerns about hearsay. See especially the Johnson excerpt at pp. 677-78. What is the Supreme Court's view about the validity of the justifications for the co-conspirator exception? Note that the Court reaffirms the exception (p. 673, 7th line). Does the Court in Krulewitch do so because the exception makes sense or only because of precedent? (The language at p. 673, 1st full ¶ seems to stress the latter notion.)

Since the Court did reaffirm the co-conspirator exception, why wasn't it applicable in Krulewitch? Was the conspiracy still in existence at the time of the statement? (Presumably, not; its main objective clearly had been attained. What was the prosecution's theory to get around this problem? Note the "subsidiary objective" approach (p. 672, last ¶). What is wrong with the prosecution's argument? Is it unrealistic to assume that the conspirators would have such an objective? Or does the Court reject the government's argument for policy reasons independent of factual plausibility? Note the Court's concern about creating a virtually unlimited expansion of an exception that the Court regards with skepticism in the first place.

Does Krulewitch keep the co-conspirator exception within reasonable bounds? If the conspiracy clearly exists, can statements such as those in Case 1 be admitted? (Yes.) But in most cases the conspiracy has not been clearly proven at the time hearsay evidence of this kind is offered. This can make it possible for evidence to be introduced on the assumption of the existence of a conspiracy which the suspect evidence itself may help to prove. The Supreme Court has held that this practice, known as bootstrapping, is authorized by the Federal Rules. See Bourjaily, p. 678, Note 4.

Apart from the hearsay problem it is worth examining other implications of a conspiracy charge. Consider:

Case 2. Suppose that taxpayer T and accountant A perpetrate a tax fraud in April, 1975. In January, 1978 A bribes an IRS agent to overlook the problem, and in June, 1980 A bribes a second IRS agent. T and A are indicted for conspiracy in January, 1983. If the applicable statute of limitations is three years, is the indictment timely?

Note that the conspiracy exists at least as of 1975, but in a conspiracy case the statute of limitations begins to run not from the time that the offense is committed (by the agreement), but rather from the time that the offense *ends* (i.e. when the last overt act in furtherance of the conspiracy is committed). See p. 678, last ¶. Was the 1980 bribery such an act? Students should see that under Krulewitch the main purpose of the conspiracy was achieved in 1975, so the 1980 act of cover-up is not in furtherance of the conspiracy to commit fraud. But is there any way for the prosecution to prevail here? Does Krulewitch leave any opening? What if T and A had established a bribery fund in 1975? Here the cover-up would be part of the objectives of the original conspiracy.

Students should see that Krulewitch does not exclude the possibility of arguing the existence of a subsidiary cover-up conspiracy but holds only that the government can't use that theory when the cover-up conspiracy is merely implicit and *uncharged.* Thus, the dangers that concerned the court in Krulewitch -- the broad possibilities for keeping a conspiracy alive almost indefinitely, with resulting consequences for hearsay, statute of limitations, venue, etc. -- still exist if the government can charge and prove an actual agreement to conceal the original object crime.

The Notes at pp. 680-84, dealing with other collateral consequences of a conspiracy charge, can be left for outside reading if necessary. Otherwise, the problem of cumulative punishment could be discussed in class. Suppose that A and B agree to import marijuana from Columbia to the United States, and that A then does so. Can A receive two separate punishments, one for importing the marijuana and a second punishment for agreeing to do so? Callanan, pp. 682-83, holds yes.

What is the justification for this result? Could A be punished separately for an attempt to import and for the successful importation? Clearly not. Then why a different result in the case of conspiracy? Note Frankfurter's argument at p. 683, 1st indented quote, that the conspiracy increases the likelihood that the criminal object will be attained. How is the point relevant? Isn't this just an argument for punishing incomplete conspiracies more severely that incomplete attempts? When the object crime *has been* committed, why is Frankfurter's argument relevant at all? Is there any other good reason for the Callanan result? Note the possibility that the conspiracy may have "ends more complex" than the commission of a single object offense. But does this argument apply in the case of A and B's importation conspiracy above? Does it apply to the facts of Callanan? Note the MPC approach, pp. 683, 2d indented quote, barring cumulative penalties for conspiracy and the object crime, *unless* the conspiracy does in fact have broad criminal objectives that transcend any of the particular object crimes.

2. Conspiracy as Accessorial Liability, pp. 684-94

Pinkerton, p. 684, shows that conspiracy is not only an independent substantive crime, but also a basis for attributing to a defendant substantive crimes committed by others. What is the Court's justification for holding Daniel responsible for crimes committed by Walter while Daniel was in prison? Consider especially p. 685, last 2 lines. The Court appears to be arguing that Daniel could be convicted as an accomplice (for aiding or encouraging). But if this is so, what does conspiratorial liability really add? Consider carefully whether Daniel <u>could</u> be convicted as an accomplice. Under the expansive conception of accomplice liability accepted in cases like Luparello, p. 615, this would be easy, since foreseeability alone is enough. But could Daniel be convicted as an accomplice under the traditional approach? If Daniel was in prison, how could he aid? Did the record show that he aided or encouraged any of the specific offenses? The answer is no, as the dissent makes clear. Thus, despite the Court's claim of an <u>analogy</u> to accomplice liability (as traditionally understood), the only substantive requirements are that the principal's acts be in furtherance of the conspiracy and reasonably foreseeable (p. 686, last ¶ of the majority opinion).

Even if the test for vicarious conspiratorial liability differs in theory from the traditional test for vicarious accomplice liability, do the two tests produce different results in practice? Given Daniel's part in the overall conspiracy, can't it be argued that his participation encouraged Walter to commit the substantive offenses? Yes, there may have been some encouragement, but what was Daniel's mens rea? Is it enough that the accomplice should have foreseen that his actions could encourage the principal? (This was the precise issue in Hicks, p. 606; the answer, of course, is No.) Even if Daniel contemplated the specific offenses committed by Walter, did Daniel have a purpose (stake in the venture) with respect to those offenses? If not, Daniel cannot be held as an accomplice under the traditional approach. In contrast, to hold Daniel vicariously liable as a conspirator, only foreseeability (negligence) is required with respect to the substantive offense.

Discussion should make clear the ways in which conspiratorial liability under Pinkerton is easier to establish than accomplice liability under the traditional standard. To help students master the distinctions, problem 3(a), p. 690 is worth sorting through. Applying the tests of complicity and of conspiratorial liability with respect to each party yields results indicated by the chart on the page that follows:

Liability for Crimes of Co-conspirators

Party Liable	Pinkerton Theory	Complicity Theory
A	Yes.	Yes. (A purposely encouraged their commission.)
B (for C's robbery)	Yes. (Both robberies in furtherence of common conspiracy and foreseeable.)	No. (Can it be shown that merely entering into conspiracy was sufficient to encourage the other's robbery? Can it be shown that any such encouragement was purposeful or that each had a stake in the other's venture? If not, no liability.)
D (for robbery of bank 2)	Yes.	No. (No aid or encouragement of that crime.)
D (for robbery of bank 1)	Yes.	Yes.
B (for D's theft) C (for D's theft)	Yes, _if_ they could have reasonably forseen a stolen car might be necessary to rob a bank.	No. (Neither agreement to rob nor the robbery itself aided the theft. Even if B and C, by those acts, "encouraged" the theft, they presumably did not do so knowingly. But query whether test of reasonable foreseeability can be used for accomplice liability.)

Does <u>Pinkerton</u> also expand the possible scope of vicarious liability where the <u>Luparello</u> approach is accepted? Because foreseeability is sufficient under <u>Luparello</u>, accomplice theory presumably would produce the same result as conspiracy theory in problem 3(a). But what result in problem 3(b) (i.e. <u>Luparello</u> itself) and in problem 3(c)? In both cases, vicarious liability was upheld under an accomplice theory. Is there liability in these cases under <u>Pinkerton</u>? Students should see that in both cases, the killings, though foreseeable, were not in furtherance of the conspiratorial objective. Thus <u>Pinkerton</u> liability is broader than traditional accomplice liability, but narrower than liability under the <u>Luparello</u> approach because <u>Pinkerton</u> still requires that the principal's crimes be in furtherance of the conspiracy.

Is it proper to impose vicarious liability when the parties could not be convicted on ordinary complicity principles? In other words, is the <u>Pinkerton</u> doctrine sound? <u>Bridges</u>, p. 687, and <u>Alvarez</u>, p. 691, provide useful testing cases.

Is the conviction in <u>Bridges</u> justified in terms of general principles of liability? Note that the shooting by Bing and Rolle was in furtherance of the conspiratorial plan. And the possibility of gunplay was clearly foreseeable. But what was Bridges' level of culpability? (Negligence; possibly recklessness.) What is his offense and sentence? (1st degreee murder, with a sentence of 30 years to life. See p. 687, end of the 1st ¶ of the opinion.) The problem (as discussed in connection with <u>Luparello</u>, p. 615) is liability greatly disproportionate to fault.

Is the result in <u>Alvarez</u> appropriate? The defendants do not appear sympathetic, but <u>Pinkerton</u> easily blurs culpability distinctions by legitimating a kind of guilt by association. What exactly was each defendant's culpability? Discussion can usefully focus on the role of Hernandez, the motel manager. What did he actually know? Did he intend a killing? Was he consciously reckless?

Is murder liability in such cases (<u>Bridges</u> and <u>Alvarez</u>) justified by the same principle that supports the felony-murder rule? Yes and no. Deterrence theory might suggest an affirmative answer, and the defendants' commission of a lesser wrong might suggest that they are no longer entitled to the benefit of a finely calibrated system of grading. But could they be convicted of murder under the felony-murder rule? No: In <u>Bridges</u> the predicate felony would merge; in <u>Alvarez</u>, the predicate felony might not qualify as inherently danagerous, especially when assessed in the abstract. (See the parallel discussion

of these problems above in this Manual, in connection with Luparello, p. 615.)
The concern to keep liability in proportion to fault has produced tight restrictions
on the felony-murder rule, but Pinkerton liability can be much broader.

[Teachers who have discussed Gordon, p. 659, may wish to compare that
case to Pinkerton. In both situations the prosecution attempts to hold a principal
responsible for acts of his agent carried out in furtherance of a common
enterprise. Gordon holds that the agency relationship is not enough for liability
(even if the acts of the agent are foreseeable, as they presumably were in Gordon
itself). Isn't the Supreme Court's decision in Pinkerton (1946) fundamentally
inconsistent with its later decision (1954) in Gordon? If Gordon is right, then isn't
Pinkerton necessarily wrong?

[The agency rationale central to Pinkerton does seem directly in conflict
with the rejection of vicarious liability in Gordon. The only distinction is that in
Pinkerton the joint enterprise is not in itself an illegal one. In effect, Pinkerton
reflects a kind of lesser wrong theory - - the law normally rejects vicarious
liability of a principal for the acts of his agent, but prevailing law is willing to
accept just this sort of vicarious liability if the joint enterprise between principal
and agent is an illegal one. Why should the principal's commission of one crime
(perhaps a relatively minor one) expose him to vicarious liability for far more
serious crimes that co-conspirators might commit?]

The concern to keep liability in proportion to fault has led a number of
jurisdictions to reject Pinkerton. See, e.g., McGee, p. 693, Note 2, and the MPC at
p. 693, Note 3. Similarly, the Alvarez court, though bound by Pinkerton,
suggests the possibility of limiting the Pinkerton doctrine in the context of
"reasonably foreseeable but originally unintended substantive crimes" (p. 692,
n.27) when the co-conspirator plays only a peripheral role. Compare the defense
of the full Pinkerton doctrine at p. 692, Note 1.

3. The Actus Reus, pp. 694-704

Interstate Circuit, p. 694. Students should be sure to understand that the
obvious agreements between Interstate and each of the eight distributors are not
sufficient here. The government had to prove a conspiracy among the eight
distributors. (See p. 695, end of the 1st ¶). What is the basis for concluding that
the eight conspired together? Was the action of each distributor independent, or
did it result from an agreement among them? What is the Court's conclusion?
Note two alternative ways to read the opinion.

(a) The Court seems to say that a finding of agreement is not necessary.
See especially 696, 1st sentence of the 2d full ¶. Is that the holding of Interstate

Circuit? If so, what is the meaning of the qualification in that sentence: "in the circumstances of this case"? If the Court really means that agreement is not necessary, what does the crime of conspiracy consist of? Presumably, the cited sentence at p. 696 has to mean only that "in the circumstances of this case" an *express* agreement was not necessary because *there was* a (tacit) agreement.

(b) The alternative interpretation of the holding, therefore, is that there was a tacit agreement on the facts of this case. But how can there be a tacit agreement here if the Court admits that the supposed conspirators never communicated with each other and never explicitly agreed to anything? Students will need to understand the dynamics of the economic situation, especially the circumstances indicating that the terms accepted by each distributor were strongly against its own economic self-interest, unless *all* the others agreed to the same terms. See p. 695, last full ¶. Thus, Interstate Circuit shows that agreement need not involve any express understanding between the parties and can be inferred from parallel or complementary actions, provided there are circumstances making such actions improbable without a prior tacit understanding.

To test student understanding of Interstate Circuit, consider Problem 3(a) at p. 697. What result under the Interstate Circuit principle? Is there an explicit agreement here? Among the four teenagers, possibly yes, but not between the two passersby, nor is there any express agreement between the passersby and the teenagers. Given Interstate Circuit, can we say that there is a conspiracy even without express agreement, on the basis of the parallel actions of the parties? Under the narrow reading of Interstate Circuit, he question is whether we can infer from the parallel action that the parties must have had a tacit agreement. In Interstate Circuit the behavior of the parties would not have been in their own self interest in the absence of an agreement that would assure them that others would behave likewise. Is that true here? Arguably, a single teenager would be at risk if he or she tried to loot the store alone - - safety in numbers. (Similar reasoning might support a finding of conspiracy in Problem 3(b), p. 698.) But that reasoning becomes attenuated as applied to a passerby - - he can loot without joining the teenagers' conspiracy or caring what the first group of looters may do. And in any case, the actions of the two passersby are in no way dependent on one another, so a finding of conspiracy between them would be especially tenuous.

Alvarez, p. 699 deals with the question of how much evidence is necessary to establish the conspiratorial agreement. Is the problem that the defendant had only *promised* to unload? Even if Alvarez had performed, that act would be at best only *evidence* of a prior agreement to do so. Can't the jury infer such an agreement among Alvarez and the others from his making the promise? This is what the en banc opinion concludes. (p. 700, 1st full ¶). Is this persuasive? Compare the 2d ¶ of the dissent: a smile and a nod may be enough to send a person to the penitentiary, but not here. (p. 700) Why not? The dissent says that there was no other evidence to show Alvarez knew of the conspiracy and agreed to join it. But given A's admitted *intent* to unload the marijuana, the dissent's refusal to infer that he must have *agreed* to do so shows an especially strict insistence on proof of the particular agreement charged in the indictment. Clearly the dissent is moved by "the potential for injustice in conspiracy cases" (p. 700, last ¶ of the dissent).

The majority's decision in Alvarez may seem somewhat counter-intuitive. Do the sweeping incidents of conspiracy justify the dissent's strict approach? Or do the practical difficulties of proving an illicit agreement (see James, p. 694) justify a more flexible standard? Shouldn't the prosecution's burden of proof require it to exclude, beyond a reasonable doubt, the possibility that the complementary acts occurred without agreement? Compare Williams' view that, at least in England, it is permissible to infer an agreement unless there is evidence suggesting that the concurrence of acts was accidental (p. 697, 2d indented quote).

Students could be asked to apply these approaches to the Problem at p. 701. Are the crew members of the COWBOY part of the marijuana importing conspiracy? Is conspiracy liability here fair? (Intuitions may differ on this. Liability may seem appropriate since the crew clearly knew what was up. But what could they do about it? In any case does it make sense to treat them as part of the *conspiracy*? What if one of the confederates in Miami kills an informant - - would it make sense to hold that the crew members, as co-conspirators, are liable for murder?)

Analytically, in the COWBOY Problem, how should the "agreement" issue be resolved? Note that the crew members seem to meet the Murphy requirements (p. 697, Note 2) of performing complementary actions that promote the conspiratorial goal. But does this exclude, beyond a reasonable doubt, the possibility that the complementary acts occurred without agreement? Here, Prof. William's caveat (p. 697, 2d indented quote) seems especially pertinent - - the concurrence of acts could perfectly well be accidental or independent of an agreement. Realistically, what could a crew member like Freeman (the cook) have done? Judge Godbold's dissent in Freeman (p. 701, 2d indented quote) therefore seems persuasive in suggesting that there was insufficient evidence to hold the crew members for conspiracy. The court's contrary result in Freeman illustrates the breadth of conspiracy law and the potential unfairness that can result from flexible evidentiary rules for finding "agreement."

The Note beginning at page 701 explores conspiracy as an inchoate crime and considers the extent to which conspiracy doctrine pushes the line of criminality back into the early stages of preparation involving few if any "acts." Is conspiracy a crime without any actus reus at all? Some statutes require an "overt act," but at common law there was no such requirement, and modern statutes often do not require an overt act for conspiracies to commit the most serious crimes. See MPC Section 5.03(5). When no overt act is required, is the crime purely mental? Note <u>Mulcahy</u>, p. 701, Note 1, holding that the agreement itself is the act. Does it make sense to view the agreement alone as an act sufficiently substantial to warrant criminal punishment?

Reconsider <u>Alvarez</u>, p.699, in this connection. Since Alvarez's conduct clearly did not go far enough to warrant conviction for attempt, why should his nod of the head render him punishable for a conspiracy? Note the justifications offered in the MPC comment at pp. 703, 2d indented quote: that agreement shows an unequivocal purpose and an increased likelihood that the offense would be committed. Are these arguments persuasive as applied to a case like <u>Alvarez</u>? Are concerns about an insufficient actus reus be met by the requirement of an "overt act" (i.e. an act beyond the act of agreement)? Note how trivial the overt act can be. See Holmes at p. 702, 2d indented quote. A possible solution is to require a "substantial step" instead of just an overt act. See p. 703, 1st full ¶.

4. <u>Mens Rea</u>, pp. 704-14

At the outset of the mens rea discussion, it is helpful to reiterate the formal elements of the offense: an agreement by two or more people to commit an unlawful act. (As to agreements to commit lawful acts, see p. 680, Note 1.) Note that the parties must intend *to agree*. But there is a second level of mens rea questions: Must the parties have some particular level of purpose, knowledge or awareness with respect to the objective or results of that agreement? <u>Lauria</u> explores the dimensions of the problem.

<u>Lauria</u>, p. 704, raises the question whether a true purpose is necessary to satisfy this mens rea requirement, and if so, how that true purpose can be established. The former issue recalls that considered in <u>Gladstone</u>, p. 611; if previously covered in that connection, it can be covered briefly here.

What was the nature of Lauria's activity? Did he have any "agreement" with the prostitutes? If so, what was his mens rea? Did he intend to agree with them? (Yes). Did he intend to further their criminal acts? In what sense? Should knowledge alone be sufficient to constitute intent? Consider:

Case 1. Suppose that Lauria knew a customer was using his answering service to relay messages concerning a bank robbery operation. Should that knowledge be sufficient for conspiratorial liability?

In connection with Case 1, consider first whether Lauria could be convicted of robbery as an aider and abetter. Where purpose is required (e.g. the MPC), presumably not. If knowledge is held sufficient for aiding and abetting, should it also be sufficient for conspiracy? Is there any reason to treat conspiracy differently? Recall the extensive collateral consequences of conspiracy and the broad vicarious liability for the acts of co-conspirators. If Lauria's aid should be punishable in Case 1, isn't it adequate to convict for aiding and abetting robbery? Even in the case of the most serious crimes, conspiratorial liability, with its broad "agency" implications, arguably should require a true sharing of the criminal purpose.

Where does the law now stand -- when is a true purpose required? Even under Lauria, purpose is required for conspiracy to commit a misdemeanor. What about a conspiracy to commit a felony offense of price fixing or water pollution? Under the Lauria reasoning, is there a "duty to take positive action to dissociate oneself" (p. 708, 1st full ¶) in such cases? Does the misdemeanor/felony line really work? What result under the MPC? Students should see that under § 5.03(1), knowledge alone is insufficient no matter how serious the conspiratorial objective; a true purpose is required in all cases.

How can purpose be established? Consider Thomas, p. 706, 4th full ¶; the grossly inflated charges gave the defendant a direct participation in the illegal activity. But compare Bainbridge, p. 708, 1st 2 lines, where the court says that knowledge can support an inference of intent. But how does knowledge alone establish *participation* in the scheme? Students should see that such reasoning amounts to saying (on policy grounds) that knowledge alone is sufficient and that intent simply is not required.

Where an actual purpose is required, can it be established in the absence of direct profit-sharing or some other direct stake in the success of the venture? What about Direct Sales, p. 707, 4th ¶? Were there inflated charges there? (No; in fact the seller actually gave a quantity discount to the purchasers. See p. 707 n.c.) Inflated charges can establish a stake (Thomas), but here *reduced* charges also establish a stake, on the ground that the high volume of sales, which the seller encouraged, made the seller a participant in the illegal venture. But on this basis wouldn't Direct Sales have had a stake in the venture even if they had refused to extend discount prices? If Direct Sales had a normal quantity discount schedule, but had refused to make those discounts available to purchasers involved in illegality, would that action have helped or hurt their case? (Discount sales are taken as incriminating, but a refusal to extend a discount for sales in volume would in effect amount to "inflated" prices and thus would be incriminating too!) Discussion of such problems should bring out the difficulties of neatly separating "mere" knowledge from a stake in the venture.

Why can't the <u>Direct Sales</u> approach be applied in <u>Lauria</u> itself? Whether he charged high prices, discount prices or normal prices, didn't Lauria have a stake in the success of the prostitutes? If the prosecution could establish an unusually high volume of business with them, the court recognizes that this argument clearly could be made. See p. 707, 1st sentence of the 4th ¶.

Ultimately, the line between purpose and mere knowledge becomes quite thin, at least in the case of a supplier who has repeated dealings with a wrong-doing customer. Nonetheless, there exists a clear difference in principle (and also, for one-shot transactions like <u>Gladstone</u>, p. 611, in practice) between knowledge coupled with indifference on the one hand, and a stake in the venture on the other.

If time permits, student mastery of this framework can be tested by working through the problems at p. 710, Note 2.

Problem 2(a). Does Lawrence have a stake in the venture? (Note, incidentally, the importance of conspiracy as a doctrine of inchoate liability here. Because the "cook" was never carried out, there is no liability on a complicity theory, and because there were apparently few "substantial steps," liability for attempt would be unlikely.) Is Lawrence a conspirator? The fee - - $1000 - - sounds like a grossly inflated rent, but is that clear? What if we take into account the risk of damage to the trailer? Perhaps surprisingly, the court in <u>Blankenship</u> (per Easterbrook, J.) reversed Lawrence's conviction, largely on this ground.

Problem 2(b). The sales price here looks grossly inflated, but does this reflect a kind of participation in the illegality, or just a seller's attempt to strike a favorable bargain with two young and unsophisticated buyers? Why is it relevant that the aircraft had seats removed to facilitate hauling cargo?

The remaining Notes, pp. 710-14, pose the question whether the mens rea for conspiracy should track the mens rea for the underlying substantive offense. In other words, if the defendant has the required purpose to promote particular conduct, and any other mens rea required for the offense, is that mens rea sufficient (i.e., symmetry with the mens rea for the substantive offense), or should liability as a conspirator require a higher level of mens rea?

Case 1. <u>Gormley</u>, p. 711, line 2. Note the charge: conspiracy to violate the election law. Note the defendant's mistake - - there was no opposition candidate and the defendant therefore thought that his actions in recording the votes too soon were not illegal. Would his mistake be a defense in a prosecution for the substantive offense? (No). The why should the mistake nonetheless be a defense to a conspiracy charge? One way to put it is that the defendant never agreed to violate the election law. But he did agree to engage in the conduct that violated the election law. Should that be enough?

As a matter of culpability, the result in Case 1 should depend on whether the defendant's mistake goes to a *material* element of the offense. Does it? Ordinarily knowledge of the law is <u>not</u> a material element; like a purely jurisdictional fact (p. 712, note 4(a)), knowledge of the law is irrelevant to the wrongfulness or gravity of the offense. See § 2.02(9). Symmetry here therefore makes sense as a substantive matter, even if symmetry should not be imposed automatically in every situation as a matter of logic. See MPC Comment at p. 711, 2d indented quote.

Case 2. <u>Freed</u>, top of p. 713. What should have been the result here? Consider the nature of the defendant's mistake. Is the mistake here more like one of a purely jurisdictional fact or of a fact relevant to the wrongfulness of the conduct?

The Court in <u>Freed</u> treated the defendant's claim as if it were an argument that he did not know it was a crime to possess grenades. Should such a claim constitute a defense? No, see Case 1 - - to the extent that the defendant is claiming that he did not agree to violate the law, that claim should not be a defense. But isn't the unregistered status of the grenades a material element? In this respect the defendant is claiming that he never agreed to do the *act* made criminal by the statute. His claim should have been allowed as a defense.

Is <u>Freed</u> an aberration, or does it foreshadow a symmetry approach even when, on the acts as the defendant believes them to be, his conduct is not wrongful at all. Consider:

Case 3. Commuters A and B agree to form a carpool to drive to work. On Monday driver A goes through a red light without seeing it. Can passenger B be convicted of conspiracy to drive through a red light? Does symmetry analysis require us to say that he can be? Intuitively, a conspiracy conviction seems absurd. But don't the policies that support strict liability for the substantive offense apply with equal force to the conspiracy charge?

Case 4. Consider the Alan-Mary hypothetical, p. 713, Note 4(c), 1st ¶. Can Alan and Bill be convicted of conspiracy to commit statutory rape? Why not extend strict liability to the conspiracy charge? In this connection consider whether Alan can be convicted of attempted statutory rape. (Possibly, see p. 563, Note 7(b). If A commits statutory rape, can B be convicted as his accomplice? (No, see Johnson v. Youden, p. 622, Note 1.)

In cases like Case 3 (the traffic light) and Case 4 (statutory rape) there is an argument for symmetry, on the ground that the competing policy considerations relevant to strict liability (or negligence) have already been resolved in facing the mens rea issue for the substantive offense. But query whether reduced mens rea requirements in connection with the substantive offense reflect in part a retributive impetus and a desire to short-circuit possible defenses in order to assure punishment when certain harms have actually occurred. If so, it seems a peculiar sort of bootstrapping to adhere to a symmetry approach and dilute mens rea requirements when the proscribed harm has *not* occurred and when the defendant may not even have gone far enough to have committed a punishable attempt. In view of the sweeping collateral consequences of conspiracy doctrine and the much earlier liability for preparatory acts, the argument for preserving an intent requirement (with respect to *material* elements) is even stronger for conspiracy than for attempts. In any event discussion should bring out the ways that a careful mens rea analysis (for both the substantive offense and the conspiracy) will depend on the nature of the mistake allegedly made -- whether it relates to a jurisdictional fact, to a material fact, or to the penal law.

5. Scope of the Agreement, pp. 714-23

To introduce this section, consider:

Case 1. Smuggler S delivers to distributors D1 and D2. D1 then delivers to retailers R1 and R2; D2 delivers to retailers R3 and R4. The situation can be diagrammed as shown on the page that follows:

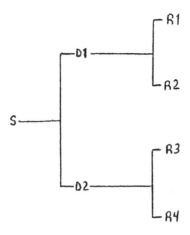

How many conspiracies are there here? Specifically, is R1 in a conspiracy with S? With R2 or even with R3? Is R1 in a conspiracy with D2?

Before sorting out the issues, it is helpful to consider first what difference it makes. From a defendant's point of view is it better to establish one inclusive conspiracy or numerous separate ones? (Usually, defendants will want to split up the conspiracy, to limit their vicarious liability for the acts and statements of others. See especially Anderson, at p. 718, where an outlying conspirator was held liable not only for abortions performed on women she referred to Stern, but also for abortions performed on women referred by others whom she did not even know.) Will a defendant ever want one all-inclusive conspiracy? See Braverman (1st ¶ of the Note on p. 721) where the government alleged several separate conspiracies, and the defendant claimed only one, in order to avoid consecutive sentences for allegedly separate offenses.

The upshot is that a defendant in the center of a conspiratorial relationship may benefit from treating the entire operation as a single agreement; he is in any event vicariously liable for the acts of those he joined with, whether in single or multiple conspiracies. But those on the fringes will usually prefer to split the conspiracy up. In any event, whatever the defendant's preferences, how should the issue be resolved?

Kotteakos, p. 714. Note the relationship among the parties. Brown is at the center and each of the defendants deals with him. How many conspiracies are there? Why does the Court conclude there were eight or more *independent* groups? Note that the purposes were similar, and each group committed the same kind of crime. But the success of each group was not dependent on that of the others, i.e. in the Court's metaphor, p. 715, last full ¶), there was a wheel without a rim to enclose the spokes.

On what kind of evidence could the prosecution have established a single conspiracy in Kotteakos? Consider:

Case 2. Blumenthal, p. 717. How many conspiracies were there here? Clearly the salesmen F and B were in a conspiracy with distributors W and G; W and G were in a conspiracy with the identified owner O. But consider two problems:

(a) Why are F and B part of the conspiracy with O? The Court notes that F and B "must have known that others unknown to them were sharing in so large a project" by playing other roles in the scheme. (p. 717, 11 lines from the bottom). This is the "chain" aspect of the conspiratorial relationship.

(b) Why are F and B in a conspiracy with each other? Couldn't the defendants have argued for two groups comprised of O, W, G and F on the one hand, and O, W, G and B on the other? Why is this situation different from Kotteakos? Note that there "each loan was an end in itself" (p. 718, line 3), while here the Court assumes the entire lot had to be sold and therefore that each salesman's efforts were necessary to the success of the plan. See p. 718, 1st full ¶.

Case 3. Anderson, p. 718. Is this case more like Kotteakos or Blumenthal? The court treats it as being like Blumenthal, but is the result correct? Where is the "rim" of the wheel? The court appears to treat knowledge of the mere *existence* of others as sufficient. That is surely inconsistent with Kotteakos. Absent evidence of *interdependence*, the result seems incorrect.

Query also whether Anderson had the mens rea necessary to convict of membership in the larger conspiracy. Did she have a "stake" in the success of the others? Students should see that the interdependence requirement for defining the scope of the conspiratorial agreement is consistent with the mens rea requirement of a true purpose.

Bruno, p. 718, illustrates the application of these principles to a complex narcotics smuggling ring. Since the smugglers, middlemen and retailers are in a chain relationship, each depends on the others; whether or not they actually communicate with one another, all are in the same conspiracy. But why aren't the two groups of retailers in separate conspiracies? Note again the analysis invoked in Blumenthal: the court assumes that the success of the venture depends on being able to unload the entire lot. See p. 718, last 3 lines of the opinion.

In a narcotics case is this assumption realistic? What if the Texas retailers were constantly pressuring the middlemen to give them a larger share of the total supply? Isn't it likely that the Texas and New York retailers are essentially in competition with one another? At least in today's drug markets, the assumption of competition among retailers seems far more plausible. Thus, as Borelli indicates, p. 719-20, the chain metaphor is misleading as applied to this aspect of Bruno. In effect, there were arguably two separate chains (or one chain ending at the middlemen and then two independent spokes to the two groups of retailers). Discussion of fact situations like that in Morris and Torres-Ramirez, pp. 720-21, can help students develop familiarity with the various ways that the required interdependence among conspirators can be established (or refuted) under the prevailing judicial approaches.

The cases primarily focus on complex but more-or-less static organizational structures. What result if a new retailer joins an existing scheme? Consider:

> Case 4. In Case 1 above, suppose D2 dies and is replaced by a new distributor D3. The conspiracy, in operation for a year, has already distributed six shiploads of heroin. Is D3 a member of the original conspiracy? Can he be convicted of the substantive smuggling offenses committed before he joined?

The hornbook answer is that where a conspirator joins an ongoing conspiracy, he held responsible for all statements previously made in furtherance of the conspiratorial objective (see p. 689, Note 1). The problem here, however, is whether D3 *did* join that larger, pre-existing conspiracy? Did he have any stake in that venture?

As Borelli shows (p. 720, 1st full ¶), the concept of a single conspiratorial agreement becomes difficult or impossible to apply to the conduct of an illegal business over an extended period. What is the proper solution to this problem? Why not simply abandon conspiratorial notions and prosecute the parties solely for their individual crimes (which usually are numerous)? Or should conspiracy doctrine be made even more flexible, to permit effective prosecution of complex criminal organizations? The MPC and RICO represent contrasting responses to these questions.

Consider how Bruno would be decided under the MPC approach, explained at pp. 722-23. How many conspiracies are there? Note that the Code permits no single answer to this question. Since the culpability of each participant is examined separately under the criteria of §§ 5.03(1) and (2), the smugglers might be in a broad conspiracy including all the retailers, while each retailer might be in a narrow conspiracy not including any of the smugglers.

What are the advantages of the MPC approach? The MPC avoids the artificiality of looking for "spokes" or "chains" in a complex, ongoing relationship. But given this unilateral approach, what is the liability of retailers for the acts of the smugglers and vice-versa? Note that the Code abolishes most of the collateral consequences of conspiracy, by restricting vicarious liability to normal accomplice principles (§ 2.06), and by establishing separate principles to determine joinder and venue (§ 5.03(4)).

6. Parties, pp. 723-30

The material on accomplice liability explores the specific problems that arise when one of the parties is a victim of the offense or merely a feigned participant. The conspiracy cases raise similar issues. Students should note the differences between the solutions to these problems under accomplice doctrines and under conspiracy doctrines.

Gebardi, p. 724. Note the reversal of the woman defendant's conspiracy conviction. Since the Mann Act was intended to protect those in her position, convicting her seems absurd. If she had been prosecuted as an accomplice, the same result would be reached. See Tyrell, p. 642, Note 6(a). Now what result as to the male defendant? If the woman is not guilty of conspiracy, doesn't his conviction necessarily have to be reversed, too? (The Court so held.) But does it make sense for the defendant to escape punishment on the ground that the statute was intended to *protect* his victim? The problem lies in the effort to prosecute the male defendant for conspiracy. Presumably, he can be convicted on a substantive Mann Act charge, but the added dangers of group activity are not implicated unless there is a third party helping him to transport the victim.

What if neither party is a victim. Suppose that A and B (both married to other parties) agree to rent a hotel room so that they can spend the night together there. Can they be convicted of conspiracy to commit adultery? Under the Wharton rule (p. 725, Note 2), the answer is no. But note the erosion of the Wharton rule in Iannelli, p. 726, 1st full ¶.

Is the Wharton rule sound? What is its rationale? Since the substantive offenses necessarily contemplated two parties, there appears to be no aggravation of the danger when those two parties plan to commit it. But what about the function of conspiracy as an inchoate offense? See MPC Comment at p. 725, 2d ¶ of the 2d indented quote. But if the conduct would not be punishable as attempted adultery, why should the agreement (inevitable in this context) trigger criminal liability at an earlier point? Why not deal with these problems as matters attempt or solicitation doctrine? Compare the MPC solution to these problems in §§ 5.04, 2.06(5), 2.06(6)(a) & (b).

Garcia, p. 726 raises a problem analogous to that raised by Hayes (p. 633) in the accomplice context. Under traditional conspiracy law, could the conviction be upheld? (No, because there was no meeting of the minds and thus no true "agreement.") The MPC's unilateral approach (p. 727, indented quote) solves this problem. But compare Foster, p. 729, Note 2, where the court held that the traditional bilateral concept should be preserved even under a statute using language patterned on that of the MPC.

Is there a practical need for the unilateral approach? Is conspiracy doctrine really necessary in order to convict a defendant like Garcia? Note that under many modern penal codes, Garcia could be convicted of solicitation. See, e.g., MPC § 5.02.

Even if the unilateral approach is not strictly speaking necessary, are there any serious problems posed by adopting it? As indicated in Escobar De Bright, p. 729, Note 3, the danger of group activity is arguably absent if the only co-conspirator is a government agent. Beyond this, if the feigned conspirator makes statements highly incriminating to the defendant, should these statements be admissible against the defendant under the co-conspirator exception to the hearsay rule? If the feigned conspirator commits additional criminal acts in furtherance of the "conspiracy," should the defendant be chargeable with these additional substantive offenses?

The vicarious responsibility of co-conspirators, highly problematic at best, seems defensible only when there is a true community of purpose among the parties. But is this a defect of the unilateral approach under the MPC? Note that under the MPC and many other modern codes, vicarious responsibility for acts and statements is restricted or abolished in any event. Thus, under a well thought-out modern code, it may make little or no practical difference whether the bilateral concept is retained or abandoned.

Discussion of such questions should help students see the functional significance of different approaches to conspiracy doctrine and the value of separating collateral issues (e.g., hearsay rules and accomplice liability) from the conceptual question whether a "conspiracy" exists.

7. <u>Criminal Enterprises and RICO</u>, pp. 730-48

The text of the RICO statute, pp. 730--32 and the Notes following, pp. 732-35, introduce the basic RICO concepts. Students should be sure to note:

(a) the wide list of eligible predicate offenses (§1961(1));

(b) the important expansion of federal jurisdiction [note the many §1961(1) offenses that are not normally federal crimes]; and

(c) the steep penalty enhancement triggered by RICO [§1961(1) offenses punishable by just over 1 year under state law become RICO offenses punishable by up to 20 years under federal law if the RICO elements are satisfied.]

The Notes at pp. 732-35 set out and explain the principal elements of a RICO violation - - the enterprise, the pattern, and the "conduct" or "participation." Each of these elements is now becoming the subject of its own complex body of law. For purposes of a first-year course, it will normally be sufficient to indicate the ambiguous but undoubtedly far-reaching character of all the key concepts. (See, e.g., the comments of Judge Sentelle, p. 744.)

In addition, students should be sure to see the multi-layered manner in which RICO extends the coverage of traditional conspiracy concepts that would otherwise be available for prosecuting a criminal organization - - RICO enterprise liability under §1962(c) is itself a kind of conspiracy liability for participating in a criminal enterprise, and in addition, §1962(d) makes it a crime to conspire to violate §1962(c), in effect an offense of conspiring to engage in a conspiracy. <u>Elliott</u>, provides an opportunity to examine the meaning and significance of the new conceptions embodied in the RICO statute.

<u>Elliott</u>, p. 735. Students should be clear on the specific acts charged against the defendants. (See pp. 736-36.) Note particularly the limited allegations against Elliott, Delph and Taylor.

Against that background consider first whether all defendants could be charged with a single conspiracy under pre-RICO law. Why not? Is this just a hub (revolving around J.C. Hawkins) without a rim? Or were these crimes financially interdependent (unlike the frauds in <u>Kotteakos</u>). Why can't this rationale be invoked here? The court implies that the answer is that the crimes here were "not truly interdependent" (p. 737, 2d full ¶). But is this true? Why wasn't there strong financial interdependence here?

Another suggested reason is that several parties had "no contact" with each other (p. 737, 3d full ¶). But is contact a necessary prerequisite? (Clearly not. See Blumenthal and Bruno). Then why is traditional conspiracy law inadequate to reach the conspiracy in Elliott?

The main problem may be the diversity of activities and the difficulty of showing that each participant was *aware* of those activities (p. 737, 3d full ¶). The weakness in Elliott is the flip-side of that in Kotteakos: in Kotteakos there is awareness (see p. 716, 1st carryover line of the footnote), but no interdependence; in Elliott there may be enough interdependence but there is not sufficient awareness. RICO helps avoid this problem by defining a broad object offense (participation in the affairs of an enterprise). Under Elliott, the various parties can be linked together in a single conspiracy, so long as each defendant was aware of the enterprise; he need not be aware of the particular ways in which other parties participate in its affairs.

Even under the court's broad interpretation of RICO, was the conviction of Elliott himself proper? Note the need to show that each defendant agreed to participate in the affairs of the enterprise, rather than merely agreeing to commit independent thefts (p. 740, 1st sentence of the last ¶). Given this requirement, some awareness of the role of others apparently is still required.

What if Elliott, knowing that J.C. Hawkins was the center of an on-going criminal enterprise, agreed to steal some meat for him to help raise money. Would Elliott then have become a co-conspirator with the others, even if he didn't know specifically about the drug activities involving Delph and Taylor? The discussion on p. 738, 1st full ¶, implies an affirmative answer. But compare Sutherland's requirement (p. 742, at the end of the 2d ¶ of the 2d indented quote) that "each defendant must necessarily have known that others were also conspiring to violate RICO." In view of this limitation, how much does RICO actually expand the traditional conspiracy doctrines? Discussion should help indicate the difficulty of pinning down just what RICO accomplishes. Much depends, obviously, on how liberally RICO itself is interpreted and on how narrowly the requirements of awareness and interdependence are interpreted under traditional doctrines.

As a matter of policy, it is sound to insist on clear proof of mutual awareness and interdependence? If so, does prosecution of a complex operation like that of J.C. Hawkins become impossible as a practical matter? Or is it the prosecution just forced to focus on the particular crimes actually committed by each defendant? What would be wrong with that approach? (Reconsider the debate about the potential unfairness of vicarious liability under Pinkerton, pp. 692-94.)

Under the expansive interpretation reflected in <u>Elliott</u>, are traditional requirements of personal responsibility adequately respected? Consider the court's answer at pp. 738-40. First, is it true that there is "no significant extension of a co-conspirator's liability" (p. 739, end of the 1st full ¶)? Consider first the penalties for a RICO conspiracy. Suppose defendant D commits two acts of mail fraud. The maximum penalty (five years on each count) becomes twenty years for the RICO conspiracy (plus the possibility of consecutive sentences for the predicate offenses).

Second, how does RICO change the problem of guilt by association? Note that in <u>Elliott</u> four defendants charged with thefts and drug transactions were forced to stand trial as confederates of a deliberate killer. The court concedes that this "ups the ante" (p. 740, 1st full ¶). If doing so is not unconstitutional, is it unwise as a matter of legislative policy? Is the prejudice limited to the indirect taint of undergoing joint trial? If Delph and Taylor are part of the enterprise conspiracy (as the court holds), why can't they be convicted (presumably in a state court) of the murder committed by R. Hawkins? Given both RICO and <u>Pinkerton</u>, the prospects for vicarious liability without personal participation (or even awareness) can become extensive.

Discussion of these issues should bring out the tension between the need, on the one hand, for effective means to prosecute complex organizations and well-insulated individuals, and the need, on the other, to avoid guilt by association and punishment disproportionate to personal participation and fault.

Competing with the approach of RICO, as well as that of the state RICO statutes (p. 746, Note 1), and the increasingly common antigang statutes (p. 747, Note 2), is what Professor Lynch calls the "transaction-bound" conception of crime (p. 744, last 2 lines). The article by Prof. Lynch (pp. 744-46) draws attention to the more traditional paradigm, and can help students get a better appreciation of the traditional approach to defining crimes, to see its virtues as well as its practical limitations. (The article by Prof. Brenner, cited at p. 746, Note 1, is also extremely useful in this connection.) For purposes of class discussion it may also be worthwhile to raise the question of the extent to which the crime of conspiracy itself, especially in the light of its attendant doctrines, represents a comparable departure from the transaction-bound conception of crime. The Lynch article, therefore, can be profitably used for several purposes: (1) to help teach important aspects of RICO; (2) to assist reflections on the character of the more traditional crime of conspiracy; and (3) to draw together the essential features of the main approach to the definition of crimes characteristic of the Anglo-American tradition.

Chapter 8
Exculpation

In a one-semester course, this Chapter normally warrants three to four weeks or roughly twelve classes: for example, two classes on protection of life and person, one on protection of property and law enforcement, one on necessity, one on euthanasia, one each on duress and intoxication, four on mental disorder and the related Robinson-Powell material (pp. 929-940), and one class on the concluding material (pp. 940-49) that helps provide an overview of the course. Where more abbreviated treatment is required duress, intoxication and/or the concluding material can be summarized or, if necessary, omitted.

    A. Introduction: The Concepts of Justification and Excuse, pp. 749-750

    B. Principles of Justification, pp. 750-842

    1. Protection of Life and Person, pp. 750-96

Peterson (p. 750) and Goetz (p. 751) introduce the basic elements of self-defense doctrine, with emphasis on necessity, imminence, the reasonableness of the apprehension, and the special requirements related to use of deadly force. The Goetz case provides a vivid and contemporary setting in which to introduce the subject of the justified use of defensive force, particularly where the defensive force is deadly in character. The primary legal issue in the case is the proper definition of the mens rea of a justified self defensive killing. Is it enough that the defendant truly believed he would be killed if he did not kill his adversary, a subjective approach, or must he in addition meet an objective test, namely that a reasonable person in his circumstances and situation would have so believed? And if the latter, what features of the circumstances of the defendant's situation should be taken into account? This latter issue in the law of self-defense recurs in connection with cases dealing with the battered woman defense and elsewhere. The Goetz case provides an interesting set of facts to explore that issue. (pp. 759-61, Notes 1 & 2 provide further grist for such a discussion.)

The conclusion reached by the court in Goetz (that there is an objective component to the rule) is the law generally. But given the New York statutes, was the court's interpretation correct? How much force was there in the view of the court below? And in terms of justice and public policy, which test is to be preferred? The court concludes: "We cannot lightly impute to the Legislature an intent to fundamentally alter the principles of justification to allow the perpetrator of a serious crime to go free simply because that person believed his actions were reasonable and necessary to prevent some perceived harm. To completely exonerate such an individual, no matter how aberrational or bizarre his thought patterns, would allow citizens to set their own standards for the permissible use of force." (pp. 754, 5th full ¶)

Is that conclusion irresistible? The Goetz case presents a setting in which the application of this approach is very appealing. Yet the quotation from Glanville Williams, p. 759, Note 1, and the excerpt from the Restak column that follows it suggest arguments in behalf of a subjective test. The student might be alerted to reserve final judgment until reaching the battered women cases that follow.

If an objective test is to be employed, how should it be applied in a case like Goetz? And how wholly objective should the test be? Must it not include some of peculiar features of the defendant's situation. For example, shouldn't the jury be told to take into account that Goetz had been mugged before in deciding whether his action was reasonable? But how about the fact that Goetz is an especially apprehensive person? Should they be told to consider that as well? See p. 761, Note 2. Should the jury be told that not only Goetz, but also subway riders in New York generally, or many of them, tended to be acutely apprehensive of the danger of mugging? That in assessing the reasonableness of Goetz' fear of the four young men they may consider that young blacks commit disproportionately more crimes of violence than young whites? (On this point, consider Armour's argument at pp. 757-58).

How would the student have applied the law as stated by the N.Y. Court of Appeals to the facts of the case insofar as they appear in the court's opinion? On the facts as there stated isn't it clear that Goetz by his own admission went beyond the limits of legitimate self-defense by shooting the young men even after there was no longer a threat to himself? The jury acquitted him of all charges having to do with his shooting the men. How can this be understood? Must it be understood as a flagrant instance of racism? Was it based on the notion of the jury that the men got what was coming to them? Is there any possible and acceptable formulation of the law of self-defense under which Goetz would be properly acquitted? Is it sound that the defense of self-defense should prevail even if it can't be justified in terms of the standard of the reasonable person, so long as the defendant's actions are found to be understandable and excusable, given the circumstances? Again the student might be advised to hold final judgment until discussion of the battered woman issue.

The Notes on Reasonableness, p. 759, pursue various aspects of the mens rea issue. The Problem (p. 762, Note 5) provides a way to work through the MPC approach (p. 762, indented quote), which is easily misunderstood. The MPC presents an interesting solution to the problem of finding a middle ground between the objective and subjective tests; namely, allowing for conviction of a lesser homicidal offense when the defendant truly but unreasonably believed he had to kill.

State v. Kelly, p. 763, and the cases and materials that follow provide a basis for discussing the legal problems raised when the "battered woman" resorts to deadly force against her persistent batterer and claims self-defense. It will help to point out the range of factual settings in which the final, fatal episode may occur, since the setting may have an important effect on the legal analysis. Several illustrations are provided: Kelly, (p. 763); Norman (776); Jahnke (p. 784, Note 7).

The facts of Kelly provide a suitable starting point for discussion. What was the defendant's version of the fatal confrontation? On her testimony, were the elements of self-defense made out? If so, which elements of the self-defense claim were problematical? Was the battered woman evidence relevant to them? In exploring these questions, it may be helpful first to note that the "battering" claim can be broken down into two kinds of evidence: (i) the defendant's own testimony about the background, and (ii) the expert's testimony about the battered woman "syndrome." Consider the former evidence first. Should it be admissible? How is it relevant? Note the importance of determining whether the defendant really did fear great bodily harm and if so, whether that fear was reasonable. On both questions prior assaults are plainly of great relevance. That being so, is there any possible objection to the admissibility of the defendant's testimony? Note the potential prejudicial effects, involving possible devaluation of the life of an unappealing victim or the legitimation of violent solutions whether strictly necessary or not. How should the balance between relevance and prejudicial effect be struck?

Given its strong relevance for the central issues in Kelly, prior assaultive behavior would without doubt be held admissible. But how far should this principle be carried? In a case like Jahnke (p. 784, Note 7) a court conceivably might rule inadmissible even the defendant's own testimony about prior assaultive behavior.

Consider next the admissibility of the expert testimony. Once the defendant's own testimony is admitted, why does the defendant need the expert at all? Why was expert testimony needed in Kelly? Note the attack on the credibility of defendant's testimony and the relevance of the battered woman theory for explaining why such testimony is not inherently implausible. It serves to dissipate the juror suspicion that if she in fact were telling the truth about the past beatings and threats, she surely would left him long ago. One important caveat: If relevance outweighs prejudicial effect, does the battered woman syndrome evidence automatically come in? Note the requirements for the admissibility of expert testimony in general (p. 773, Note 4) and the limited holdings in Kelly at the end of the opinion, p. 768.

A more controversial question is whether the expert's battered woman testimony has any legal relevance beyond tending to establish the credibility of the woman's account of her abuse at the defendant's hands in the light of her continuing to remain with him. The language in the Kelly case is a bit confusing, but its likeliest reading is that the test is not what a battered woman would believe, given her disabilities, but whether the jury finds that a reasonable person would believe that danger to her life was imminent if the testimony of the expert were believed. As the court states at p. 767, 2d full ¶: "The crucial issue of fact on which this expert's testimony would bear is why, given such allegedly severe and constant beatings, combined with threats to kill, defendant had not long ago left decedent." The prevailing view, reflected in cases like Humphrey, p. 770, Note 2, insists that the proper standard is that of the reasonable *person*, not the reasonable battered woman.

It is worth considering the challenges to this position to see whether it stands up. The material from p. 770, last 2 lines, through p. 773 is devoted to this issue. Is the claim for a "reasonable battered woman" standard different in principle from a claim for a standard of the reasonable intoxicated person, or the reasonable person with a clinical depression? Note that the drunk, unlike the battered woman, is partly responsible for his situation, but we can't distinguish in this way the situation of the person who is clinically depressed. Are battered women who suffer from the "syndrome psychologically impaired by definition, so that their behavior is no longer that of a healthy person? Students might be asked to consider whether the Holocaust Syndrome and the variety of other syndromes referred to the Werner case, p. 775, Note 6 should also be eligible for a special individualized standard of reasonableness. If not, why not.

In <u>Norman</u>, p. 776, isn't any self-defense claim insufficient as a matter of law? How can the defendant meet the related requirements of necessity and imminence? Consider <u>Ha</u>, p. 783, Note 4(b), where the court acknowledges that a reasonable person would have feared death or serious physical injury, but nonetheless denies a self-defense instruction. Same result in <u>Schroeder,</u> p. 782, Note 4(a), upholding the refusal to give any self-defense instruction where the victim was stabbed while sleeping. But isn't the dissent's argument persuasive?

Note how the MPC modified the traditional requirement of imminent necessity. P. 783, Note 5. If that provision were applicable wouldn't it have required a different result in <u>Schroeder</u>? If so, can it be invoked in a battered wife context? Are the cases distinguishable? <u>Schroeder</u> was physically trapped, but in Norman isn't the defendant psychologically trapped? Arguably the jury should at least be allowed to consider whether the wife (even in <u>Norman</u>) is in effect in a <u>Schroeder</u> situation. But compare the result in <u>Jahnke</u>, p. 784, Note 7. Wasn't the defendant (a minor) even more likely to be trapped, psychologically and legally, than the typical battered spouse? Why did the court exclude the evidence? And how about the case where the woman hires a killer to do away with her batterer? Is the argument based on her being psychologically trapped any weaker in this case? Or is it stronger, since arguably she wasn't sufficiently free to do the act herself?

Why is the law would allow the claim of self-defense in this situation? One important factor may be suspicion of claims based on largely unverifiable premises that run counter to popular perceptions of human behavior. Is that kind of intuitive suspicion well grounded, or is it just the result of ill-informed psychological premises?

<u>Deadly Force</u>.

The use of deadly force in self defense is generally limited to cases where life or extremely great bodily aggression is at stake. See p. 785, Note 1. Does the law thereby put too great a value on preserving the lives of aggressors?

Consider this hypothetical: A, while drinking in a bar, is taunted by B, C, and D. B pours beer on A's shirt, and B and C then shove A off the bar stool. B lifts a beer pitcher and threatens to empty it over A's head. A then pulls his gun and warns the three aggressors to back off. If they do so would he have a good defense to a charge of assault with a deadly weapon? Yes, under the Model Penal Code § 3.11: "A threat to death or serious bodily harm, by the production of a weapon or otherwise, so long as the actor's purpose is limited to creating an apprehension that he will use deadly force if necessary, does not constitute deadly force." But if they refuse to back off and continue to jostle and bully him in this way may A shoot in self defense?

Working through the elements of the traditional common law analysis, the threat is imminent and use of deadly force is the only effective way that A can protect himself: non-deadly force is not likely to be effective when it's three against one and retreat may be impossible. But the common restriction on use of deadly force to cases where great bodily harm is at stake leaves him with no other options. Apparently the judgment is that it is better for A to suffer this invasion of his rights than for him to kill in order to stop it. Is this right? Is it realistic?

Retreat.

Abbott, p. 788, explains the arguments for and against a retreat requirement and the circumstances under which the retreat obligation arises under the New Jersey-MPC approach. Is the obligation to retreat sound in principle? Is it sensible in practice? Consider the following applications:

Case 1. An Olympic track star T, waiting on a street corner, is confronted by a knife-wielding assailant K. If T uses a gun to protect himself and seriously wounds K, can T be convicted of aggravated assault? (Yes.) What if T uses judo, throws K to the ground and causes a fracture that leaves K paralyzed for life? Note that unless judo is considered "deadly force," there is no obligation to retreat and T therefore escapes conviction. Query: If the retreat obligation is sound at all, why limit it to cases of "deadly" force?

Case 2. T is again confronted by K, this time in T's home. What result? Note that T is no longer required to retreat. Is this home exception sound? What is it based on? See Tomlins, p. 791, Note 3, relying on Hale's notion of the inherent danger of flight. Is this rationale still valid today? Why take life if it is not strictly necessary to do so? Is the home exception based on sound moral principle or rather on a concession to pragmatic law enforcement realities?

Case 3 . Same situation as Case 2, except that K is T's wife. They are arguing in the kitchen, K picks up a carving knife and approaches T, who is standing next to the kitchen door. If T kills K, does he have a valid claim of self-defense? What result under the MPC? (T wins. See § 3.04(2)(b)(ii)(1).) Is it sensible for T to have a privilege to kill in this situation?

Case 4. While at work in his office, T is confronted by L, another knife-wielding assailant. Does T have to retreat if he knows he can do so? Note the MPC answer. (No.) But why does the rationale of the home exception extend to an office? What result under the Code if L is a co-worker? (T must retreat.) If a home is like an office, why should T have to retreat from a co-occupant in the latter but not in the former? If these rules are based on moral principle, what is that principle? If they reflect a concession to practical realties, does it make sense for them to be so complex?

Discussion should help bring out the difficulties posed by strictly adhering to the principle that the taking of life (even that of the "culpable" aggressor) can be justified only when absolutely necessary, and the problems of translating that preference for life into workable standards that do not diverge too much from prevailing morality.

The Initial Aggressor.

Peterson, p. 792, explains the prevailing common law rule. The factual sequence is complex but worth analyzing: violent assaults seldom fit the polar model of a wholly unprovoked aggressor and a purely innocent victim.

Who was the initial aggressor in Peterson? Wasn't it Keitt? Students should see that if the events are to be subjected to a fine-tuned analysis (as the court does), P did not have to retreat --he was on his own property. Nonetheless, K broke off the encounter; Peterson then became the "initial" aggressor. (See his threat to shoot at p. 792, 2d full ¶ of the opinion.)

Even when P is viewed as the initial aggressor, does it make sense for him to forfeit his right to self-defense? Note the court's rationale that the right of self-defense is granted only to those who are "free from fault in the difficulty" (p. 793, 1st full ¶). But once K returned with the lug wrench, what should P have done? Allowed himself to be beaten? Run inside? What if P had chased K with a knife instead of a gun, and K had then returned with the lug wrench? Would P have to submit to a beating if he couldn't manage to run away? (Under the common law approach, apparently yes.) What result if K attacks, P resists, and each seriously wounds the other? Note that K is probably punishable for his unnecessary attack. But P is also punishable for resisting; since he was initially at fault he has no right to defend even against unlawful force.

How would these variations on Peterson be resolved under the MPC? See p. 795-96, Note 3. Note that the Code avoids the common law rule's automatic forfeiture of the right of self-defense and attempts to preserve a closer proportion between fault and the defendant's loss of rights. But is the MPC approach workable? Note the fine tuning required to determine rights and liabilities in the MPC examples.

Does the initial-aggressor rule apply to one who provokes an assault without actually striking the first blow? Consider:

Case 5. Consider the David and Uriah hypothetical at p. 795, Note 2. How should the situation be analyzed? Should David be considered the "initial aggressor"? Note that even if Uriah has a defense of adequate provocation, his assault is still unlawful. Should David lose the right to defend? Is this a rational way to "punish" David for his transgression with Beth-Sheba, Uriah's wife? Or is it again a pragmatic concession to commonly prevailing assumptions that the defender should have "clean hands"? Is it intuitively unacceptable for David to have the right to kill Uriah under these circumstances?

The initial-aggressor problems, like those connected with retreat, bring out the conflicts between prevailing standards of everyday morality on the one hand, and the law's normal preference for nonviolence and the maximum protection of human life on the other. Discussion should help indicate the difficulties of giving legal form to standards of conduct that are theoretically sound and can, at the same time, be workably and evenhandedly enforced.

2. Protection of Property and Law Enforcement, pp. 796-809.

The common law rules applicable to protection of property can be clarified by beginning with a simple situation:

Case 1. Student S sees thief T cut the chain of S's bike, get on it and start to ride off. Can S shoot at T to stop his flight?

Note the common law approach: deadly force could be used to stop a felony but not a misdemeanor. Which is it here? The result might turn on the value of the bike. But assume a valuable racing bike, so that T had committed a felonious theft. Now can S shoot in Case 1? Under the traditional common law approach (perhaps still followed in some states), yes. But note that although Cal. § 197(1) reflects this approach with its unqualified "felony" language, Ceballos (p. 796) reads in a limitation: the felony must be an "atrocious" crime. See pp. 798, last full ¶. Non-violent property offenses are clearly excluded. What if the offense is violent? Consider:

Case 2. Muggers M and N push S against a wall and start punching. Assume that M and N have committed a felonious assault. If M and N are much stronger than S, can S pull a gun (his only weapon) and shoot? On what theory?

If Case 2 is analyzed as a prevention-of-felony case, the question is whether the felonious assault is an "atrocious" crime. Note Jones, p. 798, holding no, unless there is a threat of GBH; otherwise S has to submit to the attack. Does this make sense? Consider what should be the result in Case 2 if S invokes a self-defense theory. Note again that S must submit to the attack unless there is a threat of GBH. (See Case 1 in the self-defense discussion above.) The restrictions of the kind imposed by Cebellos on the kinds of property crimes and other felonies against which a defendant can use deadly force avoid the anomaly of granting a broader privilege to defend property than to defend against a personal attack.

Ceballos, p. 796. How do the above principles apply here? Note the facts and the crime committed by the intruders (residential burglary). Why isn't the defendant entitled to use deadly force in defense? Is it because these burglars were young and unarmed? Would that mean that a homeowner cannot shoot at a burglar unless he knows that the burglar is armed? Or, alternatively, is the holding based on the fact that the defendant was not personally present? Consider two variations that test these interpretations:

Case 3. C sets up a spring gun at his front door. Intruder I, who was carrying a loaded gun, forces the door open and is shot dead. Does C have a valid defense? Note first the rule in Gilliam, p. 797, 6th full ¶, which reflects a common approach. Under that analysis C wins. What result under Ceballos? Note the rejection of the Gilliam approach; thus C would be convicted even though the burglar was heavily armed. Does this make sense? Note that the Gilliam approach does not lay down any intelligible standard to guide behavior. See MPC Comment, middle of p. 798, 1st full ¶.

Case 4. Same facts as Ceballos, except that instead of using a spring gun, C sits in the garage and fires at Stephen and Robert just after they force their way in. What result under Ceballos? Assuming that the homeowner is present when the intrusion occurs, is residential burglary a forcible and "atrocious" crime? Note the Ceballos analysis: murder, robbery and rape are automatically presumed to involve threats of death or GBH (p. 799, 1st full ¶), but with respect to burglary, a reasonable fear of death or GBH must be established in light of the "character and manner" of the particular burglar . Presumably C would have no defense in Case 4.

Is the Ceballos approach realistic? Consider a variation on Case 4: Homeowner H is surprised in his bedroom by a nighttime burglar. Is the applicable rule that H cannot shoot until he has a particular reason for considering the burglar armed or dangerous? Or can a nighttime, residential burglary be considered sufficiently dangerous per se? See p. 800, 2d & 3d ¶'s, apparently leaving this question open. Compare a second variation: Storeowner S is asleep at the back of his shop when he hears breaking glass and sees an intruder crawling through the broken window. Does S have a reasonable basis for believing that the intruder is armed? Can he shoot in any event, on the ground that he is in his "dwelling"? Is S's position more like that of C in Case 4 or that of H in the first variation?

Compare the treatment of burglary under the MPC, Cal. and N.Y. provisions (pp. 800-01, Note 2. What result for homeowner H in N.Y.? Note the absence of any requirement of a fear of GBH (§ 35.20(3)). Presumably, therefore, H is privileged to shoot. But is this really "necessary" to prevent the burglary? (Why can't H just fire in the air?) What result for storeowner S? Doesn't § 35.20(3) still apply? Is this going too far? Is it reasonable to presume a danger to the person in any burglary of an "occupied building"?

For a contrasting approach, see MPC § 3.04(2)(b) and § 3.06(3)(d). What result for homeowner H and storeowner S? Note the absence of any special presumption of danger for residential burglaries. Does the Code require concrete evidence, or in practice are the requirements of §3.06(3)(d)(ii)(2) always met in the case of a residential burglary?

As a practical matter, does it make any difference how these standards are formulated? Even under a strict interpretation of the MPC, will the homeowner ever be prosecuted or convicted? If not, is it better to enact strict restrictions on the use of deadly force and then rely on prosecutorial discretion to avoid injustice? Or does this approach carry too many risks of unequal enforcement? Discussion should help students see the difficulty here, as in the self-defense area, of formulating clear, workable rules that, at the same time, do not legitimate unnecessary violence.

If time permits, the MPC, N.Y. and California standards should also be applied to other protection-of-property situations, especially where the offense is robbery rather than burglary. The following situation is much more likely to result in prosecution than those involving residential burglary:

> Case 5. A and B, after arguing in a bar, decide to step outside to settle their differences. Afterwards B is found, lying face down, with a knife between his shoulder blades. A admits stabbing B but claims he did so to stop B from getting away after B had attempted to rob A's watch. Does A have a valid defense? What result in California? In N.Y.? Note that in both states, deadly force is automatically permissible to prevent robbery. See Ceballos at p. 799, 1st full ¶; N.Y. § 35.15(2)(b).

Compare the analysis of Case 5 under the MPC. First, can A claim a privilege to effect the arrest of B? (No. See §3.07(2)(b)(ii).) Can A then claim a privilege to protect his property? Note the limits in §3.06(3)(d)(ii). What facts would A need to establish a defense under this provision? If A is stronger than B or if others are nearby to stop B, can A meet the requirements of subsection (d)(ii)(2)? (Probably not.) But consider two variations on Case 5:

> Case 6. Suppose B pulled a knife on A, but then dropped it as he started to run. Does A have a MPC defense here? (Yes). But assuming that A can't otherwise meet the requirements of subsection (d)(ii)(2), does the result in this variation make sense? Why should B's prior use of deadly force in itself give A a privilege to kill? One answer may be that A does not have such a privilege because § 3.06(1) (third line) still must be satisfied. But then doesn't subsection (d)(ii)(2) have to be met in all cases?

> Case 7. What if B pulled a knife on A, grabbed A's watch, and started to run. When A pulled his own knife, B dropped the watch but kept his own knife and kept running. If A stabbed B while in hot pursuit,

does he have a defense under the MPC? Note that the threshold requirement of § 3.06(1)(b) is no longer met. Even though B poses a clear threat of GBH, A loses his privilege because he is no longer attempting to prevent consummation of a robbery.

One further problem can be brought out by comparing Case 7 and Case 5. If B can't otherwise be stopped, A can stab or shoot to kill in Case 5, but not in Case 7. What accounts for the difference in results? Just the fact that B has A's watch? Does this justify the taking of life? Note that if B pulls a knife and tells A to get out of sight, A must retreat rather than stand his ground and kill. But if B commits robbery, A can actually pursue B and kill him if necessary to get back the watch. Does this make sense? Is § 3.06(3)(d)(ii)(2) consistent with §3.04(2)(b)(ii)? In this connection recall the facts of the Goetz case. When four teenagers, in a threatening manner, asked Goetz for $5, Goetz pulled a gun and shot them. What result if Goetz had handed over the $5 and then shot the fleeing teenagers in the back? See N.Y. § 35.15(2)(b). Does $5 justify this difference in results?

Durham, p. 802, introduces the rules applicable to the use of force to effect an arrest. The use of force by police officers should be considered first. Why is the Durham conviction reversed? Does the court permit the use of deadly force to effect the arrest of a misdemeanant? If Long had broken away and started to run, could the defendant shoot? Note the distinction drawn between flight and resistance; deadly force can be used (*if necessary*) to overcome resistance, but if the misdemeanant flees, deadly force cannot be used, even if it is the only way to prevent escape. Does Durham grant the police any privilege, with respect to misdemeanants, that they would not have under ordinary rules of self-defense? Note that under self-defense, the deputy in Durham would have to retreat if he could; under Durham he can stand his ground and kill if necessary to protect himself, but he can't kill just to prevent the suspect's escape. Consider a variation on Durham:

Case 8. Long breaks away and starts to flee. Durham correctly determines that in this instance the game law violation was a felony. Now can Durham shoot to prevent Long's escape? Under the common law rule, yes. See MPC Comment at p. 808. Until recently, this per se approach was apparently still dominant. Does the per se approach make sense? But what is the appropriate alternative? Compare the MPC proposal at pp. 808-09.

Tennessee v. Garner, p. 804. Why was the use of deadly force here constitutionally "unreasonable"? In addition to the victim's obvious interest in life, note society's interest in imposing punishment by orderly procedure. But what about the law enforcement interests? Note first the offense allegedly committed by the victim. Would it be constitutionally permissible to impose the death penalty for this offense? (Probably not; see Coker v. Ga, p. 502, Note 3(a)). If not, how can it be justified to impose that penalty without even having a trial?

One answer is to note the additional offense involved: the victim apparently was also guilty of illegal flight. But what is the penalty for this offense? If the suspect can't be killed for the burglary and can't be killed for the escape why is he being shot? The argument has been made by George Fletcher in *A Crime of Self-Defense* (1988) that killing as punishment and killing to prevent a crime are distinguishable situations, because while the principle of proportionality limits the former it does not in the same way limit the latter. Consider the acknowledged right of a woman to kill to prevent herself from being raped, even though the Supreme Court held that the death penalty "is grossly disproportionate and excessive punishment for the crime of rape and is therefore forbidden by the Eighth Amendment." Coker, at p. 502.

Does reasoning from the principle of proportionality that limits the imposition of legal punishment lead to the conclusion that deadly force can't be used even to prevent the *escape* of a robber or rapist? If the suspect is heavily armed, shooting him might be a lesser evil than allowing him to endanger others. But suppose a situation in which husband H kills his wife in state that does not authorize the death penalty for murder. Can an officer shoot to prevent H's escape? Under Garner, yes. But how can this result be justified, if there is no reason to believe that H poses a continuing threat of violence to the community? Is the problem that too many murderers may go unpunished? If so, why isn't this problem equally (or more) applicable to the many burglars who might escape if police can't use deadly force to apprehend them? If it were shown that the Garner result would sharply reduce the burglary arrest rate (or double the number of burglaries committed), would the decision still be justified? How can we weigh the loss of life for minor crimes against the broader effects of hampering or preventing the apprehension of large numbers of suspects? Note the sources relied on by the Court. Are these persuasive on the policy question? Are they adequate to support the rule as a *constitutional* matter?

In concluding the discussion of this section, it may be helpful to consider why the rules relating to the use of force need be so detailed and so doctrinally compartmentalized, with separate standards for defense of self, others, property and law enforcement. Is there a single standard that could capture the appropriate principles of conduct? Note the recurrent tension between the desire to minimize resort to violence and the desire to enact workable, widely accepted standards (desires that may be incompatible in our society). If some compromise between these objectives is necessary, shouldn't it at least be one that is clear and consistent over the various contexts in which these issues arise? Is the complexity of current standards self-defeating?

3. Choice of the Lesser Evil, pp. 809-32 and pp. 135-40

This material could be covered in about one class if the instructor concentrates on the basic MPC balancing principle and its various contemporary applications (pp. 809-22). Coverage of the uncommon but more troubling issues involving the propriety of utilitarian balancing with respect to such fundamental personal interests as life itself (pp. 135-40 and 822-32) would require an additional class.

Unger, p. 809. Before examining the doctrines of necessity and duress, consider whether a prisoner can raise a self-defense claim in situations comparable to Unger. For example, suppose the prisoner had to flee in order to avoid being burned to death in a prison fire. Why isn't a self-defense claim available? Note the traditional limitation of self-defense to a defendant's response to *unlawful* force. Why isn't self-defense available in Unger itself, where the other prisoner's threat clearly was unlawful? Note also that self-defense traditionally must be exerted *against* the unlawful attacker. Given such restrictions, a separately defined privilege must be invoked in a situation like Unger. A continuing issue, of course, is whether such compartmentalization of the various justifications is necessary or desirable.

The Unger opinion illustrates a further complexity -- the difference between necessity and compulsion (duress). Why isn't the latter available? Note the court's reasons at p. 810, last full ¶. Would duress be available under the MPC? See § 2.09, arguably suggesting a comparable limitation. Does it make any difference, if necessity will be available even when duress requirements can't be satisfied? This issue is better delayed until the student reaches the Duress material, specifically Note: Necessity and Duress Compared at p. 852.

Should a necessity defense be available in Unger itself? Should Unger be able to qualify even without meeting the Lovercamp conditions (p. 862-811, 3d full ¶)? Note especially conditions (2) and (5). Without these elements, was Unger's conduct really necessary? But note the language of the Illinois statute (p. 811, indented quote). Doesn't the defendant qualify in Illinois even without meeting the Lovercamp standards? If so, is the Illinois formulation too loose? Compare N.Y. § 35.05, p. 817, and MPC §3.02, p. 816.

· What result in Unger under the N.Y. formulation? Under the MPC? If the result is the same, in what respects do the formulations differ? Students should note such issues as whether the necessity is limited to emergency situations (why should it be, if the other requirements are met?), whether the harm avoided must "clearly" outweigh the harm caused, whether the harm avoided must *in fact* outweigh (N.Y. and MPC) or must instead only be reasonably believed to do so (Ill.), and the relevance of the defendant's fault in bringing about the necessity (defeats the defense in Illinois and N.Y. but not under the MPC).

Should there be a necessity defense at all? Does it open too wide a potential loophole? How can courts determine whether the harm avoided "outweighs" that caused? Consider for example the Williams, Leno, and Hutchins cases, pp. 813-15. How do we evaluate the precise harm caused by the defendant's conduct? In Williams, why does the harm done to the property owners by the trespass "outweigh" the harm suffered by the homeless if they were not allowed to trespass? In Leno, how to weigh the encouragement to the use of illegal drugs if the needle exchange program were permitted against the possible saving of lives the program is designed to produce? And in Hutchins, was the court right in rejecting the medical necessity defense to the crime of illegal possession and cultivation of marijuana? If equally effective lawful medication is available, presumably the marijuana use is not "necessary". But what if no alternative lawful medication is equally effective? What precisely is the harm caused by the defendant's possession and use of marijuana? Does such harm "outweigh" the pain that the particular defendant avoids by using the drug?

Such cases suggest the difficult problems posed by a balancing-of-evils defense; but what problems would be presented by complete rejection of this kind of defense? Consider a prison fire which forces prisoners to flee for their lives. Would it be tolerable to punish such conduct under an escape statute? Can such a result be justified, despite its unfairness to the individual defendants, simply on the ground that consideration of necessity claims would involve too much discretion? One response may be that jury nullification will prevent harsh results in situations like that of a prison fire. But if the law refuses to recognize necessity as a defense, wouldn't the prosecution be entitled to have any references to the fire ruled inadmissible? And wouldn't the prosecution be entitled to a jury instruction that any alleged "necessity" was not a defense to the charge?

With respect to cases like Williams, Leno, and Hutchins above, note that juries deal with such balancing problems all the time in connection with crimes of recklessness or negligence. Is the necessity issue appropriate for jury resolution as well? Or would this create too many possibilities for frustrating the legislative intent? Compare the Illinois and N.Y. approaches on this point.

Case 1. Narcotics addict N, facing severe pain and possible death from withdrawal, takes heroin to relieve his symptoms. Assume that no help for his condition is available through lawful medical channels. Should N have a necessity defense? If not, is this because the harm avoided (pain and suffering) is really less than the harm caused? How can a court make this judgment?

Consider first the result that should be reached under the Illinois statute. Even if the harm avoided is deemed less than the harm caused, doesn't N reasonably believe the contrary? Or, given the legislative judgment reflected in the drug laws, would the court hold that such a belief was not "reasonable"?

What result in Case 1 under the N.Y. statute? Note first that reasonable belief here is insufficient (see the last sentence of § 35.05). But how should a *court* balance the evils here? Isn't N's death from withdrawal clearly a greater evil than his use of heroin? Should there be a Lovercamp-type requirement of seeking help at the first available opportunity? But even if N met this requirement, what is the significance under the N.Y. statute of the second sentence? If the statute's application to a particular class of cases (e.g. severe addicts) cannot be questioned, then doesn't Unger lose automatically? Doesn't the prisoner lose automatically even in Case 1? If such results were not intended, how can the language of that sentence be confined? Presumably the sentence was intended to bar the defense in situations contemplated by the legislature at the time the law itself was passed. Presumably the legislature did not contemplate application of the prison escape statute to a case where a raging fire threatens the lives of all the prisoners. But even on this narrowed interpretation, the addict loses in Case 1.

Discussion of such problems can help indicate that the main (and arguably exclusive) role for a necessity defense is to provide a safety valve for unusual situations where the legislature itself would not have intended the statute to apply. See p. 817, last full ¶ of the MPC Comment. Case 2 probably fits this requirement. <u>Unger</u> and Case 3 seem more problematic. In principle the court in these cases should be attempting to determine whether the legislature itself would have written in an exception, if it had anticipated the problem. But often, as in <u>Unger</u>, this narrower judgment may itself be impossible to make with confidence.

<u>Schoon</u>, p. 820, raises the problem of determining the extent to which necessity can be invoked as a defense in a civil disobedience situation. What was the defendants' claim? The evil their conduct was designed to avoid was America giving financial and other support to one of the parties to a civil war in El Salvador. Did that evil "outweigh" the harm caused? What was the harm caused? The vandalism and temporary disruption of the IRS office?

The trial court relied on part on the absence of an imminent harm, a ground the Court of Appeals, as well as most courts that have faced this kind of situation, agree is sufficient to reject the defense. See Note, p. 822. But why should the immediacy of the peril be crucial, so long as the harm avoided outweighs the harm caused? Presumably the answer is that non-emergency situations afford alternative solutions. But suppose the alternative solutions are not adequate?

The <u>Schoon</u> opinion goes further than most courts have so far gone in concluding that "necessity can never be proved in a case of indirect civil disobedience. . . even if the protested harm is imminent." The distinguishing feature of *indirect* civil disobedience, according to the court, is that the harm protested is not the law that is being broken, but some other law or policy. Why should this fact alone make the defense unavailable?

One reason the court gives is that in a democracy "the mere existence of a constitutional law or governmental policy cannot constitute a legally cognizable harm" whose avoidance could ever be a lesser evil than violating a law. Is this sound? What assumption seems to make it inexorable? Another reason given by the court is that the law violation alone can not possibly abate the action simply by its doing since the only way the protested law or policy could be abated is by subsequent legislative action. Is this an independent reason, or is it altogether dependent on the first? Why should it matter that the law violation itself can not abate the action? The final reason given by the court is that so long as the legislature might change its mind there is always a legal alternative that renders the law violation unnecessary. Is this persuasive? Might there be cases where there is the remedy of political action exists in theory, but not in reality?

Consider:

Case 2. A group of right to life advocates seek to disrupt an abortion clinic by such tactics as chaining themselves to equipment and blocking passageways. Charged with criminal trespass, the protestors raise the defense of necessity, claiming that their actions were justified by the need to save the lives of the fetuses that otherwise would be killed. How should the claim be analyzed? Does the harm caused (trespass) outweigh that avoided (the deaths of numerous viable fetuses)? If not, why isn't the necessity defense available? Isn't the requirement of an immediate peril satisfied here? What alternative means do the defendants have to pursue their protest? Given Roe v. Wade, is peaceful dissent and the ballot an available solution? If not, then why isn't a necessity defense available?

One answer may be that the harm caused must include the interference with the woman's privacy rights as defined in Roe itself. Does this harm outweigh the harm avoided? Roe presumably holds that it does. But what result in Illinois, where the outcome turns on the defendant's "reasonable belief"? After Roe, is a belief that the harm to the fetus outweighs the harm to the privacy rights automatically "unreasonable"?

Where does the Schoon decision leave the protestor who engages in civil disobedience out of a sincere conviction that the law in question is profoundly evil? Suppose, for example, that protestor P attempts to block a train carrying Japanese-Americans to concentration camps as part of the forcible relocation program during World War II. Does P have a necessity defense? If the answer, under the foregoing principles, is no, then is the necessity defense too narrow to capture a proper assessment of moral culpability? Courts tend to limit the choice-of-evils defense remains largely to balancing from the perspective of the values and priorities that the legislature itself is presumed to hold. Even if morally justified, P would not have a "legal" justification under the necessity defense as it is typically defined. But should courts allow suspension of the law when they believe it serves some purpose they regard as higher?

Dudley and Stephens, p. 135, was introduced in connection with the preliminary discussion of the purposes of punishment. Students should now be in a position to focus more rigorously on the theories available to determine whether the defendants should have a defense. Recall first the reasons given by the court. Is the court's objection that the victim was not singled out in a fair way? (Apparently not, see p. 138, 1st 7 lines.) Then is the court's objection that the killing was not really necessary? But how could they possibly have known whether a ship would appear in time? Was their estimate of their chances at all unreasonable? Consider also p. 139 n.1. Grove's point apparently is that it would be wrong to kill three to save one. But is that the relevant choice? Isn't the relevant question whether it is wrong for three to die rather than all four? If the latter is the only issue that can be relevant to Dudley and Stephens, what justifies the court's conclusion? Isn't it clearly better for some to survive than none at all? Doesn't the court in effect reject the choice-of-evils defense, at least with respect to homicide? But if the choice-of-evils principle is valid, why isn't there just as much (if not more) reason to apply it when the value to be maximized is human life?

In examining this question, consider how Dudley and Stephens would be decided under the MPC. Note the MPC Comment at pp. 824-25. Since the killing of P produced a net savings of lives, D and S presumably would have a § 3.02 defense. But is this a fair result? Can the net savings justify the stronger men in singling out the weakest to die? Arguably, P was so weak that he would have died anyway. But suppose all had the same chance of survival, and that D decided to strangle P because the latter was too small to offer effective resistance. Wouldn't D still have a defense under the MPC? If so, isn't that an intolerable result?

Presumably, some requirement of fair procedure has to be read into the Code. But even with this modification, is the MPC approach workable? What is a fair procedure for minimizing harm? In the following cases, consider whether the passengers should be required to draw straws, or whether the person to be sacrificed should be selected on some other basis:

Case 3. D and S each has a family to support, and P has none. Can D and S single out P on the ground that his death will cause the least harm? Why must the life of each individual be assumed to be of equal value (MPC Comment at p. 825, lines 4-5)?

Case 4. D is a corporate executive who earns $500,000 per year; S is a concert violinist who earns $200,000; B is a research biologist who earns $60,000 working on a cure for cancer; and P is an unemployed alcoholic who is a loving parent to three small children. Should the value of each life be determined by earning capacity or on some other basis? If so, what basis? Is the MPC presumption of equal value based on a utilitarian judgment that each life really is of equal value to society, or solely on the administrative difficulty of making distinctions?

Case 5. D is 45 years old, S is 32, and P is 19. If all are otherwise in comparable physical condition, shouldn't D be killed in order to maximize the total savings in expected person-years of life? If so, why not consider other factors also bearing on life expectancy. What if D is in perfect health, but S has cancer (eight-month life expectancy), and P has a heart condition (ten-year life expectancy)?

Discussion of Cases 3-5 can suggest both the awkwardness of assuming that all lives are truly equal in value, and the difficulty of making a selection on any other basis. But do these problems result solely from the difficulty of making comparative judgments? Consider one other aspect of these issues:

Case 6. A, B, C, D and E are all adrift in an overloaded boat. A minimum of 500 pounds must be jettisoned if any of the passengers is to survive. A, B and C each weigh 170 pounds, D weighs 200 pounds and E weighs 300 pounds. Under the MPC approach, should all five draw straws? Or would A, B and C be justified in throwing D and E overboard? Here even assuming strict equality in the value of each life, the maximizing principle seems to grant approval for singling out some individuals to save others. But shouldn't D and E be granted some chance of survival?

Case 7. K is undergoing minor surgery when his doctors learn that an injured motorist M, just brought into the emergency room, urgently needs a kidney transplant to survive. K's wife, who is in the waiting room, refuses to consent to the transplant of one of K's two healthy kidneys in order to permit the survival of M. Can the doctors remove one of K's kidneys without consent? Do they have a necessity defense? Assume that K is best situated to provide a kidney in the fastest and least complicated way, and that the alternatives are either the certain death of M (without a transplant) or a 30% reduction in K's life expectancy (if the transplant occurs). What result under the MPC if the transplant is performed?

Cases 6 and 7 help suggest why there may be something wrong with the Code's balancing analysis? Aren't there situations in which the individual's right to autonomy and bodily integrity should trump the utilitarian advantage of society as a whole? But if so, then should Parker have a right to keep his very slim chance of survival rather than being forced to die for the benefit of Dudley and Stephens? Should Mary, the twin who has no chance of long term survival (p. 825), have the right to live for a few more weeks rather than be killed to permit the survival of her sister? For discussion, see the Note on Rights and Lives at pp. 830-31.

Public Committee Against Torture, p. 826, poses essentially similar issues, but unlike Dudley and the related hypos, the context of PCAT is highly realistic and could recur frequently. Accordingly, students will probably find the issues, as they arise in that context more immediate and more difficult. The utilitarian balancing approach may lead to condoning severe shaking and, for that matter, even more brutal methods of torture (and torture of innocent but knowledgeable bystander, p. 830, note 3) if the number of innocents to be saved is great enough. Is this a tolerable result? Are there hidden costs to society of endorsing such brutalities?

If the right answer is that such methods are to be condemned because they violate rights, regardless of aggregate social cost, then does it follow that the "milder" methods of harsh interrogation also are out of bounds, even when a known terrorist is the subject and the lives of many hundreds of innocents (e.g. Oklahoma City, p. 829, Note 1) are at stake?

Students should see that some of the fundamental dilemmas of the choice-of-evils approach result not only from the extreme difficulty of evaluating and comparing various interests (including life itself), but also from the inherently problematic character of any utilitarian calculus that may, by definition, require the sacrifice of some for the benefit of others. The problem, here posed from the viewpoint of the victim of aggression, is analogous to the problem posed by utilitarianism from the perspective of the defendant facing a punishment that can be justified by reference to social welfare though not by reference to personal fault.

4. Euthanasia, pp. 832-42.

This material is not usually included among the subjects covered in a Criminal Law course. Its current timeliness and controversiality, plus its intimate connection with the concept of a justified killing in our culture, seem to us to warrant its inclusion if time can possibly be made for it. As we have presented the subject, there are two principal themes, one doctrinal and the other broadly policy.

Cruzan, p. 832, is the starting point for the development of a doctrinal jurisprudence of justified mercy killing. The court upholds Missouri's refusal to withdraw Cruzan's life support system. Does this mean that there are no constitutional limitations here? What is the principle that underlies the Court's holding? Note that the Court holds that a competent person has a "constitutionally protected liberty interest" in refusing medical treatment. P. 833, last full ¶. Thus, the Missouri decision to continue life support is upheld only because the patient in this case was not "competent" and there were doubts about her actual wishes.

Given Cruzan's holding that the constitution protects a competent person's liberty interest in avoiding unwanted medical treatment, what further propositions follow? Is that "liberty interest" absolute, or can a state ever override that interest even though a clearly competent person clearly wants to refuse treatment? Is the right to refuse life-saving treatment confined to the terminally ill? Is it confined to those who are presently competent, or does it extend to those who express their wishes clearly, before becoming incompetent? Does the right extend not only to the refusal of treatment but also to an affirmative right to medical assistance in implementing a choice to end life? The issues are addressed in the Kadish excerpt, p. 841, and the Kamisar excerpt, p. 842.

The Glucksberg case, p. 834, provides a concrete setting for probing the issues. If a person has a right to refuse to permit his life to be extended, does it follow that he has a right to end it? Regardless of the circumstances? Only when his life has become intolerable? When he does have such a right, if he is not able to end his life by himself, does he have a right to the assistance of one who is willing to help him? Does it make a difference whether the other person actually does the killing or only helps him? The majority refuses to accept a constitutionally protected right to assistance in committing suicide. What is the principle that distinguishes that result from the holdings in Cruzan and Casey? Can the principle that supports Cruzan be fairly limited as the majority asserts?

The second major theme is the broad policy question of whether the law should move in the direction initiated by Cruzan and the successful Oregon initiative, p. 838, Note. What precisely are the fears of those who oppose these laws? The excerpt from the New York State Task Force, p. 839, and the Kamisar excerpt, p. 842, express these concerns. Does the Oregon law (p. 838) contain enough safeguards to protect against abuse?

A helpful article by Alexander Capron in the Hastings Center Report, January-February 1995, at p. 34 discusses the potential loopholes in the Oregon "limitations":

(1) The initial determinations must be made by the patient's "attending physician." Does this requirement prevent an impersonal determination by an MD who is essentially a stranger and insure a significant doctor-patient relationship? (Capron notes that any MD assigned to treat the patient is an "attending physician" and therefore is apparently authorized to make the initial determination that the circumstances justify prescribing the lethal medication.) Does this allow a physician to set up a practice specializing in assisted suicide? Should some established prior relationship with the patient be required?

(2) The initial diagnosis must be confirmed by a consulting specialist. Does this requirement provide a significant check on abuses? Who selects the consulting MD? Note that under the statute (last of the enumerated duties of the "attending physician," p. 838, indented part of the quote) it is the "attending physician" who refers the patient to a consultant. Capron notes that there is no requirement that the two physicians be independent of one another. Should there be? Apparently, under the Oregon law, the two key roles could actually be fulfilled by MD's who are partners in a specialized "suicide-assistance" practice.

(3) Does the requirement of psychiatric counseling for patients suffering from psychological disorder provide a significant safeguard? (Capron points out that there is no assurance that the two physicians who make the final judgment will qualified to determine whether the patient is suffering from a psychological disorder or from a depression causing impaired judgment.) Is this a serious concern, and what should be done to address it?

On the other hand is the Oregon law unduly restrictive of which patients qualify? Why only terminally ill patients? How about patients suffering from intolerable pain? How about Alzheimer patients who suffer awful deterioration over an extended period? Is it just to exclude these groups of patients? And how about those physically unable to administer the drugs without help? Why should they be denied the opportunity to end their lives solely because of their physical disability?

B. Principles of Excuse, pp. 842-949

   1. Introduction, pp. 842-45

   2. Duress, pp. 845-61

Toscano, p. 845, introduces the principal requirements of the duress defense, and summarizes the main areas of controversy concerning the scope of the defense. At the outset, the relationship between necessity and duress is worth exploring. See the Note at pp. 852. In many jurisdictions necessity can be invoked as a defense only when the threatening circumstance is a natural event. Toscano therefore would have to claim duress rather than necessity. But in such jurisdictions both necessity and duress are *justifications*, available only when the defendant has chosen the lesser evil. Can Toscano succeed in a claim of duress *as a justification*? Is the harm avoided more serious than the harm caused (fraud)? If so, would such threats justify continued participation in the fraud? Perjury to cover it up? Perjury to cover up a homicide? The balancing analysis required by the necessity defense can become problematic when broad interests in the administration of justice are involved in the balance.

   Can Toscano avoid these balancing problems -- can he establish some defense even if his choice was not the lesser evil? Consider first whether, given the severity of the threat, he can argue that his act was not voluntary. Does he meet the MPC requirements? Apparently not -- see § 2.01. But under the MPC and jurisdictions that follow its approach duress may be available in cases where the conduct is not technically involuntary and the harm avoided does *not* outweigh the harm caused. Under this approach, necessity (a justification) attempts to show that the conduct was desirable; duress seeks only to excuse.

   But if, by hypothesis, the conduct was not desirable, why should a defense be allowed at all? Does the defense make sense from a deterrence viewpoint? Is punishment useless because the defendant subject to duress is undeterrable? Or would rejection of the defense at least serve to deter those who might hope to feign such a defense? Logically, shouldn't we *increase* the punishment for defendants subject to duress? But even if punishment of the compelled defendant would be useful, wouldn't it violate the requirement of moral fault? How can legislators and judges condemn behavior in which they themselves would engage under similar circumstances? See the MPC Comment at p. 850, 3d full ¶. The impulse to allow the duress defense probably rests on the notion of moral blame as a prerequisite to punishment more than it rests on any straightforward deterrence calculus.

If that is the rationale of the defense, how should it be defined and limited? The four principal issues are whether the threat must be imminent, whether particular kinds of threats should be required, whether the defense should in any case be excluded for particular offenses (e.g. homicide), and whether the standard should be subjective or objective. At this stage in the course, the last issue will be familiar to students and may not require further exploration in class. (For discussion in the duress context, see p. 850, Note 2.)

With respect to *imminence*, return to the facts of Toscano. Why was the duress defense rejected at trial? Was the threat too vague? There may be a legitimate credibility question for the jury here. But the sole problem *as a matter of law* was the lack of "imminence". But if imminence is not required for a necessity defense, why should it be required for duress? So long as the other stringent requirements for duress are satisfied, why should it matter whether the threat will be carried out immediately or only in a couple of hours? Arguably, lack of imminence suggests that the defendant had an alternative (e.g. going to the police). But does that alternative provide effective protection against threats like that in Toscano? What if one of Toscano's co-conspirators had sought police protection under similar circumstances and had been found the next day at the bottom of the river? Or consider whether non-imminence mitigates the seriousness of the threat in Fleming, p. 855. Why do courts say that lack of imminence in such situations establishes the inadequacy of the threat as a matter of law? Compare Contento-Pachon, p. 856, and Ruzic, p. 857. Is that a more realistic approach? Or does it open the door to easily invented duress claims? What impact will the Contento-Pachon holding have in the "war on drugs"?

What *kinds of threats* should suffice? Consider:

Case 1. Suppose that in Toscano the caller had "merely" threatened to chop off Toscano's arm? In some jurisdictions, this threat would be insufficient! (See p. 847, n.8). Why such an arbitrary limit? What accounts for these efforts to confine the defense? Is there special reason to fear exploitation of this defense by defendants? Or to fear exploitation of human weakness by the wrongdoer who exerts duress? In practice most jurisdictions probably have abandoned the strict limitation to threats of death.

Case 2. Suppose the caller had threatened to blow up Toscano's office and destroy his medical practice. What result in New Jersey? What result under the MPC? Note under both formulations the requirement of force against the person. Does this make sense? If, by hypothesis, the person of ordinary firmness would be unable to resist, why should the threat be ruled insufficient as a matter of law? Is the problem that protection of property interests should be handled under the balancing analysis of the choice-of-evils approach? But is this an adequate solution? Consider:

Case 3. Suppose that an impatient gangster threatens to blow up a cabdriver's vehicle unless the driver takes him to the airport at 80 mph. Can the driver, if charged with speeding, successfully assert a choice-of-evils defense? (Probably not: consider the dangers attendant upon high-speed driving.) But is there a good reason to rule out duress as a matter of law in this kind of case? The widely prevailing exclusion of threats to property or reputation seems highly debatable. Compare Lord Simon dissenting in Lynch, p. 860, Note 5.

Case 4. Consider the problem case at p. 854, Note 1(b). What result? Note the requirement that the coercion stem from *unlawful* force. But why should the defense be denied in (b) if it is allowed in (a)? Does the unlawful force limitation reflect another effort to avoid problems of manipulation and uncertain proof? Is there a desire to reserve the defense for situations where at least some party will be punishable? Is the latter consideration a legitimate one, or just a vestige of unjustifiable notions of retaliation?

With respect to *offenses*:

(a) Why should duress automatically be unavailable in homicide prosecutions? Couldn't some threats (e.g. torture of a loved one) force the ordinary person to kill under some circumstances? Compare the argument of Lord Salmon in Abbott, p. 859, top. But doesn't this argument confuse justification (not available when there is a net loss of life) with *excuse*, which should be available if the reasonable person couldn't be expected to do otherwise.

(b) What if the defendant's participation is relatively minor and probably would not be crucial to the success of the killing in any case? See the dissent in Brown, p. 859, Note 4.

Class discussion of the various traditional limits on the duress defense can bring out the tensions that are ever present in the law of excuses. Students should see that in the case of each limitation there is a conflict between, on the one hand, the effort to identify and generalize the underlying logic of situations involving lack of fault, and on the other hand, the continuing concern to avoid weakening incentives for compliance.

   3. Intoxication, pp. 861-75.

A basic question here is why intoxication should not always be a defense if the jury is satisfied that the defendant would not have committed the crime had he been sober. There are two situations where this question might arise.

The first situation, the more common, is where the defendant becomes drunk voluntarily. The law here is beyond doubt: so long as he has the mens rea required for the offense, the fact that intoxication lowered his inhibitions, which would have kept from committing the crime had he been sober, does not constitute a defense. "Voluntary temporary intoxication does not excuse one for the criminal consequences of his conduct." Booth, at p. 864, 1st indented quote.

Why should this be? Can we say that the effects of alcohol are so well-known that the defendant was culpable in getting drunk? Is this assumption valid, or does it depend on the prosecution's ability to show that the defendant had some special reason to anticipate that his intoxication would be dangerous? See Hall at p. 864. Even if the intoxicated defendant should be considered culpable, culpable *for what*? Does Glanville Williams (p. 864) have a point in arguing that "if a man is punished for doing something when drunk that he would not have done when sober, is he not in plain truth punished for getting drunk"?

Kingston, p. 861, presents the second situation, that is, where there is not even the voluntary action of the defendant in getting drunk on which to hang responsibility. The law is uniformly held to be the same as in the first situation -- so long as the defendant has the required mens rea, the fact that he would not have committed the crime if sober is no defense, even though he became drunk through no fault of his own. Kingston is interesting because the intermediate decision of the Court of Appeal made a rare (and short lived) challenge to this general rule.

The case for allowing a defense in this case is strongly put by the Court of Appeal, p. 862, middle of page. Why isn't the court right when it says (p. 862, 3d full ¶): "If the sole reason why the threshold between [having criminal inclinations and putting them into practice] has been crossed is or may have been that the inhibition which the law requires has been removed by the clandestine act of a third party, the purposes of the criminal law are not served by nevertheless holding that the performing the act is guilty of an offence"? How does the House of Lords answer this challenge? Lord Mustill at p. 862-63 points out some practical difficulties of administering such a defense: the danger of fabrication; the difficulty, if not impossibility, of reliably determining whether the defendant would not have done the deed if he had been sober; the perverse effect of such a defense - - it being easier to establish, the more susceptible the defendant was to the temptation to commit the crime.

But are these practical considerations invoked in Lord Mustill's opinion sufficient if it is *unjust* to hold the defendant liable in this circumstance? Interestingly, Lord Mustill says "justice makes no such demands," p. 863, last full ¶. Why not? Because the trial judge can better assess the play of the various relevant factors by tailoring the sentence. P. 863, last sentence of opinion. Is this satisfactory? Does the possibility of a lesser sentence eliminate the injustice? Or is the possible injustice in these situations no greater than the law typically accepts in its doctrines of liability and excuse?

Compare the commentary of the MPC at p. 863, 1st ¶ of the Note: "The actor whose personality is altered by intoxication . . . is treated like others who may have difficulty in conforming to the law and yet are held responsible for violation." But suppose the involuntary intoxication not only reduces his normal inhibitions, but has the effect of rendering the defendant in a temporary condition equivalent to a person who is legally insane? The MPC, and it is fair to suppose jurisdictions generally, would allow the defense. See P. 863-64, Note on Intoxication and Responsibility.

Roberts, p. 864, introduces the other major issue: not whether, because of intoxication, the defendant should be excused for a crime that was committed, but whether, because of the intoxication, the defendant lacked the mens rea required and so committed no crime at all. What is the holding in Roberts? Note that since the offense charged required a particular intent (to kill), the court concludes that the jury must be directed to consider intoxication to determine whether the defendant could and did entertain this intent. What's the basis for this common position? The student should see that it follows logically from the definition of the offense. If the required mens rea is not present, then the crime has not been committed; the fact of intoxication may, depending on the mens rea, have an evidentiary bearing on whether the defendant acted with the required mens rea. Does this position raise difficulties in practice? In the cases that follow, consider how the difficulties in applying this logical principle have led to its erosion.

Hood, p. 865. Note the offenses charged here (assault with a deadly weapon and assault with intent to murder). Does the court permit evidence of intoxication to be considered? (No. See the last sentence of the opinion.) Would the Roberts court have reached the same result? Note the need under Roberts to determine the mens rea required for the offenses. What mens rea is required here? The definition of assault is at p. 867 n.6. Since assault is a kind of attempt, what mens rea is implied? Recall the usual requirement of a purpose to achieve the particular result. Doesn't this mean that assault with a deadly weapon is a specific intent crime? The court recognizes this possibility (p. 867, 1st full ¶), but in the end holds that assault with a deadly weapon is a "general intent" crime.

In what sense does the court really mean that assault with a deadly weapon is a general intent crime? Does the court mean that recklessness would be sufficient for conviction? Suppose A, who is chopping wood, knows that B is standing behind him, but carelessly hits B with the ax. Is A guilty of assault with a deadly weapon? Would he be convicted in California? (No, see Carmen, p. 867, line 3). Students should see that although the California court calls assault with a deadly weapon a "general intent" crime, this label is misleading: functionally the court holds that the required mens rea is still (as in any attempt) the particular intent (knowledge and probably purpose) to effect a battery.

Given this holding with respect to the mens rea, how would the intoxication issue be handled under Roberts? Discussion should make clear that under the Roberts approach, intoxication is relevant whenever (as in Hood) the statute requires proof of a particular (i.e. "specific") intent. The Hood court decides first that intoxication should not be a defense and then labels the offense one of "general intent" in order to justify that result. But students should see that in effect Hood represents an ad hoc approach, deciding case-by-case whether intoxication should be relevant as a policy matter, regardless of whether the statute requires proof of a particular intent.

Is the court's analysis in Hood persuasive? Why is intoxication irrelevant if — as the court concedes — the statute requires proof of intent? Consider p.

867, 2d full ¶. What precisely is the court's argument? Is it true that evidence of intoxication would "relieve a man of responsibility"? Or is the issue simply whether he is responsible in the first place, i.e. whether he did the acts with the mental state required by statute? Is the argument that intoxication (short of unconsciousness) can *never* preclude "an intent to do something simple"? If this isn't *invariably* true as an empirical matter, why not let the jury decide it on a case-by-case basis?

What result in <u>Hood</u> under the MPC? Note the structure of §2.08. The material thus illustrates three distinct approaches: the general intent/specific intent analysis (<u>Roberts</u>): the ad hoc approach (<u>Hood</u>); and the approach that considers intoxication where factually relevant, *except* in crimes of recklessness (MPC). What is the justification for excluding crimes of recklessness in the MPC approach? Compare the arguments at p. 872, last ¶, with the critique by Prof. Morse, p. 873.

<u>Stasio</u>, p. 867. Note the charge here (assault with intent to rob). What result under the three approaches previously considered? Students should see that evidence of intoxication would be admissible under all three. What are the court's reasons for rejecting that result? If the legislature prescribes a particular punishment for assault with intent to rob, what is the justification for applying that punishment to a defendant who did not in fact intend to rob? Why is a defendant who lacks that intent because of intoxication punished, when one who lacks that intent for other reasons is not punished? The arguments developed by the court are worth examining. Will allowing an intoxication defense undermine the law's social protection function (p. 868, 1st full ¶) any more than any other refusal to impose strict liability? Note also the <u>Stasio</u> court's refusal to extend its approach to first-degree murder cases (p. 868, 2d full ¶). Why this exception? If the court's arguments are valid, why don't they apply in the first-degree murder context too?

4. <u>Mental Disorder</u>, pp. 875-929

<u>Organization and time allocation</u>

This section normally warrants extended discussion; two to four classes may usefully be devoted to the topic. But because instructor preferences and scheduling imperatives at this late point in the course vary widely, we have structured the material in segments that will permit the topic to be covered adequately in just one or two classes if necessary. Before turning to a detailed discussion of the content of each class, a few comments on how to divide and pace the material are warranted.

a) Where time is running very short at the end of the semester, it is possible, if necessary, to cover the insanity material in just one or two classes, by assigning pp. 875-90 for the first class [see ¶(c) below] and pp. 890-905 [see ¶(d) below] if there is time for a second class.

b) Where the class schedule does not require such abbreviated treatment, we find that students can benefit from having time for more extended reading and discussion of the insanity issues, especially since background reading and a feel for the "texture" of the cases can be especially important here. Depending on the preferences of the instructor, three to five classes can be allocated to the material. These can be selected from the segments described in ¶'s (c) through (g) below.

c) First two classes: For the first class, the Introductory Note, M'Naghten, and the material following (pp. 875-85) provide the background concerning the nature and operation of the insanity defense and offer a basis for discussing two fundamental questions: should there be an insanity defense at all; and if so, how should it be defined? A second class, focused on pp. 885-96, can provide an opportunity for an appraisal of the Model Penal Code alternative and of the debate about whether to retain the volitional branch of the insanity defense. Teachers who must cover both the M'Naghten and MPC formulations in a single class can do so by skipping pp. 890-96, which deal with the debate over the volitional branch of the MPC test.; the first class would then cover pp. 875-90.

d) Follow-up classes: The book also offers several options for the teacher who can devote an additional class or two to the material. The issues most warranting attention are:
  (1) the debate over the volitional branch (pp. 890-96);
  (2) the question whether the insanity defense should be abolished completely (introduced at pp. 902-05, and made concrete by examples such as Green, pp. 896-900; and
  (3) the consequences of an insanity acquittal for the actual disposition of the defendant (pp. 882-84, Note 2, and the related problem of Automatism, pp. 914-19).
  We find that student discussion of the abolition and disposition-after-acquittal issues can be lively and profitable, so where scheduling permits the teacher to allow more time for such discussion, each of these topics can be allocated a full class. For exposing students to the core issues, with perhaps less time for give-and-take debate, all three topics can be covered in a single class hour.

e) The material on the disease requirement (pp. 909 to 912 or to 914) is interesting in its own right, and it can offer a useful way to introduce the "disposition" issue, because the breadth of the concept of "disease" is a major factor in determining whether law achieves the right "fit" between the criminal and mental health processes, or whether instead there are problematic gaps. Thus, these pages can be used as part of the introduction to the disposition issue, or where (as in most courses) such time will not be available, these pages can be assigned as background reading to introduce students to a concept that is central to all the different insanity defense formulations.

f) A final class can be profitably devoted, if time permits, to the problems of diminished capacity (p. 919-29).

a. <u>Introduction and the Traditional Test</u>, pp. 875-85

At the outset, students should understand the relationship between insanity and other excuses. Compare duress to intoxication: do these excuses involve a claim that the defendant lacks mens rea in its narrow sense (the mental elements required for the particular offense) or do they involve a claim that punishment is inappropriate even if mens rea is satisfied? Note that voluntary intoxication is the former type of excuse (when it is available at all) and that duress is the latter type. Where does insanity fit in? Suppose a defendant, because of hallucinations, thinks he is squeezing a lemon rather than someone's throat, and therefore does not "know the nature and quality of the act he was doing" (<u>M'Naghten</u>)? Here insanity would negate mens rea in the narrow sense. But was this the situation in M'Naghten's case? The defendant knew perfectly well he was killing a human being. There the insanity defense involved a claim of the latter type.

How is insanity defined? Students often think first of the <u>M'Naghten</u> or MPC definitions, but note the definitions of insanity for purposes of competency to stand trial (p. 876, Note 1(a)) or execution (p. 876, Note 2, especially at p. 877, Note 2(c)). Why do these definitions differ from <u>M'Naghten</u>? From each other? Plainly such definitions grow out of the purposes they serve in different contexts. (In terms of current law, note that on March 26, 2001, the U.S. Supreme Court granted cert. in McCarver v. North Carolina, No. 00-8727, a case posing the question whether the Eighth amendment prohibits execution of the mentally retarded. The issue is expected to be decided during the 2001-02 Term).

What *is* the purpose of insanity as a substantive criminal law defense? What is the view of Justice Dixon in Porter, p. 880? Is it true that it is "perfectly useless" (p. 880, 3 lines from the bottom) to punish the insane? Is it true that the insane can't be deterred at all? Even if it is, can't punishment of the insane deter some sane people who might otherwise hope to feign an insanity defense? (For the classic argument to the effect that deterrence considerations alone cannot explain the law's acceptance of insanity and other excusing conditions, see H.L.A. Hart, Punishment and Responsibility, pp. 40-43.) Presumably, the claim about the lack of any utilitarian value in punishment is at best only partially true (i.e. not "too much" deterrence is lost). The crucial point must be that punishment seems to be unjust. But why is this so?

In light of the asserted purposes of the insanity defense, how should that defense be formulated? Students should be clear first on the language of the principal alternative tests. Consider an example:

Case 1. X suffers from a behavioral problem that a psychiatrist describes as "pyromania." X experiences an intense drive to set fires and cannot control his compulsion to do so. If the jury finds such testimony credible, does X have an insanity defense? Under which test?

Discussion should help insure that students understand the basic verbal formulations and their apparent consequences. X presumably does not have a defense under M'Naghten (insanity is limited to cognitive impairment), but probably does have a defense under the irresistible impulse approach (adding volitional impairment, see p. 889, 3d full ¶) and under MPC §4.01 (extending to substantial as well as total impairments).

How might the prosecution challenge the insanity claim even under the most flexible (MPC) standard? Is pyromania really a "mental disease"? Students should see that this crucial threshold concept is central to all the insanity tests. It is explored at pp. 909-14.

Preliminary discussion of Case 1 can help students identify the leading issues involved in the formulation of any insanity test: (1) whether the impairment must be total or only substantial; (2) whether impairment of control is included or only impairment of cognition; and (3) whether the defense is limited to impairments resulting from "mental disease," and if so, how "mental disease" is to be defined.

Criticism of M'Naghten, pp. 885-90

Blake, p. 885, provides a basis for discussing the pro's and con's of M'Naghten. Does the M'Naghten test properly identify those who cannot be blamed? What are the criticisms of M'Naghten? Blake and the MPC Commentary (pp. 888-90) focus on three problems: M'Naghten's requirement of *complete* impairment, its restriction to impairment of *cognition*, and overall its artificial restriction on the scope of expert testimony. The MPC formulation is designed to remedy all three defects.

The MPC Commentary can be used to make clear the main goals of the MPC reform. These were, as just mentioned, to cover partial as well as complete impairments, to cover volitional as well as cognitive impairments, and to avoid artificial restrictions on expert testimony. These points can usually be conveyed most efficiently by a brief summary at the outset of class, so that class time can be devoted primarily to the controversial issues about volitional impairment raised by Lyons (p. 890).

Volitional impairment, pp. 890-96

Lyons, p. 890, develops this issue and is worth examining in detail. Note first the facts. Is narcotics addiction a mental disease at all? If not (p. 890. Last full ¶), why not? (This puzzle can be explored in more detail later, in connection with Moore, p. 940.) But if narcotics addiction is not a mental disease, how could Lyons have any claim here at all? Note Lyons' allegation of actual physiological damage to the brain. If Lyons did suffer such brain damage, and if such damage prevented him from controlling his behavior, how can he be justly punished? The crucial point is the court's conclusion that volitional impairment (inability to control) should not afford a defense.

What are the court's objections to the volitional prong of the insanity defense? Note the various objections and the response to each in Judge Rubin's dissent. Which view is more persuasive?

(1) Is it true that there is no distinction between those who "can't" and those who "won't"? Or is the problem that there is no objective method to *verify* claims of those who say they are in the former group (p. 891, 3d full ¶)? Why can't ordinary psychiatric methods of diagnosis and treatment shed light on the issue? Is the problem any more elusive than that of determining which defendants suffer from impaired *cognition*?

(2) Alternatively, is the real fear that too many defendants might be able to present *genuine*, persuasive evidence of impaired control? Is this a realistic fear? Compare Judge Rubin's view at p. 892, 5th full ¶ & n.8. Even

if the fear is realistic, does it justify the result in <u>Lyons</u>, or does it suggest only the need for some other public safety measure not entailing criminal condemnation of the blameless?

Students should be asked to evaluate the relative merits of the MPC test and the new generation of insanity proposals (pp. 894-95, Notes 1-3). Precisely how does the federal statute (p. 895, Note 2) modify the MPC formulation? Note the stricter requirement of a "severe" disease and the elimination of the volitional prong. Would either of these changes prevent the swearing contest among experts that the court condemns in Lyons (p. 891, last ¶)? (Probably not: see the comments by Prof. Stone, p. 901, Note 3.)

Discussion should provide a basis for drawing out two sets of problems that parallel those discussed in connection with duress and intoxication: first, that of articulating the factors that play a part in judgments about blameworthiness (including especially the relative importance of cognition and control), and second, that of assessing the degree to which such factors can be incorporated in a readily administrable (but not manipulable) standard. Does the MPC approach reflect the best effort to resolve these issues, or does it devote too little attention to the second set of problems? Does the new federal statute go too far in the opposite direction?

<u>Abolition and Related Issues</u>, pp. 896-905

<u>Green</u>, p. 896. Note that this case was tried under the most flexible insanity standard (the MPC test) and that the prosecution had to prove sanity beyond a reasonable doubt. On what possible basis could the jury have convicted here? Was Green deterrable? Morally at fault? Arguably, the jury disbelieved the psychiatric testimony and credited the lay witnesses who described Green as just "a little bit different" (p. 899, 1st full ¶). But is this a justifiable evaluation of the evidence? Does the jury's verdict more likely reflect concern that Green may be dangerous and should be kept under control? But how can a just system of criminal law *punish* someone as disturbed as Green?

Even if the jury verdict seems hard to justify, was it proper for the appellate court to overturn it? Wasn't the jury entitled to resolve the credibility questions in favor of the prosecution? Note the court's argument that the prosecution witnesses, even if believed, did not offer testimony *inconsistent* with insanity (p. 900, indented quote). But given the court's understanding of the "encapsulated" nature of schizophrenic delusions (p. 899, indented quote), how could the prosecution *ever* produce evidence inconsistent with insanity? Isn't the real problem that the police witnesses (and perhaps the jurors) had a very different conception than the doctors did of what it means to be "nuts"? A helpful approach suggested by Prof. Herbert Fingarette (*The Meaning of Criminal Insanity* 137-142 (1972)) develops the intuition that the absence of moral responsibility results from the lack of a capacity for conduct that is rational in light of the relevant circumstances of a situation.

Abolition jurisdictions (p. 902, Note 4) no longer attempt to preclude an insanity defense for defendants who had no mens rea at all, as state courts in the early 20th Century held that approach unconstitutional. Abolition statutes today typically make clear that lack of mens rea due to mental disease remains a complete defense.

Assuming that it is constitutional to abolish the insanity defense, is it just to impose criminal punishment on a defendant who knew he was killing, but because of utterly irrational thought processes could not understand that such an act was wrong? Should it be permissible to impose criminal punishment on a defendant like Steven Green (p. 896), or a defendant like Cameron (p. 909, Note 2) who believes he is killing in response to the command of God?

Whatever the constitutional constraints, abolition desirable as a matter of policy. Note that abolition proposals have attracted the support of both liberals and conservatives. (See the MPC Commentary at pp. 904-05.) What accounts for this situation? If liberals assume that the "defense" causes defendants to face *longer* incarceration, and if conservatives assume that the defense causes shorter (or no) incarceration, which group is right? Does it depend principally on the law of civil commitment?

It may be worth mentioning to the class that the 1973 Nixon proposal (p. 904, 1st ¶ of the MPC Commentary) came at a time when due process attacks on automatic commitment threatened to curtail sharply the commitment of insanity acquittees. As the casebook materials indicate (p. 882, Note 2), such attacks are now much less likely to succeed. When long-term commitment is automatic (see, for example, Judge Rubin's dissent in Lyons, at p. 892, last ¶), should the insanity defense be attractive for conservatives? Conversely, does that approach strengthen the claims of some liberals that defendants would be better off without the insanity defense? The resolution of these questions may depend heavily on the state of civil commitment practice in particular jurisdictions and in particular, on the extent to which the state's mental health system tends to retain custody over defendants perceived to be dangerous.

Other considerations affecting the desirability of the insanity defense can be explored if time permits. How much does the insanity defense really interfere with the administration of criminal trials? Consider, for example, the Lyons dissent, and the Morris article at p. 904. How much does the insanity defense impair the deterrent effect of the criminal law? As a matter of justice, would criminal law be tolerable without recognition of this kind of an excuse? See especially the comments of Professor Wechsler at p. 903, and the MPC excerpt at p. 905, 1st full ¶.

Discussion of the abolition issue provides an occasion for students to reflect on the broader problems of identifying the prerequisites for criminal responsibility. To what extent is moral fault to be measured by the capacities and limits of the individual rather than the ordinary person? To what extent is moral fault a prerequisite to just punishment? To what extent should the requirements of just punishment (viewed as fairness to the individual) give way to the requirements of social survival, effective enforcement, or simply cheaper enforcement?

The preceding questions can be put with respect to each of the doctrines of actus reus, mens rea, justification and excuse considered throughout the course. As students begin to review the course (as they may be doing at this point!), these issues can be flagged, so that students can consider whether the answers are the same in the various doctrinal areas. If not, are there good reasons for the differences? Can we (or should we) develop unified, coherent principles of criminal responsibility? Discussion can not only provide a brief overview of the course material as a whole, but can help students appreciate some of the reasons for the complexity of the legal and policy issues they have been considering.

The Meaning of Wrong, pp. 905-09

Crenshaw, p. 905, provides an opportunity to appraise, in the setting of a concrete case, the abstract debates about how to formulate an insanity test. Students may be asked whether, as jurors, they would vote to acquit. Would the answer depend on how the instructions are framed or would their vote (and their instinctive sense of justice) be the same no matter how the rule of law was articulated? (The same questions may be usefully posed with respect to Serravo, p. 908, and Green, p. 896.)

Students who would be inclined to acquit Crenshaw may be asked why the jury reached a different result. Was Crenshaw really mentally ill? Did he understand what he was doing? How would they attempt to persuade jurors of an opposing view? Do Crenshaw's actions prove he knew his acts were legally wrong? Probably yes: Note the effort to cover up. But why should knowledge of the law be controlling? The implication, presumably, is that such a defendant is deterrable. See p. 906, right before the 2d indented quote. But is this always true? No, see the quote from Stephen, at p. 907, Note 1. In any event, does such a defendant necessarily have sufficiently rational thinking to warrant moral blame?

If the legal wrong requirement is sound, when should the "deific decree" exception (p. 909, Note 2) come into play? Was Cameron (p. 909) really "crazier" than Crenshaw? Or does the difference between the cases turn on Crenshaw's failure to choose the right words ("command" of God rather than Muscovite "religion"). Was Cameron (or his psychiatric experts) just better schooled in the legal requirements? (In Cameron the emphasis on a deific command occurred in the expert testimony, not in Cameron's own statements.) Does this mean that the deific decree exception is untenable and that both Crenshaw and Cameron should have an insanity defense? If so, what of the anarchist who also believes his acts are legally but not morally wrong? Is there an important distinction between the anarchist and Cameron? The important point should be not the presence of a "deific decree" but the fact that the anarchist is not mentally ill; his thought process is perfectly rational. From this perspective the anarchist can properly be denied the defense while both Crenshaw and Cameron prevail on it.

If knowledge of the law shouldn't automatically defeat an insanity claim, should Crenshaw nonetheless lose because he also knew his acts were morally wrong? The court so holds, p. 906, last full ¶. But did the jury convict on this basis? (No: Note that the trial judge's instructions (p. 906, 1st indented quote) did not require the jury to find that Crenshaw knew his acts were morally wrong from society's viewpoint.) Apart from the procedural flaw in this arguments, do the facts support it? Compare Dr. Belden's somewhat ambiguous comment (p. 906, last indented quote) with Crenshaw's comments to the hitchhikers (p. 905, last full ¶), where he freely admits the crime to several perfect strangers. Was that the behavior of someone who knows that his actions are morally wrong?

<u>The disease requirement</u>, pp. 909-14

The material in this section helps underscore for students the significance of the "disease" requirement as a regulator of the breadth of the insanity defense. Not all mental or emotional impairments provide a basis for acquittal, *even if* such impairments result in lack of cognition or lack of control, because the impairment must result from *disease*. The reading, which can be assigned for background reading if necessary, illustrates this point in a number of interesting contexts, and also shows the complete failure of courts and legislatures to articulate a meaningful test for determining whether an impairment rises to the level of "disease."

<u>Guido</u>, p. 909, is particularly fascinating because at first it seems so dated -- today we would view this as a classic situation for battered spouse syndrome. But if the defendant cannot qualify for self-defense (recall the imminence and retreat problems when, as here, the battered spouse has shot a sleeping husband), should she have a defense of insanity? This can't work, unless battered spouse syndrome is considered a "mental disease." What does this depend on?

Consider first whether the mental disease issue is a medical question? (Presumably it is not; otherwise defense counsel's effort to change the doctors' diagnosis would indeed seem highly improper). But if it is a legal question, what is the test?

Students should be asked to examine the three suggested legal definitions (p. 911, Note 2), to see whether they help answer the issue presented in <u>Guido</u>. Should we just leave this issue to the jury's sense of fairness? Are there any dangers in that approach? What happens if a jury acquits on grounds of mental "disease," but psychiatrists regard the defendant's problem as a mere personality disorder and therefore discharge him from confinement in the mental health system? Part of the difficulty of defining disease seems to be the simultaneous need to have this concept governed by legal concepts of responsibility and blame, but also to retain its links to medical standards for diagnosing mental disorder.

<u>Disposition after acquittal</u>, pp. 882-84

This material raises the question of what should be done with persons acquitted by reason of insanity (BRI). Why are insanity acquittees treated differently from defendants acquitted for any other reason? Is it really accurate to describe insanity as a "defense"?

Note that in <u>Jones</u>, p. 882, last full ¶, the defendant was charged only with shoplifting, a mere misdemeanor. He pleaded NGRI, the prosecution conceded insanity, and he was automatically committed, pending the 50-day hearing (p. 882, last 3 lines.)

For a defendant like Jones, who "successfully" invokes the insanity defense, how long does the commitment last? Just 50 days? What if defendant fails to invoke the 50-day hearing? If the defendant is presumed insane, does it make any sense to permit him to "waive"? Consider <u>Fasulo</u>, p. 883, 1st 4 lines. Whether presently sane or insane, many acquittees may be heavily medicated while detained, and they may no longer be represented by counsel. Students should see that there may never be a 50-day hearing. (The Court in <u>Jones</u> acknowledged as much.) Thus, the initial commitment is not just a temporary detention for observation; it is an indefinite commitment.

If the defendant does request a hearing, what has to be shown to justify continuing confinement? (This is almost a "trick" question; actually *nothing* has to be shown to continue the detention. The detainee has to make a showing to obtain release. See p. 882, last full sentence.) Substantively, the crucial issues are mental illness and dangerousness. But what happens if the evidence on these issues is unclear? Since the "acquitted" defendant has the burden of proof, the initial commitment is not just a temporary detention for observation. In effect the initial commitment in jurisdictions like D.C. (<u>Jones</u>) is indefinite; insanity acquittees remain confined until they can prove their eligibility for release.

What is the justification for this indefinite commitment? As a matter of due process, the deprivation of liberty must be supported by a legitimate purpose. Here the purpose is treatment and social protection. But how does *acquittal* of a criminal charge establish the need for treatment and social protection? Note the Jones Court's argument - - that the NGRI verdict establishes insanity and dangerousness. Are these facts sufficient to establish the need for treatment and social protection?

Consider first the finding of mental illness. Why is there any need for a new hearing on this issue? (a) Does the BRI verdict actually involve an affirmative finding of mental illness? In D.C. it does because defendant had the burden of proving insanity at the criminal trial. (A separate problem (considered below) may be posed where a BRI verdict indicates only a reasonable doubt as to sanity.) (b) Note the timing problem: Even if insanity is established beyond a reasonable doubt (or admitted by both sides, as here), how does that show *present* mental illness? The Court's answer is that it is reasonable to assume that the condition of insanity continues. (See p. 882, last full ¶.) Is this convincing? (Recall that inevitably, the defendant was recently found competant to stand trial.)

If the notion of continuing insanity is plausible, what follows? Does this notion mean that the state should be able to rely on an evidentiary presumption in meeting its burden of proving present insanity? Why should the notion of continuing insanity justify *shifting* the burden of proof to the defendant? Jones does not use the notion of continuing insanity simply to support a shift in the burden of proof - - under Jones, the presumption of continuing insanity is in effect *conclusive* because it eliminates the need for any initial commitment hearing at all. How can the possibility of continuing insanity, however plausible, support this result? (The Court's answer relied essentially on administrative efficiency.) Should such convenience considerations be adequate to support the complete elimination of a hearing in this context?

Similar issues should be considered with respect to the relevance of the criminal trial verdict to the question of dangerousness. Does a violent criminal act necessarily support an inference of continuing dangerousness? Even if the violent act does support such an inference, does it justify a shift in the burden of proof? Does it justify eliminating the hearing entirely? Isn't there a need for a hearing to determine how relevant the particular act is to the possibility of future dangerousness?

Consider, in addition, the "dangerousness" of the criminal act in Jones itself. In what sense is a non-violent property crime dangerous? Is it *sufficiently* dangerous to justify indefinite confinement? What if a defendant has an uncontrollable (and uncurable) tendency to write bad checks (e.g. the facts of Lynch v. Overholser, 369 U.S. 705 (1962))? Should it be permissible to confine such a person for life? The Court in Jones gives, in effect, an affirmative answer. In contrast, many states limit such commitments to defendants who are considered potentially violent.

Assuming that the initial commitment is justified without a hearing, should there be any outer limit on the time that a defendant can be held? Should it make any difference that the offense charged carried a one-year maximum prison term? The Court's answer in Jones is that since the commitment is for treatment and social protection, there is no reason to assume that the maximum prison term indicates the appropriate period of confinement. But this argument returns us to the issue whether the determinations of illness and dangerousness can be justified *without a hearing*. Consider:

Case 1. Suppose that Jones had a codefendant Smith, identically situated in all respects, who had pleaded guilty and served a one-year term. Thereafter, the government decides that Smith is still dangerous and should be held for treatment and social protection. Can the government hold Smith without a hearing? If not, what must be shown at the hearing in order to justify continued confinement of Smith? Who will have the burden of proof and by what standard?

Students should see that Smith cannot be held unless the government can meet the civil commitment standard by proving, by clear and convincing evidence, that Smith is still mentally ill and dangerous. See Addington, p. 882, 2d full ¶. Is there a good reason for continuing to hold Jones, if Smith cannot be held?

Tactically, what does Case 1 suggest about the desirability of pleading NGRI? If a defendant pleads guilty, the trial judge normally is not permitted to find him NGRI over the defendant's objections. See p. 881, Note 1. (Alternatively, if a judge does enter a verdict of acquittal BRI over the defendant's objection, the *automatic* commitment procedure cannot be invoked. See Lynch v. Overholser, supra.) Thus after Jones, the defendant must, before choosing a plea, make a difficult calculation about whether confinement is likely to be longer after conviction or after an NGRI acquittal. Does it make sense for condemnation of the mentally disturbed to turn on that kind of calculation?

Consider the tactical and legal situation in a jurisdiction where an NGRI verdict requires only a reasonable doubt about sanity. Can a defendant found NGRI in such a jurisdiction be committed indefinitely without a subsequent hearing? Consider whether the reasoning of Jones applies. Is it relevant that the defendant *pleaded* insanity? (Or should his plea be interpreted only as a claim that there is a doubt about sanity?) Note that the reasoning of Jones turns in part on the fact that mental illness has already been established in the criminal trial. Thus, Jones arguably does not govern in a "reasonable doubt" jurisdiction. But if there is uncertainty whether a defendant should be confined in prison or in a mental hospital, should it follow that the defendant should not be subject to confinement in either place? This concern may suggest that the Court would not insist on proof by a preponderance (at the criminal trial) as a precondition for automatic commitment; the defendant's plea of insanity might be interpreted to bar a subsequent inconsistent plea that he was not insane at the time of the offense.

The approach of automatic commitment without a hearing (which Jones holds constitutionally permissible) may seem illogical, but what is the alternative to this approach ? Even at the time of Jones, a large group of jurisdictions treated defendants found NGRI just like defendants acquitted on any other ground. Commitment was permitted only under the same standards applicable to any other civil commitment. See p. 882, Note 2(a). Perhaps surprisingly, Jones apparently has NOT led more states to follow the automatic commitment approach; a survey conducted several years after Jones (see the Brakel article cited in Note 2(a)) found that several states had REPEALED their automatic commitment statutes in the wake of Jones and that only 10 states authorized automatic commitment.

What problems arise when a state has no special regime applicable to defendants acquitted BRI? Consider:

> Case 2. The defendant, clearly mentally ill, poses a serious risk of continued shoplifting. What happens if the defendant is charged with shoplifting and found not guilty BRI?

> Case 3. The defendant has killed three people and is clearly dangerous, but psychiatrists are divided about whether his problems are the result of a mental disease. What happens if the jury finds mental illness by a preponderance and therefore acquits BRI, but the evidence is not strong enough at the civil commitment stage to establish mental illness by clear and convincing evidence?

In many states, it is not permissible to civilly commit a person like the defendant in Case 2. Similarly, the defendant in Case 3 is not civilly committable because there, even though dangerousness is clear, the proof of mental illness doesn't meet the Addington requirement of "clear and convincing" proof. (See also Foucha v. Louisiana, 112 S. Ct. 1780 (1992), making clear that mental illness is a constitutional prerequisite to continuing civil commitment).

The upshot is that in states without any special regime applicable to persons acquitted BRI, defendants like those in Cases 2 & 3 may escape *both* civil commitment and criminal conviction. Such situations apparently have not posed serious problems in practice in states that have chosen to rely solely on the civil commitment approach. But such situations could conceivably result in many offenders (including some very dangerous offenders) slipping through the cracks. Is that a problem? Or is it the right result when the defendant is not morally blameworthy and is not sufficiently dangerous or mentally ill to warrant civil commitment?

If cases like Case 2 and Case 3 do pose a serious problem, how could a state deal with it? Would it be better to expand the grounds for civil commitment that apply to persons *not* charged with criminal conduct? Or should the state instead take steps to make acquittals BRI harder to win? (The GBMI verdict, pp. 883-84, Note 2(c), may represent one strategy of this sort.) Or alternatively, should a state preserve its commitment to not imposing criminal punishment in the absence of moral blame but abandon its commitment to treating insanity acquittees the same as all other members of the general population?

Discussion should help students appreciate some of the reasons for society's ambivalence about the insanity defense. On the theory that criminal condemnation requires proof of blameworthiness beyond a reasonable doubt, the defendants in Cases 2 & 3 appear entitled to an acquittal and should be treated thereafter no differently from any other member of the general population (each of whom is subject to civil commitment only on clear and convincing proof). But many courts fear that full acceptance of that approach would yield inadequate controls over dangerous individuals. Jones may reflect a judgment that it is better to compromise on the safeguards afforded to defendants after acquittal BRI than to dilute the standards of responsibility in the criminal trial itself. But even on this approach, shouldn't the initial commitment of the insanity acquittee require some kind of hearing? And doesn't a commitment implemented *for that reason* become irrational after the period of maximum criminal confinement has been reached?

b. Automism, pp. 914-19

This section presents the issues that arise when mental abnormality produces unconsciousness or involuntary muscular movement. What defenses can the defendant invoke? (Lack of mens rea and lack of a voluntary act are possible options.) Does it make any difference which defense is applicable? The material, which can be assigned as background reading if necessary) provides another concrete example of the practical bite of the issues involved in Jones. If the dispositional consequences of an NGRI acquittal differ from those of other kinds of acquittals, then it may become necessary to distinguish precisely between insanity and other defenses related to a defendant's awareness or control.

The prevailing American approach permits the defendant to choose his defense (or rely on several in the alternative). See p. 917, Note 1. In contrast, under the English approach (Bratty) and American statutes like Wyoming's (p. 917, 1st indented quote), if the condition is caused by mental disease, insanity becomes the *only* available defense. Why should this be? If the defendant lacks the required actus reus, how can the question of any affirmative defense arise at all? See Grant, p. 918-19, Note 2(c), rejecting the Bratty approach.

Under the prevailing American approach, illustrated by Grant, what happens to the dangerous defendant who prevails on a mens rea or automism defense? Reconsider Cogden, p. 178, where a mother who had subconscious hostility toward her only daughter killed the daughter during an episode of sleepwalking. Should Mrs. Cogden be free to return home after her acquittal? (What if she has another daughter?) Students should see both the problem posed (the dangerous defendant at large) and the solution normally available (civil commitment). Why isn't civil commitment an adequate solution? (The problem, presumably, is that either mental illness or dangerousness may not be sufficiently clear to support civil commitment. But then in such a situation, what is wrong with outright acquittal and release?)

Under the Bratty approach (insanity as the exclusive defense), how should insanity be defined? The problem can be important in automatic-commitment jurisdictions, since that approach enhances the incentives for defendants to cast their defense in terms other than insanity. Should a brain tumor (Charlson, p. 918, 1st indented quote) be considered a mental disease (or defect)? What about brain injury (Fulcher, p. 917, Note 2(a)) or epilepsy (Grant, p. 918, Note 2(c))?

Students should understand the various possible definitions of what is a mental disease for this purpose.

(1) Consider Lord Denning's test: whether the problem is likely to recur p. 918, 1st indented quote, and Fulcher p. 917, 2d indented quote. Does this suggest that a non-recurring problem is *not* a mental disease? Why is recurrence relevant to the legal test under M'Naghten?

(2) Compare the Quick approach (p. 918, 2d indented quote): transitory conditions may or may not qualify. The test is whether the cause is external or internal; only internally caused conditions can constitute mental diseases.

Is the Quick approach satisfactory, or is it ultimately arbitrary as well? The real problem here may not be the particular definition of mental disease but the entire idea of insisting that mental disease (however defined) precludes reliance on other defenses that may be established by the facts. Compare the approach of MPC § 2.01(2)(b) and Grant, p. 918, Note 2(c), leaving the choice entirely up to the defendant. But if the epileptic and Mrs. Cogden should not face automatic commitment, why not take the same approach for defendants who rely only on the insanity defense? Arguably, the logic of the matter requires either rejecting automatic commitment (i.e. rejecting Jones and MPC§ 4.08) or on the other hand extending automatic commitment to situations like Bratty and Cogden.

Discussion should help students appreciate the persistent sense of differences in culpability (and dangerousness) between psychological disorders and other factors that may negate actus reus or mens rea. A continuing question is whether such perceived differences are sufficiently significant to warrant differences in penal treatment. In any event students will grasp the tactical significance and practical implications of casting defense claims in different doctrinal terms.

c. Diminished Capacity, pp. 919-29

This section deals with the admissibility of evidence of mental disorder when offered to rebut mens rea rather than to establish an insanity defense. The material helps make clear the different kinds of psychiatric testimony that may be available in a criminal case and the different ways that such testimony may arguably be relevant to criminal responsibility. The material also helps students appreciate the administrative difficulties entailed in handling such testimony and in dealing with dangerous offenders who may use it to win acquittal. To bring the issues into focus, an introductory hypothetical may be helpful:

> Case 1. Defendant D is charged with first-degree murder. A psychiatrist retained by the defense finds, after examining D, that he is suffering from profound cognitive disorientation, and at the time of the offense, D thought he was squeezing a lemon rather than his brother's throat. Will such evidence be admissible? For what purpose? On what theory should the defense seek to present it?

Discussion of Case 1 can begin with the question of what tactical preferences the defense should have here. Is it desirable to rely on an insanity defense?

> (a) The obvious disadvantage of an insanity defense is the prospect of commitment. But suppose defense counsel thinks that after a mens rea acquittal D will face civil commitment with virtually

the same prospects for confinement as he would face after acquittal BRI. Is there then any reason to rely on a mens rea defense instead of insanity?

(b) Note next that the result of a mens rea defense may be conviction, but only of a lesser included offense; in that event D might face a considerably *shorter* period of confinement after conviction than after acquittal BRI.

(c) What if experts are divided about whether D's hallucinations are the product of "mental disease"? Note that a mens rea defense may succeed where an insanity defense could not, because with respect to the former, D need only raise a reasonable doubt.

In sum, asserting a mens rea defense instead of, or in the alternative to, an insanity defense offers several tactical advantages. (If D chooses to rely *solely* on mens rea, can the trial judge nevertheless find him not guilty BRI, and if so can the regime of automatic commitment be invoked? On these questions, see p. 881, Note 1.)

What *should be* the result in Case 1? Is the evidence admissible for purposes of rebutting mens rea? If so, is it admissible only to rebut premeditation, or can it rebut intent to kill and malice, so that D might be acquitted entirely? Students should understand the different approaches indicated in the materials.

(1) What result under <u>Brawner</u>, p. 919? Note the court's emphasis on logical relevance (p. 920, 1st ¶). On this basis the evidence arguably could be considered for purposes of negating not only premeditation but all criminal intent.

(2) Compare the <u>Wilcox</u> approach, p. 921 (such evidence is never admissible), and the various intermediate positions, i.e. <u>McCarthy</u>, p. 925, Note 3 (admissible to rebut specific intent if a lesser included general intent crime is available), and <u>Wetmore</u>, p. 925, 2d indented quote (admissible to rebut specific intent whether or not a lesser included offense is available).

What is the justification for the <u>Wilcox</u> approach? If the evidence is relevant, how can it be excluded? If *voluntary* intoxication is admissible to rebut a specific intent, how can courts fairly exclude evidence of mental disorder that is not in any sense self-inflicted?

(a) Note first the <u>Wilcox</u> court's concerns about probative value and prejudicial effect (e.g., p. 923, 2d full¶). But are these concerns soundly based? If the court's doubts about the reliability and validity of psychiatric judgments are serious, shouldn't such evidence be inadmissible even for purposes of the insanity defense? Since such expert testimony is in fact deemed competent and reliable for that purpose, what other considerations account for the Wilcox result?

(b) Note next the practical consequences stressed by Prof. Arenella and quoted in Wilcox, p. 922, 5th full ¶. Why isn't the possibility of civil commitment an adequate answer? In Case 1, would D be subject to commitment? Students should see that mental illness and dangerousness would have to be established by clear and convincing evidence. But if that cannot be done, isn't the court's concern in Wilcox misplaced by definition? If D can't be proved dangerous, there would seem little ground for concern. But what happens if D is clearly dangerous but cannot be proved mentally ill? What means of social protection would be available if D's hallucinations are the result of a hormonal imbalance rather than a "mental disease"? Note that at present there would be no power to civilly commit such an individual. But is the proper solution to this problem the rule permitting conviction of a person who by hypothesis did not have criminal intent? Why not instead extend the civil commitment regime to reach dangerous individuals suffering from problems other than "mental illness"?

In jurisdictions that accept relevant psychiatric evidence (at least with respect to certain mens rea issues), the crucial question becomes whether the testimony offered *is* relevant. Is it logically relevant to the required mens rea in Case 1? Clearly yes. But consider the various kinds of psychiatric testimony that may be offered:

> Case 2. Busic, p. 926, Note 5. Is the holding correct? Is the court's reasoning sound? If the outcome depends on the fact that aircraft piracy is a general intent crime, what result if the statute had made it an offense to seize an aircraft "with the purpose of forcing it to deviate from its flight plan"? Would Dr. Diamond's testimony then be admissible to rebut this *specific* intent?

Discussion of Case 2 should make clear that the Diamond testimony does not deny that Busic knew what he was doing. But then, how can Diamond testify that Busic lacked the required intent? Note Diamond's finding that free will and choice "constitute the intent required." Is Diamond right about that? Is this matter an appropriate one for expert testimony? (Presumably this question involves a legal issue of statutory interpretation.) Alternatively, if we must assume that Busic was aware of what he was doing, can we interpret the Diamond testimony as a claim that Busic's lack of "free will" rendered his acts involuntary? Does this kind of "lack of free will" establish involuntariness in the legal sense? (No, see MPC § 2.01).

Students should see that even if *some* psychiatric testimony might have cast doubt on the required intent (e.g., if Busic had a delusion that the plane was his own car), Diamond's testimony does not. Nor does it cast doubt on voluntariness in the legal sense. Thus, the proper ground for exclusion of Diamond's testimony is that it is not legally relevant to either specific or general intent.

How would Busic come out in California? Under the revised Penal Code (p. 925, Note 4), is psychiatric testimony admissible on mens rea or not? Note the language of § 28(a). What is the distinction between offering evidence to negate "capacity to form" and offering evidence to negate whether the defendant "actually formed"? The testimony in Busic helps give content to this seemingly metaphysical distinction. Since Dr. Diamond claimed that Busic's mental state prevented him from exercising ordinary mental powers and that he "lacked the capacity" for criminal intent, the testimony would be inadmissible under §28(a), 1st sentence. Compare the result in California if Diamond had testified that Busic's hallucinations caused him to think he was seizing his own car. Here the testimony would be admissible under §28(a), 2d sentence. See also Saille, p. 926, 1st full ¶. The California distinction between capacity and actual intent may simply be an awkward way of stating that "capacity" in the psychiatric sense is not a required part of the legal concept of mens rea.

5. Changing Patterns of Excuse, pp. 929-49

This section presents material that tests the boundaries of excuse and thereby brings together several leading concerns of the criminal law: in particular those of determining when conduct involves blame and when, if ever, it is appropriate to punish in the absence of blame. If time permits, one class can be devoted to the evolution of constitutional doctrine in this area (pp. 929-39), and a second class can focus on the issues that remain open for consideration as matters of common law case analysis, legislative policy and moral judgment (pp. 940-49).

Robinson, p. 929. Students should be clear on the Court's precise holding. How far does Robinson extend? Consider:

Case 1. P is prosecuted under a state statute that makes it a crime to "be a prostitute." Does conviction and punishment violate Robinson? Is there any distinction between this statute and the one struck down in <u>Robinson</u> itself?

Several possible distinctions between Case 1 and <u>Robinson</u> can be considered.

(a) Can we interpret the offense in Case 1 as not one of "status," on the theory that conviction necessarily requires proof of repeated acts of prostitution? If so, why couldn't the addiction statute in <u>Robinson</u> itself be similarly interpreted?

(b) Is it important that prostitution is not a "disease"? (Compare p. 930, 2d full ¶). But why was it so important in <u>Robinson</u> that addiction was seen as a "disease"? Is it because a disease may be acquired involuntarily (p. 930 n.9)? But is this true of all diseases? Is it true in particular of addiction? Except for the unusual cases referred to in n.9, don't most drug users probably foresee that they run a risk of addiction? Or consider the Court's example of venereal disease. Is it clear that catching this disease (or failing to have it cured) is necessarily involuntary? If not, would the Court find criminal punishment cruel and unusual, even when the defendant could have avoided the status of "being afflicted" with this disease?

Discussion of these problems should help indicate the inherent ambiguities of <u>Robinson</u> and the difficulties of determining the precise scope of the opinion. If the involuntariness problem is crucial, then punishment presumably would be permissible in Case 1 (and arguably with respect to voluntarily acquired diseases, too). If the disease aspect is crucial, punishment again would be permissible in Case 1, but not with respect to "voluntary" diseases. Finally, if status alone is crucial, then punishment in Case 1 is unconstitutional, but punishment for involuntary *actions* (cf. <u>Powell</u>) might not be.

Which of these three aspects (involuntariness, disease or status) *should be* crucial for purposes of the constitutional determination? Why, precisely, is one day in jail a "cruel" punishment for the crime of having a common cold?

(a) Is punishment cruel because punishment cannot accomplish any purpose? Note the conceivable deterrence advantages of punishing colds or especially addiction. The Harlan opinion implies that constitutionality can be established by showing that a law is not "irrational" (p. 930, last ¶). But students should recall that cruel and unusual punishment can be found even when a law *is* rational (see the death penalty material at p. 495, 3d ¶ of the Stewart opinion.) But if punishment of addiction (or colds) can accomplish a legitimate state purpose, why is it unfair?

(b) Presumably nothing in Robinson precludes a state from civilly committing a heroin addict. But why is it any more "cruel" to confine him in a jail? Douglas gives an answer (p. 930), but is it convincing? Compare Marshall at p. 934, 2d full ¶. Does the accused escape stigma and damage to reputation if he is civilly committed as a narcotics addict? Is the crucial distinction that the *purpose* of civil commitment is treatment rather than punishment? Or is the crucial distinction that a different *kind* of stigma attaches? Does Robinson in effect imply that the distinctive stigma of *criminal* punishment (i.e. moral blame) cannot be inflicted in the absence of fault? (If this is a strong undercurrent in Robinson, what are its implications? Would the 8th Amendment then impose limits with respect to strict liability crimes?)

(c) In any event why is the status offender without fault? Recall again that the status may be voluntarily acquired. Why should it be unconstitutional to punish in the absence of an act? Consider Harlan's concurring opinion at p. 931, 1st sentence. But if the core of the problem is punishment for a mere propensity, does Robinson pose any barrier to punishment of involuntary *acts*?

Powell, p. 931. What becomes of the core principle of Robinson, as re-interpreted in Powell? Is the crucial constitutional objection to punishment for status, for disease or for involuntariness? Note first Justice Marshall's emphasis on the status interpretation (p. 934, last full ¶). Why this narrow reading? Note Marshall's justification for it (primarily that of the slippery slope, see p. 934, last 2 lines). Is Marshall's reasoning persuasive? If, as he argues, the Robinson principle cannot be kept within reasonable limits, then wasn't Robinson itself wrongly decided?

In contrast to Marshall's argument, consider how Justice Black justifies a narrow reading of Robinson. Note Black's argument that status crimes represent an evil distinguishable from criminalizing acts produced by an addiction (p. 937, 2d ¶). Is this convincing? If it cannot be a crime to have an irresistible compulsion, then how, as Justice White argues (p. 937, last full ¶), can it be a crime to yield to that compulsion? Would the Black distinction lead, as White argues, to convicting a defendant for "running a fever or having a convulsion"?

Students should see why it would not. (Neither a fever nor a convulsion is a voluntary act. See MPC § 2.01.) Under the Black-Harlan interpretation, the Robinson requirement in effect parallels (and constitutionalizes) the classic common law requirement of a voluntary act; the distinction between Robinson's situation and Powell's is thus the traditional distinction between no act and an act that is voluntary even though "the doer could not control his impulse to do it" (Bratty, at p. 177, Note 2).

Where does the law stand after Robinson and Powell? Can a state punish A under a statute making it a crime to "be an alcoholic"? Presumably not, since Robinson itself apparently remains good law. But consider the following variation:

Case 2. B is a destitute alcoholic with 70 prior convictions for public intoxication. He has no family or other resources, and sleeps on the streets or (in winter) in subway entrances. Testimony shows that whenever liquor is available to him, B has no power to resist taking the first drink and thereafter has no power to stop drinking. Charged again with public drunkenness, B asserts that conviction under these circumstances is unconstitutional. What result? Is it clear that B has no constitutional defense?

Under the narrow "status" interpretation, Robinson does not reach Case 2 because B has committed acts that are voluntary in the common law sense (e.g. drinking). But how many members of the Powell Court would subscribe to this view? (Only four. Five Justices - - White and the Fortas four - - explicitly reject it and would uphold a constitutional defense on these facts.) How many members of the *present* Court would subscribe to this view is indeterminate; the issue has not reached the Supreme Court since Powell. But it's a fair guess that most of the present Justices would subscribe to the Marshall view that was originally the minority position on the proper interpretation of Robinson.

Even if B has no *constitutional* defense, would some other defense be available in a State court? Note the solution under state constitutional law in Harper, p. 938.

What traditional criminal law defenses could B raise? Discussion of Case 2 from this perspective can provide a helpful review of the material on actus reus, justification and excuse. Students should see why such common law defenses as involuntariness, necessity and duress are not available in Case 2.

What about "insanity"? Can B meet the requirements of M'Naghten? (Probably not, because there is no cognitive impairment.) In any event, why can't B prevail where the irresistible impulse or MPC approaches are followed?

Note that B's lack of control must be due to "disease." And even if it is, the lack of control must be due to *mental* disease. But why *should* a defense be limited to impairments caused by mental disease, if all other requirements of the MPC test are met?

If "insanity" is not the right defense, why shouldn't there be a general common law defense along the lines sketched by Justices White and Fortas? These questions can be explored in the context of a class devoted to Moore (p. 940) and the material thereafter.

Moore, p. 940. Why shouldn't narcotics addiction be recognized as a common law defense? With respect to the possibility of applying a standard insanity defense, isn't it clear that drug addiction is a "disease"? Then is the problem that addiction is primarily a *physical* disease? But doesn't drug addiction have significant mental component? In any event, why shouldn't a defense be available to those who suffer from a *physical* disease that substantially impairs cognition or control? Consider first the views expressed in Powell? Do the plurality opinions rest primarily on the conclusion that a defense is undesirable (e.g., p. 934, 2d full ¶) or on the view that the scope of any such defense is best left to the states (e.g., p. 936, 1st 3 lines)? To the extent that the latter point was controlling in Powell, why shouldn't a state court recognize such a defense?

Is the problem that drug addiction is a disease that normally is self-inflicted? Even when this is true, does it afford an adequate reason to deny a defense as to *subsequent* conduct with respect to which the defendant lacks awareness or control? Compare the rule applicable to voluntary intoxication (p. 864, Booth (1st indented quote)).

What reasons for rejecting such a defense were advanced in Moore? Do the prevailing judges argue that recognition of the defense is *not* required in terms of justice to the offender? (Apparently not.) Why does it *not* "follow that because one condition (mental disease) yields an exculpatory defense..., the same result follows when some other condition impairs behavior controls" (p. 941, 2d full ¶)? Note the judges' emphasis on practical considerations:

(a) One concern is whether we can limit such a defense to possession and use of drugs, and exclude the more serious crimes. Would such a distinction be logically untenable? Compare p. 940, italicized ¶.

(b) A second concern is whether it is too dangerous to adjust legal norms to the individual's capacity to conform) (p. 941, next-to-last ¶). But don't we do this with the insanity defense?

(c) A third concern is that drug disability is not "gross and verifiable" (again, p. 941, next-to-last ¶). But is this true? How serious are the problems of verification? See those cited by Judge Leventhal at p. 941, last full ¶. But don't these problems apply with even more force to claims of mental disease? Would a drug addiction defense "tear the fabric of...social control" primarily because it is not verifiable or primarily because it could *properly* be claimed by so many offenders? Arguably, the real difference between insanity and drug addiction lies in the number of defendants potentially affected. But then, do the boundaries of the insanity defense reflect considerations of justice to the individual offender, or considerations about how much justice to the offender society can pragmatically tolerate?

If drug addiction were recognized as a defense, how much further could this sort of responsibility defense be pushed? Should there be a defense for the defendant who claims an inability to understand or control her conduct, because of severe social, economic or emotional deprivation?

Consider the facts of <u>Alexander</u>, discussed in the Delgado excerpt at the bottom of p. 944. Does socioeconomic deprivation really *preclude* choice or just make it more difficult? If the latter, does such partial impairment really prevent moral responsibility? (Arguably not.) But then, why does the MPC formulation for the insanity defense expressly reject the requirement of total impairment? If substantial impairment is sufficient for defendants suffering from mental disease, why not the same approach for those suffering from socioeconomic deprivation?

The problems posed parallel those discussed with reference to diminished capacity and drug addiction:
   (a) Would such a defense be too hard to verify? Or is the real problem that all too many defendants could clearly qualify for it?
   (b) What disposition should be authorized for a defendant acquitted on such a ground? Can the individual safely be released? On what basis could such an individual properly be confined for "treatment"? If there is no adequate "civil" disposition, does this fact *justify* criminal punishment of a person who could not understand or control his actions?

Arguably, consistency should be achieved by the opposite sort of reform: consider whether the refusal to recognize a defense of drug addiction or socioeconomic deprivation suggests that the insanity defense itself should be abolished. See the discussion of this issue *supra*, p. 902, Note 4.

The discussion of insanity and related excuses not necessarily tied to mental disorder provides an occasion for students to reflect on the broader problems of identifying the prerequisites for criminal responsibility:

- To what extent is moral fault to be measured by the capacities and limits of the individual rather than the ordinary person?
- To what extent is moral fault a prerequisite to just punishment?
- To what extent should the requirements of just punishment (viewed as fairness to the individual) give way to the requirements of social survival, effective enforcement, or simply cheaper enforcement?

These questions can be put with respect to each of the doctrines of actus reus, mens rea, justification and excuse considered throughout the course. Are the answers the same in the various doctrinal areas? If not, are there good reasons for the differences? Can we (or should we) develop unified, coherent principles of criminal responsibility?

Discussion can provide not only an overview of the course material as a whole, but also a basis for helping students appreciate some of the reasons for the complexity of the legal and policy issues they have been considering throughout the course.

APPENDIX

B (a minor) v Director of Public Prosecutions

HOUSE OF LORDS

[2000] 1 All E.R. 833, [2000] Crim. L. Rev. 403

[B, a 15-year-old boy, repeatedly asked a 13-year-old girl to perform oral sex with him. The girl refused, and B was subsequently charged with inciting a child under the age of 14 to commit an act of gross indecency, contrary to s 1(1) of the Indecency with Children Act 1960. At trial, it was accepted that B had honestly believed that the girl was over 14 years, but the trial justices ruled that his state of mind could not constitute a defense to the charge. As a result, B changed his plea from not guilty to guilty, but subsequently appealed to the Divisional Court. When that appeal was dismissed, B appealed to the House of Lords. The House of Lords held that when a person had been charged with the offence of inciting a child under 14 to commit an act of gross indecency contrary to s 1(1) of the 1960 Act, the prosecution was required to prove that the defendant lacked an honest belief that the child was aged 14 years or over. Such a conclusion gave effect to the common law presumption that a statutory offence required a mental element unless Parliament provided to the contrary, either expressly or by necessary implication, i.e. by an implication that was compellingly clear. Moreover, rejecting the "reasonable belief" qualification added by cases like Sweet v. Parsley, Casebook, p. 251, Note 2, the House of Lords ruled that where a mistaken belief would prevent the defendant from having the necessary mental element, that belief did not have to be based on reasonable grounds.]

LORD NICHOLLS OF BIRKENHEAD: . . .

As habitually happens with statutory offences, when enacting this offence Parliament defined the prohibited conduct solely in terms of the proscribed physical acts. Section 1(1) says nothing about the mental element. . . . In these circumstances the starting point for a court is the established common law presumption that a mental element, traditionally labelled mens rea, is an essential ingredient unless Parliament has indicated a contrary intention either expressly or by necessary implication. . . .

The existence of the presumption is beyond dispute, but in one respect the traditional formulation of the presumption calls for re-examination. [T]he presumption is expressed traditionally to the effect that an honest mistake by a defendant does not avail him unless the mistake was made on reasonable grounds. . . . The 'reasonable belief' school of thought held unchallenged sway for many years. But over the last quarter of a century there have been several important cases where a defence of honest but mistaken belief was raised. In deciding these cases the courts have placed new, or renewed, emphasis on the subjective nature of the mental element in criminal offences. The courts have rejected the reasonable belief approach and preferred the honest belief approach. When mens rea is ousted by a mistaken belief, it is as well ousted by an unreasonable belief as by a reasonable belief. . . . This approach is well encapsulated in a passage in the judgment of Lord Lane CJ in R v Williams [1987] 3 All ER 411 at 415:

'The reasonableness or unreasonableness of the defendant's belief is material to the question of whether the belief was held by the defendant at all. If the belief was in fact held, its unreasonableness, so far as guilt or innocence is concerned, is neither here nor there. It is irrelevant. . . ..'

Considered as a matter of principle, the honest belief approach must be preferable. By definition the mental element in a crime is concerned with a subjective state of mind, such as intent or belief. To the extent that an overriding objective limit ('on reasonable grounds') is introduced, the subjective element is displaced. . . . When that occurs the defendant's 'fault' lies exclusively in falling short of an objective standard. His crime lies in his negligence. A statute may so provide expressly or by necessary implication. But this can have no place in a common law principle, of general application, which is concerned with the need for a mental element as an essential ingredient of a criminal offence. . . .

The decision which heralded this development in criminal law was the decision of your Lordships' House in DPP v Morgan [1975] 2 All ER 347, [1976] AC 182. This was a case of rape. [T]he House held that where a defendant had sexual intercourse with a woman without her consent but believing she did consent, he was not guilty of rape even though he had no reasonable grounds for his belief. The intent to commit rape involves an intention to have intercourse without the woman's consent or with a reckless indifference to whether she consents or not. It would be inconsistent with this definition if an honest belief that she did consent led to an acquittal only when it was based on reasonable grounds. . . .

I add one further general observation. In principle, an age-related ingredient of a statutory offence stands on no different footing from any other ingredient. If a man genuinely believes that the girl with whom he is committing a grossly indecent act is over 14, he is not intending to commit such an act with a girl under 14. Whether such an intention is an essential ingredient of the offence depends upon a proper construction of [the] Act. I turn next to that question.
. . . In s 1(1) of the 1960 Act Parliament has not expressly negatived the need for a mental element in respect of the age element of the offence. The question, therefore, is whether, although not expressly negatived, the need for a mental element is negatived by necessary implication. . . . The section created an entirely new criminal offence, in simple unadorned language. The offence so created is a serious offence. The more serious the offence, the greater is the weight to be attached to the presumption, because the more severe is the punishment and the graver the stigma which accompany a conviction. Under s 1 conviction originally attracted a punishment of up to two years' imprisonment. This has since been increased to a maximum of ten years' imprisonment. . . . The conduct may be depraved by any acceptable standard, or it may be relatively innocuous behaviour in private between two young people. These factors reinforce, rather than negative, the application of the presumption in this case. . . .

The purpose of the section is, of course, to protect children. An age ingredient was therefore an essential ingredient of the offence. This factor in itself does not assist greatly. [I]t is far from clear that strict liability regarding the age ingredient of the offence would further the purpose of s 1 more effectively than would be the case if a mental element were read into this ingredient. There is no general agreement that strict liability is necessary to the enforcement of the law protecting children in sexual matters. . . Is there here a compellingly clear implication that Parliament should be taken to have intended that the ordinary common law requirement of a mental element should be excluded in respect of the age ingredient of this new offence? . . .

I cannot find, either in the statutory context or otherwise, any indication of sufficient cogency to displace the application of the common law presumption. In my view the necessary mental element regarding the age ingredient in s 1 of the 1960 Act is the absence of a genuine belief by the accused that the victim was 14 years of age or above. The burden of proof of this rests upon the prosecution in the usual way. If Parliament considers that the position should be otherwise regarding this serious social problem, Parliament must itself confront the difficulties and express its will in clear terms. I would allow this appeal.

I add a final observation. [W]ithout expressing a view on the correctness of the actual decisions in [R v. Prince], I must observe that some of the reasoning in R v Prince is at variance with the common law presumption regarding mens rea as discussed above. To that extent, the reasoning must be regarded as unsound. . . . R v Prince, and later decisions based on it, must now be read in the light of this decision of your Lordships' House on the nature and weight of the common law presumption.

LORD STEYN: . . [O]ne can be confident that the reasoning of Bramwell B [in R v. Prince], if tested in a modern court, would not be upheld: see also DPP v Morgan [1975] 2 All ER 347 at 382-383. . . . In any event, I would reject the contention that there is a special rule of construction in respect of age-based sexual offences which is untouched by the presumption as explained in Sweet v Parsley. Moreover, R v Prince is out of line with the modern trend in criminal law which is that a defendant should be judged on the facts as he believes them to be: DPP v Morgan; R v Williams [1987] 3 All ER 411 . . .

DISPOSITION: Appeal allowed.